Hare Krishna

Hare Krishna

An introduction to its philosophy, history, and fundamentals

Ivan M. Llobet

First edition: June/2021

New revised edition: January 2023

Copyright 2021 Ivan M. Llobet

ivanllobet@yahoo.com

All rights reserved. Under the penalties established in the legal system, the total or partial reproduction of this work is prohibited without the author's written authorization.

All photos used with the permission of the
International Society for Krishna Consciousness (ISKCON)

Special thanks to my dear friends Duhsala Devi Dasi (Diane Consbruck) and Krishna Balarama Dasa (Roberto De Jesus) for their selfless and dedicated effort in editing this work. May Radha and Krishna shower Their blessings upon them.

*To: My father, Arch. Santiago Llobet,
Hridayananda Dasa Goswami, my spiritual father;
Bhaktivedanta Swami Prabhupada,
founder acharya of the International Society
for Krishna Consciousness,
and to everyone who loves knowledge.
Thank you.*

AC Bhaktivedanta Swami Prabhupada

Table of Contents

Introduction 11

Part One. The Vedas: Sacred Scriptures

Chapter 1. The origin of the Vedas.. 19

Chapter 2. The books of the Vedas 28

Part Two. Vedic precepts

Chapter 3. Fundamental concepts 41

Chapter 4. The iconography and theomorphism 56

Chapter 5. The path of emancipation for each millennium 64

Chapter 6. Impersonal monism and Vedic theism 71

Part Three. The Philosophical Principles

Chapter 7. Vishnu, the supreme deity of the Vedas 80

Chapter 8. Material nature... 85

Chapter 9. The genesis of material existence 92

Chapter 10. The individual soul 110

Chapter 11. Krishna, the Supreme Person, and source of all pleasure.113

Chapter 12. Radha and Krishna: the Original Divine Couple 121

Chapter 13. Krishna: the origin of spiritual mellows (rasa).................. 126

Chapter 14. Krishna's form: inviting to spontaneous love 131

Chapter 15. Krishna: the source of the varieties of affections 138

Chapter 16. Other aspects of the spiritual mellows *(rasa)*. 164

Chapter 17. The nature of bhakti 173

Chapter 18. The dynamism of love and the spiritual emotions...........181

Chapter 19. Krishna *lila* in the spiritual and material world 191

Part Four. The Historical Framework

Chapter 20. Cultural decadence and rebirth of bhakti 218

Chapter 21. The time of the Acharyas (holy masters) 226

Chapter 22. Shri Krishna-Chaitanya: Father of the Hare Krishna Movement..238

Chapter 23. Our apostolic heritage..252

Appendix: Hare Krishna today, integration or isolation?.....................275

Introduction

On September 17, 1965, at 5:30 am, a 70-year-old Hindu elder arrived at the Commonwealth port in Boston, United States, after thirty-five days at sea. Despite his advanced age, it was the first time he had left his native India. The ship, named Jaladuta, owned by an Indian merchant company, docked for a couple of days before leaving for New York. This polite and refined gentleman was born in Calcutta in 1896; therefore, his college education coincided with the British occupation. His father was a merchant with a modest income that enabled a comfortable life for his family; his mother was the traditional Hindu wife engaged in household chores. Following his son's birth, as tradition prescribed, his father consulted astrologers to know the fate of the newborn. They predicted that the newborn would be a great exponent of religion and establish more than a hundred worship centers worldwide. Seventy years would elapse for his prophecy to unfold. Since his father was a man of deep religious feelings, he named him Abhay Charan, "free from fear due to being at the feet of the Lord." From an early age, Abhay Charan showed symptoms of being a child marked by spiritual feelings; and due to his father's effort to give him a good education, he memorized sacred texts from antiquity.

When Abhay reached adolescence, he entered college as a chemical engineering student, but in the first decades of the 20th century, India burned with nationalist sentiments in search of independence. The primary mentor in this struggle was a middle-aged lawyer who voluntarily adopted a life of asceticism to redeem his people from the economic and political dependency into which British colonialism had plunged them. His name is known worldwide: Mohandas (Mahatma) Gandhi. Being a lover of human well-being, young Abhay quickly embraced the Gandhian ideal. As part of his peaceful resistance, Gandhi urged Hindu youth not to accept degrees from British-controlled educational institutions, which Abhay Charan consented to. Abhay was also a co-student with Subash Chandra Bose, who, years later, was the leader of the Indian Army of Liberation. Although Abhay never embraced his cause, he felt sympathy for Subash, as he advocated for a revitalization of India's traditional and moral values.

Around this time, a friend who knew of Abhay's interest in religious subjects invited him to a talk that a renowned saintly person was to give in Calcutta. As of today, in those days, India overflowed with pseudo saints willing to offer their blessings and litanies in exchange for any alms. Abhay had met many of them, so he did not show much interest; however, he agreed to go only at the insistence of his friend, who assured him that this person was a truly holy man. It was there where Abhay had his first impression of the character of a true saint. Although he was 26 years old by then, something unexpected happened. As this peaceful and wise personality addressed the audience, he told Abhay that since he was an educated young man, he should preach that message in English. Abhay was somewhat shocked by the audacity of this pleasant gentleman who, without knowing him, entrusted him with such a generous but great task. Being a young Gandhinian concerned about the well-being of his country, he stated that no one would be interested in hearing the message of an oppressed nation; first, India should be free. Upon hearing his words, that honorable gentleman replied that true liberation means freeing the soul from material captivity. As long as we remain bound to nature's laws, we will have to suffer in one way or another. Therefore, this message is urgent and cannot wait for political adjustments. Years later, Abhay related how the sage moved him so profoundly that it forever changed the meaning of freedom to him.

But what is that urgent message of which that holy personality spoke? It is the need to abandon the illusion of thinking that the physical body is our true self and that our existence comes to an end with its destruction. The fallacy of thinking that this world is our true home and has been created for our enjoyment, not realizing that old age, diseases, suffering, and death haunt us at every step. It is also the message to remind us that the purpose of human life is not to increase our artificial needs in pursuit of sensual gratification. Instead, the meaning of life is to comprehend the self and reestablish our dormant relationship with God, the reason why each of our activities should be subordinate to this purpose. Those moments in his company marked the life of Abhay Charan forever, and although more than a decade passed before they met again, that extraordinary person entered the depths of his heart. This eminent saintly person came from a very distinguished family line. His father, named Kedarnath, was not only an influential magistrate in his day but also a great social and spiritual reformer who left behind an immense legacy in the field of religion in the form of a voluminous work of philosophical and theological writings. Eager to bring into the world a virtuous soul capable of continuing his reformatory mission, Kedarnath, for a long time, engaged in prayer to conceive a child of exceptional spiritual qualities. Shortly afterward, Bimala-prasad was born, the great holy person who would touch the heart of Abhay, whom his contemporaries called the prestigious title of Bhaktisiddhanta Saraswati, and who is recognized today as the most outstanding scholar of contemporary India.

The fact that in their first meeting, such an extraordinary personality entrusted him to preach, in the English language, all over the world, what he called "an urgent message" is not accidental. A sacred text from Medieval India (16th century) called Chaitanya-Mangala predicts that *a sena-pati-bhakta* (great general among the devotees) would descend to this world and spread the message of love for God in the form of chanting of the divine names of Krishna beyond the borders of India. Sometime before Abhay's birth, the great sage and spiritual reformer, Kedarnath, announced to his contemporaries that the person who was to bring the most confidential teachings of the Vedas to all corners of the world was about to appear. Shortly after, in 1896, Abhay Charan De was born in the then prosperous city of Calcutta and years later would be known worldwide as AC Bhaktivedanta Swami Prabhupada, the founding teacher of the Hare Krishna Movement.

However, we are still at the beginning of the 20th century, and almost twelve years have passed since his good friend took the young Abhay Charan to that extraordinary person who hinted to him about his life's mission. In 1932 Abhay Charan became his formal disciple receiving the name of Abhay-Charanaravinda. At that time, he enjoyed some economic prosperity. Thanks to his knowledge of chemistry, he developed a pharmaceutical business with which he supported his family. Once while visiting Vrindavana, the well-known pilgrimage site where Lord Krishna manifested His divine activities in this world five thousand years ago, his spiritual preceptor told him, "If you ever have money, print books." Despite his family responsibilities, Abhay dedicated his life to making this wish come true. Gradually, his exceptional devotional qualities and vast knowledge won him the admiration of the members of the Gaudiya-math. This distinguished religious society to which he belonged awarded him the prestigious title Bhaktivedanta, indicative of someone who knows that the culmination of Vedic wisdom is *bhakti*, devotion to God. In 1936, sensing the imminent departure of his spiritual mentor from this world, Abhay Charanaravinda wrote him a letter asking what he wanted him to do. The answer contained the same instructions he heard in their first meeting: "Preach this message in English." Two weeks later, his great mentor and spiritual guide left this world.

Despite his family duties, Abhay Charanaravinda shaped his life so that he carried the message of the chanting of Krishna's names to every place and person he visited, to the point that many spoke of him as "one who is always talking about God." Finally, in 1959, considering that his family obligations had ended, he accepted the monastic order of life and retired to the sacred land of Vrindavana under the name AC Bhaktivedanta Swami. In 1965, at 70, after much struggle, he managed to secure a ticket with an Indian shipping company.

Mr. Bhattacharya, a friend who accompanied him to embark, recounts: "He was alone. A lone fighter. When he left, there was no one on the shore to bid him goodbye. No friends, no supporters, no disciple, nobody. Even if you call me, I was not a disciple of his. I was a disciple of someone else. So I was not his follower. But due to shared love, I had very much respect for him. So, I was the only person standing on the shore to say him goodbye. No one was with me. I could not know that it was such an important event."

That was how AC Bhaktivedanta Swami arrived in New York City. He only brought a small suitcase, a handful of rupees equivalent to 7 USD, two hundred volumes of his English translations of ancient sacred texts, and an intense desire to fulfill his preceptor's request to spread in the English language the message of chanting the divine names of Krishna.

It is hard to imagine the difficulties that Abhay went through. He was a man of holy character, raised in India, in the bosom of a religious family, away from his natural environment, and alone in New York City, with its terrifying winter and the cold indifference of its inhabitants. But his perseverance soon paid off. The hippie revolution flooded American society in those days, and Bhaktivedanta Swami soon realized that countless young people wanted to break with their parents' materialistic way of life. His message, patience, and infinite compassion attracted many youngsters who gradually abandoned the hippie life and became his first disciples. The spiritual movement that the world would know as Hare Krishna had begun in the West.

Over the next eleven years, this spiritual and social reform movement grew like no other in history. It did not take long for the chanting of Hare Krishna Hare Krishna Krishna Krishna Hare Hare, Hare Rama Hare Rama Rama Rama Hare Hare, to spread throughout the major cities of the world. During those twelve years, AC Bhaktivedanta Swami, whom his disciples now called Srila Prabhupada, put aside all consideration for personal comfort and traveled extensively around the world, carrying his message of love for God everywhere. Although he was engaged in the administration of his nascent society, traveling, and acting as the spiritual mentor to thousands of youngsters, Bhaktivedanta Swami Prabhupada wrote dozens of books and translated important sacred texts into English. By doing so, he gave the world the most confidential teachings of the Vedas. Finally, in 1977, at the age of 81, sensing that the end of his stay in this world was drawing near, Srila Prabhupada asked his disciples to take him back to Vrindavana, the holy place from which he had departed twelve years earlier, to carry out his mission. During all the time he lived with his young and dedicated disciples, he taught them to live in Krishna consciousness; now, he would give them the last lesson; teach them how to die in Krishna consciousness. On November 14 of that same year, that great soul, whose birth and mission the sages prophesied more than four centuries ago, quietly left this world, his only possession being the love and affection of his disciples who assisted him until the last moment.

Today and in the days that Srila Prabhupada was in the world, many people ask: Who is Krishna? What is the Hare Krishna religion? Where does it come from? How did it come about? What are its scriptures and beliefs? This work is for those curious people who love knowledge. Its first two parts tell us about the structure of the Vedic canon and the fundamental principles of the knowledge it reveals. The rest of the work explains the philosophical concepts and history of the Hare Krishna religion. Perhaps the first thing to know is that, although this tradition is mainly known as the Hare Krishna religion or Hare Krishna Movement, its actual name in historical terms is *Vaishnava-dharma*. Yet, outside of India, this term is not very well-known. The Vedic scriptures reveal that Krishna (also known as Vishnu) is the Supreme Personality of Godhead; hence the devotees of Krishna are known as Vaishnavas, meaning "of God," "related to God." The word Vishnu means "sustainer of the universe," "the luminous one," etc., while Krishna and Rama mean "all-attractive" and "the source of all pleasure," respectively. Therefore, a Vaishnava is a devotee of God, but because Vaishnavas like to chant the names Hare Krishna and Hare Rama, in the West, most people know them as "Hare Krishnas." Therefore, we already know that when we speak of the Vaishnava religion, we refer to the Hare Krishna religion or movement.

Most thing presented in this work is spread throughout the writings and talks of AC Bhaktivedanta Swami Prabhupada. Therefore, this is nothing more than a humble attempt to synthesize the essential aspects of the history, foundations, and philosophical precepts of the Vaishnava religion (Hare Krishna) in simple language for the satisfaction of those who wish to know about it. As its presentation is the product of my imperfect and limited understanding of the subject, I do not exclude the possibility that the work does not present the subject perfectly, as expected of all human endeavors. Nevertheless, if, to some extent, it achieves its purpose, that will be our best reward.

Part One
The Vedas: Sacred Scriptures

Chapter 1
The origin of the Vedas

Although somewhat shaped by the external cultural influxes, India still endures as the oldest living culture of humanity, preserving its wisdom in sacred books of knowledge called Vedas (*veda*=knowledge). There is no universal consensus on when these texts appeared in their written form. Opinions vary according to the different sources of information that we may approach. However, most learned Indologists agree that the Rig-Veda can be considered the oldest religious text of mankind. The Vedas encompass many of the branches of human knowledge. The vast information spread throughout its many texts, both in quantity and quality, has no parallel in human society. Its origin, when and how this wisdom was compiled and written, is a subject on which there is no agreement between modern researchers and the sages of the tradition; therefore, we find two versions of it. The first falls within empirical historical research: that is, tangible evidence, such as archeology, linguistics, etc. The second comes from the Vedas and their ancient oral tradition that descends through sages and holy teachers called Acharyas.

The empirical methods cannot corroborate the antiquity

of oral transmission of knowledge. This limits anyone attempting to trace the origin of the Vedas through the hard sciences. The Vedas are written in an archaic language called Sanskrit (*sanskritam*=perfect), which modern scholars consider the mother tongue of Indo-European languages. Eminent linguists since the 18th century have devoted many essays to extolling the impeccable grammatical structure of Sanskrit, which due to its continued use in everyday religious life in India, is the most alive "dead" language in existence.

The empiric method

The Europeans made the first attempt to trace the origin of the Vedas empirically by the end of the 18th century. This attempt continues but under different parameters. These researchers, called Indologists, were primarily British and Germans. However, learning the Sanskrit language was not the main obstacle these early Indologists faced, but rather their own cultural and religious prejudices. As a product of the colonial period, these scholars saw Judeo-Christianity as the only religion capable of redeeming humanity; hence, they regarded the local culture as inferior to the European one. Although some of these Indologists were amazed at the wealth of wisdom they found in the Vedas, their biases often clouded their objectivity in trying to understand the culture and religions of India. An immensity of letters, essays, and other historical documents show that many lived convinced to be bearers of a superior culture and religion. So, they openly admitted their disgust with the scriptures and religions of India, emphasizing the prevailing need for the use of Indology as an evangelizing instrument. The result was an immense and often degrading literary production. Over time this antagonistic attitude took on such a boom that some academic circles offered monetary prizes to whoever presented the best refutation of the religious thought of the Vedas. Today's scholars recognize that despite the contributions of these early Indologists, their religious and cultural prejudices clouded their mission.

However, in the beginning, the British came to India solely for commercial purposes, although over time, the socio-political circumstances changed, and India fell under the control of a private commercial institution called "The British Company of the East Indies." Because this business relationship generated significant profits, British merchants avoided any inconvenience with their business allies over religious matters. However, in 1857 the well-known Rebellion of the Sepoys, or the Hindu-Muslim soldiers in the British service, occurred. In those days, the soldiers used their teeth to open cartridges containing pig fat. For the natives, it was an insult to their customs and beliefs, thus sparking an upheaval. In the beginning, the rebellion had some success, but the British crushed it at the cost of enormous destruction and human losses. In the aftermath, almost all of India came under the direct control of the British Crown. The new administration sponsored the study of Indology and opened the doors to Christian missionaries, who vehemently preached the superiority of Christianity over all existing forms of religion.

Since the biblical Genesis tells us that humanity descends from Adam and Eve (the first humans created by God), the Vedas' version of the creation of the world and the human race had to be wrong. Consequently, some Indologists postulated that the Vedas could not exceed in antiquity the date stipulated by Judeo-Christianity of the time for the creation of the world, some five or six thousand years before. Others considered the Hindu descendants of the great Biblical patriarch Noah, establishing a cultural dependence on Biblical Genesis. This justification for this conjecture was a theory that we still hear today in academic and educational circles known as "The Aryan Invasion Theory."

The promoter of this theory was the renowned German professor and Indologist Max Müller (1823-1900). He proposed that the Aryans were a race originating from Eastern Europe or Central Asia, which invaded the northwestern portion of India (present-day Pakistan) around the 15th century BCE. These Aryans -Müller tells us- were experts in the art of war and brought with them not only battle chariots and bronze weapons but a culture with rituals, beliefs, and gods different from that of the natives, which despite having very well-established cities, were farmers. Over time, the gods and religion of the Aryan invaders (whose rituals and praises they collected in their texts, the Vedas) gained acceptance among the conquered natives, while the Aryan priests incorporated into their religion the countless primitive beliefs of the natives of India. From this syncretism -Müller tells us- what we know today as Hinduism arose. Therefore, according to this theory, the Vedas were brought by the Aryans from Eastern Europe or Central Asia. They date from 1500 to 1200 BCE, and the Rig-Veda is the oldest due to its extremely archaic language.

However, the foundations of this theory are mainly linguistic conjectures that Max Müller justified with specific passages of the Rig-Veda, something that many of the most prominent modern scholars today invalidate due to its highly speculative nature. Today most scholars acknowledge that the European cultural prejudices of the time demanded that the Vedas neither originate from India nor could they enjoy the same divine status as the Judeo-Christian scriptures. The distinguished Professor Müller established a time frame for the composition of the Vedas, but it turned out to be so speculative that the scholars of the time rejected it. However, in 1890, in his Physical Religion, Müller himself accepted, emphasizing the purely imaginative character of his postulate:

> "... whatever date the Vedic hymns were composed, one hundred, one thousand, one thousand five hundred, two thousand, three thousand or fifteen thousand years ago, no power on earth will ever be able to determine".

Over time, with the independence of India and the subsequent social changes of the 20th century, European society entered a period of secularization, and Indology shed its religious prejudices, becoming a secular study within the academic world now characterized by skepticism. In light of new archaeological discoveries and paradigm shifts, contemporary Indology moved back many of the dates given by the first Indologists between 1000 and 4500 years, reaching times as remote as 6000 BCE for the composition of the Rig-Veda. A shred of evidence attesting to this antiquity comes from the Vedas, which mention with impressive accuracy alignments of planetary constellations, eclipses, etc., which occurred three or four thousand years ago. Contemporary experts tell us that, because of their extreme complexity, calculating these dates in such remote times would have been impossible before the computer age, which discards the possibility of forgeries to give the texts more antiquity. However, the dates given by Müller and the early Indologists for the composition of the Vedas are so petrified that we still find them in standardized study books.

Among the contributions of modern Indology, we find the rejection of the Aryan invasion theory by notable Indologists. They see it as the product of past religious and cultural prejudices. To this is added the lack of evidence of investigative rigor, the excess of speculative linguistic conjectures, and other recent discoveries. We find no mention of an invasion of such magnitude in the oldest historical texts of India, in the historical writings of the Buddhists, Jains, or any other historian or writer of ancient India. One of the foundations of this Aryan invasion theory postulates that the rapid conquest was due to the Aryans bringing horse-drawn chariots, animals hitherto unknown to the Dravidians (natives of India). However, archaeological evidence unearthed in the Indus Valley dating back to 6500 BCE, and other drawings found in caves from 4500 BCE of equestrian figures, undo this hypothesis. Other archaeological discoveries in cities of the Indus Valley show figures of sages mentioned in the Vedas cast in bronze dating from 3500 BCE, a time in which the supposed Aryan invasion had not yet occurred. Another objection to the theory raises the point that by 2200 BCE, the kingdom of the Hittites was already powerfully established in Anatolia (today, Turkey), making it impossible for invading tribes to pass through their territories. If it had happened, we should find some mention in their historical records since the Hittites kept detailed descriptions of their dynasties of kings.

Perhaps the most compelling evidence to demolish the Aryan invasion theory is the 1986 discovery of the Saraswati riverbed, considered by many to be a mythological river. NASA's space station discovered the dry riverbed of the Saraswati several meters below the arid land of northwest India. The results of the space station investigations showed that, in effect, the Saraswati was a river of immense magnitude whose flow ranged from seven kilometers in its narrowest part to twenty in the widest. This gigantic river began to disappear in 3000 BCE, and by 1500 BCE, the date of the supposed Aryan invasion, it had already vanished for reasons still debated by geologists. This evidence is essential because the Rig-Veda glorifies the Saraswati River around which the Indus Valley culture in northwestern India grew. Archaeological evidence shows that by 3000 BCE, this settlement occupied an area from Iran, through the Gujarat region (northwestern India), to Delhi and the Ganges valley, making it the largest civilization in the ancient world. If the Aryan immigrants brought the Rig-Veda to India, and if by the time the supposed Aryan invasion occurred, the Saraswati had already disappeared or was about to disappear, why would it glorify the Saraswati River as their place of cultural settlement? This indicates that the Vedas are indigenous texts from India and not imported by invaders from Eastern Europe.

Today some postulate an inverse hypothesis: the possibility that such emigration occurred in the opposite direction. The most recent evidence points to a possible dispersion between 7000 to 6000 BCE of the inhabitants of northwest India towards western Europe, taking with them the knowledge of agriculture, which is a topic of controversy within Indology. If, due to climatic changes, the desertification of the terrain, or any other cause, this immigration to Europe occurred, then the entire history of the world needs to be rewritten. The mere idea that what we learned from educational institutions at an early age may be wrong terrifies researchers and historians who have been busy writing and interpreting history for us. The anthropological and archaeological evidence suggests that in pre-historiographical times, the inhabitants of Central America, East Africa, and ancient India had cultural links until the middle of the third millennium BCE. No doubt, this adds to the ongoing controversy. The records reveal the cultural similarities between ancient India and Central and South

America. Such investigation hints at the Vedic version that, in very remote times, this area of the planet (unknown to Europeans) was also under Indo-Vedic cultural influence.

A few decades ago, the well-known historian Will Durant said that ancient India is the motherland of our race, philosophy, and much of the mathematics that came to us through the Arabs. It is also the mother of the ideals personified in Christianity, of the form of government that we call democracy, and Sanskrit is the mother of the Indo-European languages. Although this was a completely revolutionary idea in its time, today, many Indologists consider that a rigorous and impartial study of new evidence would indicate the possibility that India and its culture could have been the cradle and epicenter of human civilization.

The Vedic version

The other version of the origin of the Vedas, we find it in the pages of the Vedas and its ancient oral tradition of sages. They tell us that the collection of wisdom that we see in these sacred texts results from a long process of revelation of the Divinity to human society from ancient times. For this reason, in India, historically, the Vedas have enjoyed the same divine status that the Bible enjoys in the West. How and when this revelation occurred is impossible to verify empirically since events of this nature do not leave visible traces. The Vedas, again and again, emphasize their divine status. They tell us that such wisdom came to human society via channels of revelation beginning with Brahma and that the sages compiled it with the passing of the millennia.

Brahma is not the equivalent of the Adam of Judaism, nor is he a prophet like Moses, Jesus, Elijah, etc. The Vedas speak of Brahma as *adideva*, the first living entity created within the universe, the highest celestial being. In his heavenly abode, Brahma receives from Lord Krishna, the Supreme Divinity, the vast information of wisdom that we know today as the Vedas, which gradually spread throughout creation. Endowed by Lord Krishna with immense creative power, Brahma takes charge of the universal arrangement of the millions of heavenly bodies. Brahma manifests other celestial beings through his vast creative capacity, including the Manus (progenitors of humanity), the thousands of prototypes of species of life that gradually populate the universe. Also, other prominent universal sages that the Vedas revere. Sages such as Narada, Asita, Durvasa, Devala, etc.—many of whom there is no equivalent in Judeo-Christian angelology—are endowed with exceptional and inconceivable qualities for our puny human experience. Thus, whether through the descent of Krishna's *avataras* or the interaction between humans and the celestial sages descending from Brahma, the knowledge we find in the Vedas disseminates throughout the universe and reaches human society.

Chapter 2

The books of the Vedas

The oral transmission of knowledge was common to all ancient cultures. For example, in the well-known Spanish Reina-Valera edition of the Bible, Editorial Caribe 1980, we find the following comments:

> All the events recorded in Genesis predate Moses, which means that he certainly drew from very ancient oral and written sources available to him. (Introduction to the Book of Moses, page 1).

> It must be admitted that some of the information we find in the Bible is the result of investigations by the writers themselves. Some scripture passages have come to us from sources that cannot be identified but may have included an oral tradition. (Commentary on The Apocalypse of Saint John 1.1).

The ancient Persian culture not only possessed great wisdom —but its language was also a dialect of the Sanskrit root, from which we can intuit that ancient India once exerted significant influence on neighboring Asian cultures. According to the Vedas, in remote antiquity, social conditions and human abilities were very different from nowadays. In that distant past, there was no shortage of people capable of fully memorizing the teachings of the Vedas, however vast and complex they might be. Today this ability practically does not exist. However, we can attest to the potential of human memory in persons who can memorize with astonishing accuracy religious texts, such as the Quran, the Bhagavad-Gita, etc. It was also widespread for Buddhist monks to learn the teachings of the Buddha by heart.

Modern scholars take it for granted that the development of writing constituted an evolutionary step in the progress of humanity from a rudimentary condition to its present state, for which they consider that the societies where we find the first vestiges of writing were more intellectually advanced. However, the Vedas reveal that the emergence of writing indicates the decline of human abilities, especially memory. For the Vedic sages, the art of writing arose as a necessity and not as a symptom of intellectual progress. In other words, with the subsequent decline in memory over the millennia, the need to preserve knowledge became evident, prompting the development of writing. The Vedas glorify the great sage Vyasa as its first editor. Foreseeing the future condition of human society, Vyasa undertook the task of dividing this wisdom into different portions in a didactic way to facilitate its study. Hence, the Vyasa (compiler) is due to this contribution. Vyasa is not an ordinary sage but a powerful visionary and prophet of exceptional intellect revered by all Vedic sages. The sages describe Vyasa as a *shakti-avesha-avatara*, a soul empowered by the Divinity for this enormous undertaking. The Bhagavata Purana, a prominent Vedic text, describes him as the literary incarnation of God. After dividing the Vedas into different branches, Vyasa commissioned other sages to represent each subdivision.

Although the central wisdom of the Vedas accentuates the spiritual purpose of existence, its different branches include many other aspects of human learning, such as medicine, astronomy, musical arts, military science, moral codes, law books, etc. These texts are known as *veda-anga*, "supplementary knowledge." In this way, over the generations, the great variety of writings that today we call Vedas (books of knowledge) aroused with its many branches and sub-branches. According to tradition, this first edition of knowledge (*veda*) occurred approximately thirty centuries before the Christian era or some five thousand years ago. A fact of this nature does not leave archaeological traces, something that rules out its empirical demonstration. Although the transmission of wisdom continued to be oral, the first texts appeared over the centuries and millennia. As expected, none of these ancient palm-leaf texts from such antiquity exist today. Sometime after this first division of the Vedas by the sage Vyasa, India entered a phase of cultural decline, a difficult period for historians to outline.

The four Vedas

The term Vedas sometimes is used broadly and sometimes more specifically. When used more broadly, it refers to the great variety of books that collect this vast wisdom; when explicitly used, it indicates four fundamental texts that conserve millenary hymns used by priests to perform rituals. These four Vedas are the Rig-Veda, Sama-Veda, Yajur-Veda, and Atharva-Veda. The Rigeda (*rig*=hymn) is by far the most prominent. It contains ten books and 1017 hymns. The Sama-Veda (*sama*=melody) encompasses the proper way to intone the hymns. It comprises 1549 verses, many of which are from the Rig-veda. The Yajur-Veda (*yajur*=ritual, sacrifice) explains the adequate execution of the rituals. Finally, the Atharva-Veda contains material from the other Vedas, rites, and incantations to heal the sick and ward off spells. Because it resembles what we popularly call black magic. For this reason, the Vedas often speak of the *tri-veda* (three Vedas) as a reference to the Rig, Sama, and Yayur-Veda. The priests (*brahmanas*) viewed the Atharva-Veda with ambivalence until it became a component of the four Vedas.

The Rig-veda has captivated modern scholars because of its archaic and enigmatic language. Sometimes understanding what its hymns express can be difficult since the Rig-veda is the literary product of a highly developed metaphysical thought. Even explanatory works on the Rig-veda dating from the 5th century BCE show that by that time, due to the archaic nature of the language, many of its riddle-like expressions, paradoxes, and multiple levels of meaning, were not completely understood. Some consider that the Rig-veda is like a code from which readers extract specific meanings according to their spiritual development.

However, the success in the execution of the Vedic rituals depended on the proper chanting of these hymns and *mantras* known to the sages, which, when intoned with the appropriate accent, exhibited an extraordinary power in propitiating the descent of celestial beings to the human plane. Furthermore, the ritual's success depended on the accurate pronunciation of the Vedic hymns. This was the reason for preserving the Rig-veda's archaic language over the millennia.

Many ancient cultures attest to the interaction between humans and celestial beings. Greeks, Latins, Hebrews, Babylonians, Syrians, Persians, Africans, Chinese, Egyptians, and even the natives of America allude to ancient times when human beings interacted with divinities. However, these testimonies are not more than mythological fables for modern scholars. We cannot deny that a great heritage of mythology comes to us from the ancient world, which played a historical role in the social and literary development of human culture. Nevertheless, we should not rule out the possibility that real experiences degenerated into legends, folklore, or misleading interpretations, over time and cultural decay. Evidence abounds of extinct cultures during the times of the conquests that spoke of a very remote, undocumented, and enigmatic past unknown even by themselves, so much that they were unaware of the origin of monumental obelisks and monoliths which were ancient even for their ancestors. We should doubt that so many ancient cultures, whose vestiges reveal that they possessed great wisdom, were so imaginative as to create thousands of insubstantial and innocent fables and take them for real.

Even though the four Vedas delve more into the ritual to achieve earthly goods than into profound spiritual themes, in them, we find the seed of Vedic mysticism. Every human being yearns for some benefit in life, and it is common for pious people to invoke God and perform acts of faith, such as pilgrimages, vows, etc., to achieve them. In this primary stage of spiritual consciousness, God is not the goal but the means; in other words, the faithful are not attracted by the intrinsic value of God as much as to the gifts they can receive from Him through His satisfaction. This form of religion is known as fruitive religion since its objective is to gain something in exchange for acts of faith. Vedic rituals regulate this drive for worldly enjoyment while inducing us to develop piety since there is a close connection between pious life and happiness. By accepting that a pious action is rewarded with a greater good, whether in this world or the next, we understand that there are universal laws that we must obey and that existence continuous after death.

When the virtuous action softens the heart, the propensity to understand spiritual values develops. The Vedas attest that when flawlessly performed, the lesser divinities (*devata*) often descended to the human plane to bless the beneficiary of the ritual with the satisfaction of his wishes, either with a prosperous life or good progeny or any other gain. However, the Vedic rituals (*yajña*) also have their spiritual dimension. The offering to the Supreme Divinity (Vishnu/Krishna) or to the lesser heavenly deities that populate the universe is gratitude for all we receive to sustain life. On the other hand, the Rig-veda recognizes the existence of a supreme, divine, sensitive and undivided consciousness behind the cosmic manifestation, which is the unifying agent of everything that exists, the origin, sustenance, and rest of everything created. This means that what we call Hindu polytheism is nothing but a misunderstanding. It resembles polytheism but is not.

However, the fruitive religion does not satisfy the heart of the mystic, whose ornament is knowledge of the self and not the acquisition of sensory pleasures. Therefore, there are texts called Upanishads containing the four Vedas' spiritual essence for those with a mystic mind. While in the four Vedas, the ritual is the central theme, in the Upanishads, the ritual has a symbolic character. In the four Vedas, the ritual is about sacrificing material possessions for greater enjoyment in this life or the next. In the Upanishads, sacrifice is the pursuit of knowledge to escape worldly pleasures to attain the emancipation of the self.

The mystic tradition

The word *upanishad* means "to sit near or under" the spiritual preceptor. This indicates the respectful and inquisitive attitude the disciple must adopt if he wishes to enter mystical understanding. The Rig-veda mentions a class of men known as *munis* (mystics) living apart from the general mass of people. Although some modern scholars believe that the ritualistic tradition precedes the mystical, which arose from a long evolutionary process of spiritual consciousness, there is no evidence for such a claim. It is a fact that there have always been, there are, and there will be, human beings with different natures. Also, the date on which the Upanishads were composed has been a matter of debate. Because its language is not as archaic as the Rig-veda, scholars postulate that its composition dates from the 9th century BCE to the 6th AD. Hence the thesis is that the mystical tradition is posterior to the ritualistic.

According to the Vedic sages, the message of the Upanishads transcends human chronology; therefore, the date for their composition does not matter. For example, the language of modern editions of the Bible differs from medieval editions even though their message is the same. If we try to read works composed in the 15th century, we will have difficulty understanding certain words and expressions of old English that are now obsolete. Hence, we find contemporary English in many modern editions of old written works. Over time, it is natural that contemporary expressions replace older ones. The new generations will inevitably express ancient wisdom in their modern language. Unlike the four Vedas, preserving the archaic language in the Upanishads was not a significant factor in transmitting their message.

Another issue of disagreement lies in the name of some Upanishads because it is common to associate knowledge with people or historical moments. For example, loving God above all things and your neighbor as yourself is a universal principle. Although expressed differently, we find this principle in the Upanishads and Judaism's sacred texts.

However, since this principle was revitalized by Jesus some two thousand years ago, it has since been associated with Christian teachings. For its part, non-violence (*ahimsa*) is an essential factor in any true spiritual path. Still, because Buddha and Vardamana advocated its importance, today, we associate *ahimsa* with Buddhism and Jainism. The wisdom of the Upanishads belongs to remote antiquity; nevertheless, sometimes, they are known by the name of the sages who taught them. For example, in the Katha Upanishad, we find a conversation between Brahma and Shiva, two prominent Vedic divinities. According to tradition, the sage Katha transmitted this wisdom known as Katha Upanishad.

The Upanishads postulate that behind the physical world, there is a spiritual or divine substance called *brahman*, which, being the origin of all that exists, is not affected by the transformations of matter. *Brahman* is both transcendent and immanent; it transcends the physical world and dwells within all mobile and immobile living beings, though as a spiritual substance, it is not visible to the physical eye. As the portion of the divinity, it animates every living being; it is known as *atma* (the individual soul) and survives the destruction of the body. One of the most notable contributions of the Upanishads is the concept of the transmigration of the soul (commonly known as reincarnation); therefore, these texts speak directly about the spiritual nature of the self and incite us to take the path of enlightenment, cutting off attachments to the ephemeral, illusory world. Along with the Upanishads, we find other texts called Aranyakas, intended for the mystics who lived in the forest (*aranya*=forest).

Due to the exercise of the human intellect through the millennia, the teachings of the Upanishads may appear ambiguous. For that reason, the great sage Vyasa synthesized its message in a treatise called Vedanta-sutra (*veda*=knowledge, *anta*=final, *sutra*=to weave). This work is only understandable to highly versed scholars. The word *sutra* means "to weave," which implies that in this work, Vyasa wove or enclosed in the form of codes or aphorisms the essence of Vedic knowledge in a minimum of words. Because of its concise nature, scholars representing various schools of Vedanta philosophy have drawn different meanings from these aphorisms to fit their multiple and often opposing views.

Other philosophical, theological, and historical books

Other Vedic books of great importance are the Puranas and Ithihasas. The word *ithihasa* means history (*ithi*=thus, *ha*=time, *asa*=happened) while *purana* means "ancient event" (*pura*=previous, *ana*=happened). The Puranas contain descriptions and narratives of very ancient events. In them, we find the following topics: the process of creation, maintenance, universal destruction, genealogies of kings and sages, a history of the descent and transmission of Vedic knowledge through the millennia, cosmology, theology, descriptions of the kingdom of God as well as the relationship between the Lord and emancipated souls in the divine realm. Like the Upanishads, modern Indologists date the composition of the Puranas (at least in their present form) between the 3rd and 10th centuries AD; however, they recognize that their content dates from times so ancient that its origin is impossible to trace. Dating the Puranas is like entering a vast forest of conjecture. Nevertheless, most scholars recognize that the Puranic oral tradition is as old or older than the four Vedas. The Vedas themselves tell us that the great sage Vyasa subdivided this immensity of stories and topics of knowledge into 18 major Puranas (Maha-Puranas) and 18 minor ones (Upa-Puranas).

Among the most prominent Ithihasas are the Ramayana (The journey of Shri Rama) and the Mahabharata (History of

Greater India), both well-known in the western world. Bharata is the original name of India. The Mahabharata is an extensive work of one hundred thousand verses that summarizes part of the history of dynasties that reigned in ancient India. The central theme of the Mahabharata revolves around the appearance of Lord Krishna in this world and His relationship with the five Pandava brothers and other members of His dynasty. Much of its importance lies in the fact that it contains the Bhagavad-Gita (the Indian Bible), which some call Gitopanishad since it synthesizes the teachings of the Upanishads. Without a doubt, the Bhagavad-Gita is the most universal of all the books of the Vedas.

The rest of the Vedic texts are the Agamas, Tantras, Samhitas, Pancharatras, etc., which outline the doctrines and rituals of the different traditions. For some reason, today in the West, the word *tantra* is almost exclusively associated with some form of sexual practice from India, but this is a wrong conception. The Tantras are scriptures that expand the Vedic revelation as the term denotes. For example, the Vaishnavas (Hare Krishna) acceptance of the forms of Vishnu that permeate the spiritual creation, known as *chatur vyuha*, is not from the four Vedas or the Upanishads but a Vaishnava Tantra accredited to the great celestial sage Narada praised in the Vedas. There are non-Vedic traditions of India whose Tantra scriptures outline sexual rituals, some significantly degraded (like the *pancha-makara*, etc.). That is why the word *tantra* carries such connotation in the West.

The dates given by modern scholars for the composition of these texts in their current form vary between the 9th century BCE to the 8th AD. But as with the other Vedic books, the is a consensus that the antiquity of the material in them is extremely archaic.

What is heard and what is remembered

All these Vedic books are classified into two categories that scholars call "what is heard" (*shruti*) and "what is remembered" (*smriti*). The *shrutis* (what is heard) include the four Vedas, the Upanishads, and the Vedanta-sutra, which are conventionally considered the primal revelation. The *smriti* (what is remembered) consists of the Puranas, the Ithihasas, Agamas, Pancharatras, Tantras, Samhitas, and other similar texts. Some consider that the *shruti* (what is heard) are the most significant Vedic texts because they are the primordial, original, oldest revelation. In their opinion, the *smriti* (what is remembered) are secondary texts or of lesser status because they result from the reflection of the sages over time. However, the Vedas themselves disapprove of this hypothesis.

The Chandogya Upanishad is part of the Vedas' *shruti* or "what is heard" primal portion. This text describes the *smritis* (what is remembered) as *pancha-veda* (the fifth Veda) since they are the direct teachings of great sages praised in the Vedas, such as Vyasa, Narada, Asita, etc. Even modern scholars recognize that texts such as the Bhagavad-Gita (spoken by Lord Krishna) and the Srimad Bhagavatam (the most important among the Puranas) belong to the *smriti* section (what is remembered) and have a *sui generis* character (their own category) due to their unrivaled prominence. Because the *smritis* (what is remembered=Puranas, Ithihasas, Pancharatras, Tantras, etc.) expand and explain the *shrutis* (what is heard=four Vedas, the Upanishads, the Vedanta-sutra), many scholars recognize that they are even more important, since they explicitly elucidate what is concisely described in the *shruti*. A chart of this division of the Vedic canon would look as follows:

```
                    Books of the Vedas
                           |
        ┌──────────────────┴──────────────────┐
        ▼                                     ▼
     (shruti)                              (smriti)
   (what is heard)                    (what is remembered)
        │                                     │
        ▼                                     │
    The four Vedas                            │
      (rituals)                               ▼
        │                          Puranas, Mahabharata,
        │                          Samhitas, the Ramayana, etc.
        ▼                          Bhagavad-Gita (the
    The Upanishads  ──────────▶    essence of the Upanishads)
  (the philosophical essence                  │
     of the Four Vedas)                       │
     Aranyakas, etc.                          ▼
        │
        ▼
    Vedanta-sutra   ──────────▶    Srimad Bhagavatam
  (synthesis of the Upanishads)    (the essence of the Vedas
                                    and natural commentary
                                    of the Vedanta-sutra)
```

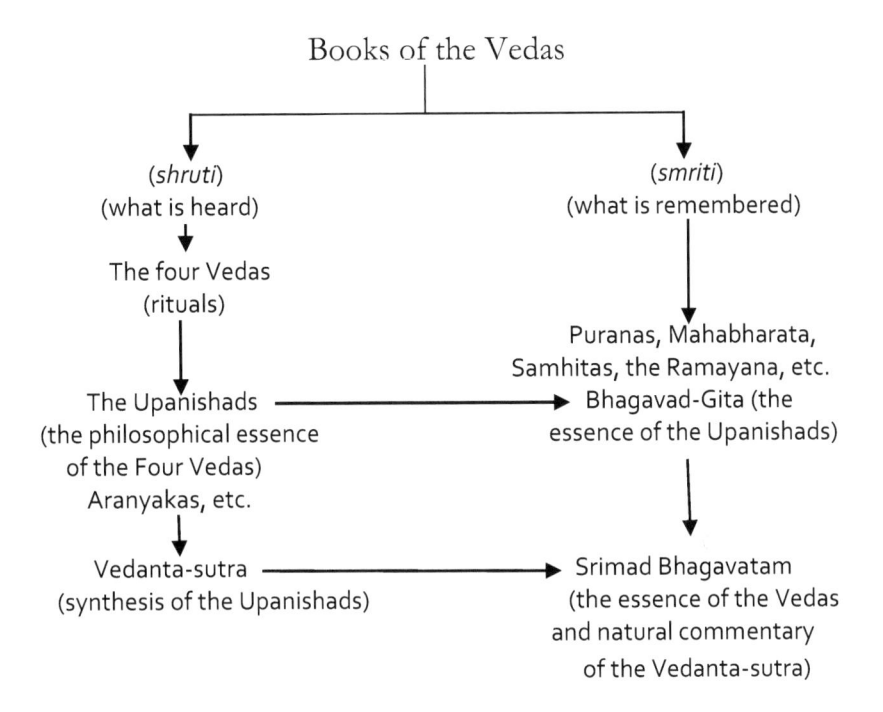

The Bhagavad-Gita and the Srimad Bhagavatam

The Bhagavad-Gita and Srimad Bhagavatam make up the essence of the philosophical thought and spiritual heritage of the Vaishnava religion (Hare Krishna). Lord Krishna spoke the Bhagavad-Gita to prince Arjuna moments before the great battle of Kurushetra, which took place among the members of the Kuru dynasty in which Lord Krishna appeared a little over five thousand years ago. Even today, Kurushetra is an important place of pilgrimage located about one hundred miles north of New Delhi, the present-day capital of India. Modern scholars hold that the Bhagavad-Gita dates from the 5th to 2nd centuries BCE. At the same time, the oral tradition maintains that its antiquity goes back to the time of the appearance of Lord Krishna about 5100 years ago. In His

Bhagavad-Gita, Lord Krishna speaks of Himself as the Supreme Person (*purushottama*). This is where its social, theological, and religious importance lies since the Gita synthesizes the different philosophical currents of ancient India and enunciates the doctrine of the *avataras* of Vishnu (Krishna).

On the other hand, the Bhagavata Purana describes the glories and activities of the different *avataras* or descents of Lord Krishna throughout different universal periods. This is why Vaishnavas (devotees of Krishna/Vishnu) call the Bhagavata Purana "Srimad Bhagavatam," or The marvelous story of the All Opulent Lord. Srimad Bhagavatam claims to be the essence of all the Vedas and the natural commentary on all Vedanta philosophy. The great sage Vyasa compiled it just after Lord Krishna departed from this world. The Bhagavatam tells us how the sages transmitted such teachings throughout the millennia. It is a fact that the Bhagavad Gita and the Bhagavata Purana are the sacred texts that have most permeated India's socio-religious psychology.

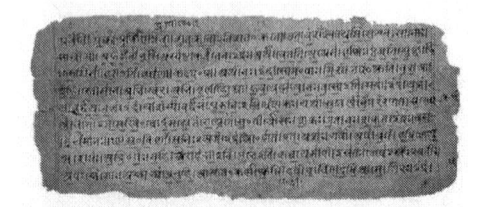

An ancient Sanskrit manuscript and a modern edition of the Bhagavad Gita

Part Two

Vedic Precepts

Chapter 3

Fundamental Concepts

India, Hindu, Hinduism

Perhaps it would surprise us to hear that qualifiers such as "India," "Hindu," and "Hinduism" are not found in any books of the Vedas. The proper term is *vadika-dharma*, "Vedic principles." The origin of the word Hindu comes from Persian phonetics. To the northeast of India (today Pakistan) runs a river called Sindhu, which the ancient Persians called Hindu for phonetic reasons. The ancient Persians spoke a dialect derived from Sanskrit, which is why they also called the land through which the Sindhu ran, Hindusthan the "land of the Hindu" (*sthana*=place, site, area, country, etc.). Later, when the Macedonian conqueror Alexander the Great invaded India in 325 BCE, the word *sindhu* was not very comfortable for the Greeks to pronounce either, who called this river Indus and the country Indica. Because of this, today, we call it India and Hindu to its inhabitants. Around the 5th century AD, the first Christians settled in India and grouped the different religious trends under the name of Hinduism.

Centuries later, the Islamic colonizers of Central Asia took up the term Hindu to refer to the land's inhabitants and

Hindusthan for the country that the locals called Bharata, the original name of India. Over time the term gained acceptance, and the inhabitants of Bharata adopted the word Hindu to refer to themselves in their dealings with the Islamic colonizers. By the end of the 18th century, the term had already established itself in the socio-religious consciousness of India.

When the British arrived, they had commercial intentions, but neither foolish nor lazy, they were quick to profit from the decline of the Mughal-Islamic empire. By the middle of the 19th century, they had imperial control almost all over India. Little by little, British cultural values and lifestyle penetrated the "Hindu" society in a way that the Muslim colonizers never did, replacing the brutality of religious sectarianism with the rationalist intellectual seduction and technological modernism that the Industrial Revolution brought about. Unsurprisingly, British modernism set the tone for the new way of life. It did not take long for India's well-to-do and educated classes to emulate the European way of life. Despite this, the British looked down on the natives, and Christian missionaries and European intellectuals systematically ridiculed their religious beliefs. Despite absorbing the European standards of life, the Indian scholars felt culturally discriminated against. Before long, a united front emerged against the British attempt to subjugate India intellectually and culturally.

This attitude provoked a reaction, and Hindu scholars educated under British rationalism attempted to stop this discriminatory intellectual offensive. They presented what they considered was the philosophical synthesis of Vedic thought, stripped of almost every religious element that did not conform to European rationalism. Shankara, the 8th-century AD Indian philosopher, was at the core of their thesis. For Shankara, the universe is an illusion, and *brahman* (the spirit) is the only reality. Therefore, the varieties of religious expressions in the Vedas are only transitory means to merge into an undifferentiated impersonal spiritual reality. For the Hindu intellectuals of the time, this was common for all India's religions and the true message of the Vedas. That is how this thesis, incorrect but attractive and convincing, spread under the name of Hindu philosophy, generating the idea of the existence of a unified thought called Hinduism despite the very different doctrines of its various religious trends. Finally, as a result of the independence of India, the term Hindu was officialized to the point that a Hindu is one who professes the religion of the Vedas. However, as we already mentioned, such a term is an import that does not exist in said scriptures.

Today what we call Hinduism is constituted by diverse paths with neither a creed, a founder or a specific scripture in common; therefore, defining it with the parameters used for Christianity or Judaism is inappropriate. Instead, the unique nature that distinguishes it must be understood. It is worth noticing that although there have been a variety of religious paths in India for thousands of years—both Vedic and non-Vedic—whose creeds and prophets differ from each other, they have coexisted in perfect social harmony. Unfortunately, with the advent of Christianity and Islam, religious intolerance and forced conversion to a single creed became known in India. This harmonious coexistence is possible because the Vedas and their infinity of sages recognize different human natures and see religious violence as a product of gross ignorance. Therefore, they prescribe different religious paths for each one of them. Simply put, God gives us free will to choose how to approach Him.

Varna-ashrama: The social and spiritual structure

The Vedas prescribe a social structure that, in its natural state, comprises four divisions that compare to the human body: 1) the thinking, intellectual or priestly class (*brahmans*) that functions as the head of society. 2) the martial or military class (*kshatriyas*) are the arms that defend the body. 3) the commercial class (*vaishya*) is the stomach that feeds the social body, and 4) the working or producing class (*shudra*) is the legs that support the social body. Society coexists peacefully and prospers when these four social classes function in harmony. The Bhagavad-Gita tells us that these social differentiations arise naturally according to the different natures and inclinations for a particular work in human beings. However, many centuries ago, in India, this system became corrupt when people considered that a person belonged to a specific social class by birth. Because of this, what was once a system of social harmony is today a powerful machine of oppression. The Vaishnavas recognize the validity of this social system in its healthy condition; however, they transcend it. For a Vaishnava, through devotion to God and proper performance of social duty, anyone can achieve perfection and act as a spiritual leader of the society regardless of the social caste, race, or gender to which they belong.

Another vital aspect of the Vedic social system is its emphasis on the gradual spiritual progress of the individual. This social system comprises four stages, beginning with the student life (*brahmacharya*), which approximately goes from 5 to 25 years of age. During this time, the young man studies under the guidance of a spiritual preceptor (*guru*) and learns the Vedas, the moral values of life, and the control of his sensory passions. Then he begins his life as a father of a family (*grihastha*), which carries with it the responsibilities of the home and which, under ideal social conditions, should diminish around 50 to 60 years of age when the children are independent. As family obligations decrease, husband and wife can pursue the spiritual path with determination. This is the stage of retirement (*vanaprastha*). By the time a man reaches 75 years of age, the intensity of his spiritual practice should increase. Finally, leaving behind the natural attachments of life, the person is expected to focus on spiritual perfection before death comes and is forced to be born again. This stage is known as the life of renunciation (*sannyasa*).

The dharma

Dharma is one of the best-known and less-understood Vedic principles. Unfortunately, there is no equivalent in modern languages for this term which encompasses a vast concept. The word *dharma* comes from the Sanskrit root *dhr* (to sustain, maintain). It means law; however, *dharma* is not a legislative law but an essential and perennial principle, prescribed conduct, a sacred law that governs the universe. *Dharma* is also often translated as a synonym for religion or to indicate a social duty or obligation. However, this does not reveal the whole meaning of the term. As a social function, *dharma* is the occupation prescribed for each person, the type of work we must engage in according to our nature. For example, the *dharma* of a teacher is to teach, that of a military man is to provide protection, that of a worker is to produce, etc. Such occupations spring from a person's nature. This is the conventional meaning of the word *dharma*. As we mentioned, human society works in harmony when each person fully fulfills their *dharma* or duty that characterizes their natural propensity.

However, in its real meaning, *dharma* indicates a vital, essential, and permanent principle—an essence that constitutes each entity's innate and unremovable characteristic. An ordinary example can help us. Fire can burn in different colors depending on the fuel we use. Although its external appearance varies, the *dharma* or essence of fire, which provides light and heat, never changes or disappears. We cannot subtract the light and heat from fire or water's humidity and liquidity. Without light and heat, the fire would not be fire, just as without moisture and liquidity, water would not be water. The Vedas call this principle *sanatana-dharma* (*sanatana*=eternal), the intrinsic and perennial function of the soul. *Sanatana-dharma* is the soul's eternal religion, transcending all interchangeable socio-religious processes, such as Hinduism, Buddhism, Judaism, Christianity, Islam, etc.

Since God and the soul are eternal principles, the relationship between the two is also eternal. It is not something that began at a particular historical moment. We have the experience that a Jew can become Christian, a Christian can become Muslim, or a Muslim can become Christian, Hindu, or any other variant. However, despite changing their religious denomination, the intrinsic function of the soul as God's eternal servant remains. Such religious designations are interchangeable labels, externalities that do not describe our actual everlasting nature. Whatever type of interchangeable denomination we may adopt, it only speaks of a particular historical moment in which a given prophet enunciated the principles of *sanatana-dharma*, to a greater or lesser degree, according to the levels of understanding of the society in which he appeared. We must not identify the name of a religious-historical process with the eternal identity of the soul. No one is eternally Hindu, Jewish, Christian, etc. For example, Jesus came to this world about 2000 years ago, but St. Augustine tells us that the religion preached by Jesus precedes what we know as Christianity. For him, its eternal essence precedes and transcends religion within the historical framework. Five thousand years ago, Lord Krishna enunciated in His Bhagavad-Gita that the purpose of His descent into this world was to re-establish the eternal religion by then lost. However, the mistaken belief that our existence began at conception is an obstacle to understanding *sanatana-dharma*. The Vedas state that the soul is eternal (without beginning or end) and pre-exists world's creation. If this is not understood, we will believe that our relationship with God began at the moment of our birth and that our conversion to a particular faith determines our eternal religious identity.

Lacking this understanding, we claim to be Hindus, Jews, Christians, Muslims, etc. The truth is that *sanatana-dharma* is present in all forms of religious expression; however, it manifests itself to a greater or lesser degree according to the depth of their teachings. The Bhagavad-Gita, Srimad Bhagavatam, and other Vedic texts present the *sanatana-dharma* in its entirety. In their pages, we find detailed information about the Supreme Personality of Godhead, our eternal identity, and how each soul eternally relates to God in His supreme abode. For this reason, a devotee of Krishna or practitioner of *sanatana-dharma* is called a Vaishnava, that is to say, "of God," "belonging to God," and nothing else. Because the Vaishnava understands the nature of both the soul and *sanatana-dharma*, whenever someone asks, "what are you?" he never claims to be Hindu, Christian, Muslim, Jewish, etc., but simply, "I am of God" (Vaishnava). To be of God is the intrinsic nature of the soul. In the Bhagavad-Gita, Lord Krishna affirms that each soul is part and parcel of Him and, as such, possesses eternal individuality. Therefore, *sanatana-dharma*, or the everlasting function of the soul, is synonymous with *Vaishnava-*

dharma, that is to say, "to be of God." Just as the occupation of the part is to serve the whole, the eternal function of the soul is to serve God. So when we speak of the Vaishnava religion (popularly called Hare Krishna), we refer to that eternal principle of the soul's relationship with the Personality of Godhead (*sanatana-dharma*).

Yuga: The Universal Eras

The Vedas present us with a concept of universal time that differs from the Judeo-Christian version, which conceives time as something linear: creation, permanence, and destruction of the world. In this model, time travels from point A (creation) to point B (destruction). Once it reaches its final destination, that is the end of history, or "the end of times." It is then that, according to their earthly conduct, each soul reaps heavenly bliss or hellish punishment.

On the other hand, the Vedas offer a circular concept of time. In this model, the creation, permanence, and destruction of the universe is not a singular act in universal history but an eternal regenerative cycle. The succession of the seasons can help us understand this cosmic pattern. With spring's arrival, we get the impression that winter is left behind as the days go by, but actually, we are getting closer to the following winter. Something similar occurs with our birthdays, the days of the week, the rainy season, and the life cycles of all living beings. The more these natural events seem to be left behind, the closer we are to them again. Material time moves circularly.

During the period that the universe remains in existence, different millennia or cosmic eras (*yugas*) elapse, each of which has its characteristics. The Vedas and other historical records tell us that human society was not always in today's deplorable conditions. For example, the ancient Greeks and even the Yorubas of Africa tell us of a Golden Age in very remote times when the qualities of human beings were much more virtuous. The Vedic texts call this Golden Age: Satya-yuga, the age of wisdom, perfection, knowledge, truthfulness, etc. According to the Vedas, the characteristics of the people in the ancient Golden Age or Satya-yuga, the first in the universal cycle, were very different from what we experience today—much so that from our limited experience, it can be astonishing. Satya-yuga has a duration of one million seven hundred twenty-eight thousand years, during which human life averages one hundred thousand years. The Vedic texts tell us that in the age of Satya, human beings enjoyed a high degree of perfection, possessed great virtue, and religious piety reigned in all its splendor, while vice was unknown.

The second era of this universal cycle is known as Treta, often called the Silver Age, and it lasts for one million two hundred and ninety-six thousand years. It is noteworthy that during each of these cosmic eras, the duration of life is reduced by 90%; therefore, the average life span in Treta-yuga is ten thousand years. It is in this period that vice enters human society. After Treta-yuga comes Dvapara-yuga, or the Bronze Age, the third era of the cosmic cycle, and lasts for eight hundred and sixty-four thousand years. By then, human life has declined to an average of a thousand years, while piety and other qualities continue to decline until they coexist alongside vice. Lord Krishna manifested in human society at the end of the Dvapara era.

Finally, we come to the fourth and last era of this universal cycle we are going through today, called Kali, or the Iron Age. The characteristic of this age is falsehood, vice, and hypocrisy. The age of Kali began at the time of Lord Krishna's departure from this world about 5,100 years ago. At that time, the great sage Vyasa, the compiler of the Vedas, realized that, in the age of Kali, human beings would be miserable, unfortunate, and impatient, and they would quarrel over even the most insignificant things. Foreseeing the corruption of the human character, the reduction in life span to scarcely a hundred years, and that memory would be impoverished, Vyasa collected and subdivided the knowledge (Veda) to preserve it for the benefit of later generations. Kali-yuga lasts for about four hundred and thirty-two thousand years, of which there are still about four hundred and twenty-seven thousand years to elapse. The Vedas tell us that the living conditions of human society towards the end of the age of Kali are pathetic.

There is a striking similitude between the story of Adam and Eve and their moral fall five or six thousand years ago and the Vedic version of humanity's fallen condition in the age of Kali. This period marks the approximate limit of historiography. The Vedas are not the only scriptures mentioning such a long life span in remote times. For example, the extreme longevity of various Biblical patriarchs seems to corroborate the Vedic version of the average lifespan for the Dvapara era, the era before the current Kali. There are ancient Babylonian historical records attesting to similar facts. The Bible mentions that Methuselah lived 979 years, Noah 960, and Adam 932. Some scholars consider that perhaps it was because, in very remote times, the conditions of life were different. In this regard, the Reina-Valera edition of the Bible, Editorial Caribe 1980, tells us:

> Methuselah is the oldest person in the scripture. The issue of longevity has been much discussed, and several possible solutions have been given; one is that men

really lived nine hundred years or more because the conditions of the antediluvian world were different... Babylonian records speak of men who lived 30,000 years... " (Commentary on Genesis 5.27).

Due to the natural human tendency to judge within according to our limited experience, such longevity may appear questionable to us. The truth is that what we call a long life varies according to species. For example, if we tell a butterfly that an animal called a dog lives for fifteen years, it would seem impossible for the butterfly since, according to its little life experience, fifteen years is an extremely long time. However, although fifteen years is a long life for a dog, it is very short for a human. What is an incredibly long time for some is extremely short for others. Since these Biblical-Babylonian narratives date back to ancient times, it could be that some of these Biblical patriarchs were people who inhabited the earth during the Dvapara era, when according to the Vedas, the average lifespan was about a thousand years.

Interestingly, modern archeology reveals a striking similarity between ancient cultures distant from each other and the sophisticated knowledge of engineering, architecture, and astronomy they possessed. Actually, to the Vedas, this is not the first time that the human race has enjoyed the achievements we see in modern society. Instead, we are another chapter in a long series of global civilizations that succumbed one after another due to natural cataclysms, leaving behind traces of advanced knowledge that today is difficult to explain. However, due to possible environmental and geological changes through periods extending for millions of years, human civilization could resurface from its ruins (that today we call the Stone Age) without necessarily being the first or the last time.

Nevertheless, the transition from one era to the other is gradual. For several thousand years, the characteristics of both universal periods overlap; just like at dawn, there are symptoms of both day and night. First, however, we could ask ourselves why there is an age such as Kali in which we see an impressive reduction of good qualities in human beings. To understand it, we need to mention two universal Vedic philosophical concepts: the law of universal compensation (*karma*) and the transmigration of the soul (*samsara*).

Karma and Samsara

The words *karma* and *samsara* are so well known in the West that they hardly need explanation. *Karma* means "action." For religious morality, our actions can be pious, impious, or a mixture of both, and all of them generate a proportional result that we reap either in the present life or in the next. *Karma* is linked to *samsara*, the continuous rebirth of the soul in different bodies and conditions of life that we ordinarily call reincarnation. The soul or the living force (*atma* or *jiva*) does not cease to exist with the destruction of the physical body; because its existence is eternal, it is neither created nor annihilated. Eternity means without beginning or end, implying that God and the souls coexist for eternity. The pain and pleasure we experience result from our pious and impious actions or a mixture of both. The same is true for the place, circumstances of our birth, and type of body we get. It all depends on our state of consciousness in a previous life.

The succession of *yugas* or cosmic ages also serves a similar purpose. Each of them facilitates the satisfaction of our propensities according to our state of consciousness. Each soul is born in a particular era, depending on its degree of piety. Therefore, there is an array of them, from the most exalted

(Satya) to the most degraded (Kali). The present age of Kali offers an opportunity to the souls prone to ungodly life to express their tendencies for worldly enjoyment. Therefore, those with little or no interest in spiritual advancement are generally born in the age of Kali. However, this does not imply that spiritual progress is exclusive to previous eras or that there is no possibility of degradation. Even though the age of Kali is so degraded, we find people who are pure-hearted and religious; therefore, those who wish to advance on the spiritual path do not have to wait for a specific moment since the Lord guides them from within the heart. Therefore, no matter what age we find ourselves in, there is always the opportunity for genuine spiritual success. According to our consciousness, we can live in the age of Satya as if we were in Kali or turn the age of Kali into Satya.

The concept of avatara

The word *avatara* is another popular Sanskrit term (*ava*=down, *tara*= to cross). *Avatara* indicates a being that crosses or descends from the world of the liberated souls to the material world, whose purpose is to redeem fallen souls. The Vedas speak of two categories of existence called *jiva-tattva* and *vishnu-tattva*. Let's explain. The word *jiva* means "living force," indicating the tiny individual soul like us. Vishnu is one of the best-known names for God (Krishna) in the Vedas, while *tattva* suggests a category of existence. Therefore, the *avataras* are basically of two categories: individual souls (*jiva-tattva*), human beings, or the category of God (*vishnu-tattva*), that is to say, the personality of God himself.

Each of us is a *jiva*, a divine spark with eternal individual consciousness and personality. We should remember that the individual soul (*jiva*) is like a golden pebble extracted from a gold mine. The gold of the mine and that of the pebble are of the same quality, although in different quantities. Therefore, we can say that both golds are qualitatively the same but quantitatively different. In other words, there is simultaneous equality and difference between the two. The same is true of the spark of fire and fire. Both possess light and heat but in different amounts. Similarly, the *jiva* (individual soul) has the qualities of the Divinity, but in a limited way. To highlight this difference, the Vedas use the terms *atma* (individual soul) and *paramatma* (supreme soul); the difference between the two is not in substance but in category (*tattva*). The soul (*jiva* or *atma*) belongs to the *jiva-tattva* or category, the minute individual soul, which is eternally subordinate to the *paramatma* or Supreme Soul, which belongs to the *vishnu-tattva* or category of God.

Just as from the flame of a candle, we can light many others, and they all have the same amount of light and heat. The Vedas describe that as the Supreme Divine Person, Lord Krishna manifests or expands many other forms as eternal, omniscient, and all-powerful as the original one. When any of these personal manifestations of Lord Krishna descends into this world, His activities are impossible to imitate and defy human reason. These *avataras* of the Lord are known as *vishnu-tattva* (God category) because they are a descend of Lord Krishna himself to the physical human plane. However, Lord Krishna often empowers a soul to descend to this world as an *avatara*, just as a president empowers a citizen we call an ambassador with special powers. In essence, the ambassador is a citizen, just like anyone else. Still, the difference lies in that the president empowers him to speak on his behalf, represent his country, and make decisions that are not within reach of the ordinary citizen. When Krishna empowers a *jiva* (individual soul) to descend into this world, he is known as *shakti-avesha-avatara*, a descending soul (*avatara*) anointed (*avesha*) with divine power (*shakti*). These types of *avataras*, although they are human beings, are not ordinary souls but liberated souls who come to the world as ambassadors of the spiritual kingdom or of some other plane of existence to spread knowledge and devotion to God.

Chapter 4

Iconography and Vedic theism

When we look at the Indo-Vedic religious model, we notice the great variety of icons and three-dimensional shapes of different divinities. In contrast, although icons are widespread, most of the Judeo-Christian culture is essentially iconoclastic; it condemns the use of icons or images, considering it idolatry. Thou shalt not worship images is a fundamental commandment of the Mosaic Law. The ancient Hebrews made a radical distinction between spirit and matter, between the creator and the creation, with the result that matter, destitute of all grace, cannot reveal its creator. Therefore, any attempt to worship God through His creation is considered idolatry. However, in the eighth century, the Christian theologian John of Damascus suggested that expressing the divine through matter is possible. Therefore, the authentic form of the Divinity that becomes visible in the world for the benefit of the faithful should not be seen as an ordinary image. For John of Damascus, the incarnation of Christ provided a solid foundation for the use of holy icons since they act as a window that offers us a transparent and closer view of the divine. According to John, since Christ became visible, his form is no more a mystery; therefore, we can make an image of him.

"Previously, there was absolutely no way in which God, who has neither a body nor a face, could be represented by an image. But now that he has made himself visible in the flesh and has lived with people, I can make an image of what I have seen of God… and contemplate the glory of the Lord, his face having been unveiled.[1]

This understanding resembles the version of the Vedic sages.

The religious icon: A sacred form or a pagan image?

The worship of the forms of Lord Krishna made of physical elements is far from idolatry since the similarity that we find between an ordinary image and His visible form is only apparent. Unlike an image that is the product of our imagination, the form of Krishna is an eternal reality. The Vedic sages call these visual forms composed of physical elements *archa-vigraha* (adorable form). These adorable forms are not the result of fertile human imagination. They are replicas of the forms in which Lord Krishna has manifested in this world and whose appearance the Vedic texts describe. Therefore, although the *archa-vigraha* externally may appear to be an ordinary image, it is not.

For example, to the ordinary vision, a murderer and a surgeon are similar: both have masked faces, and their hands are stained with blood; both hold a sharp object, and before them lies an unconscious and bloody body. Despite sharing such similarities, there is a fundamental difference: while the murderer takes our life, the surgeon saves it. Thus, appearances may deceive us. Often, idolatry exists in the eye of the beholder. Even religious societies that condemn the use of icons recognize their emotional value without realizing it since, in their publications, we see colorful illustrations about

---

[1] The Christian Theology Reader, Alister E. McGrath Blackwell Publishers 1995. p150).

the life and work of Jesus and other biblical passages. Iconography is natural to human beings. When the faithful observe the graphic representations of these stories, their feeling of communion deepens. It is hard to deny that iconography positively impacts spiritual awareness. A cross may be an ordinary piece of wood for someone outside of Christianity, but seeing it, a Christian will feel communion with the life and work of Jesus. The truth is that icons, symbols, graphic depictions, and three-dimensional representations that we ordinarily call images function as something more than simple didactic mechanisms.

When we say that God is the Absolute Truth, we acknowledge that everything that exists emanates from and depends on Him and that there is no other source of existence outside or independent of Him. According to the Vedas, the Supreme Lord and His energies are simultaneously one and different. They are one with Him because they are the same in quality, being spirit, but they are also different because God is the creator or energetic source, and His energies are the emanation of the created. Therefore, God and His energies are a single unit. For example, the sun and the sun rays form a single unit, but there is also a difference between them: the sun is the sun, and its rays are its rays. The sun's rays emanate from the sun; they are its potency, its energy.

This means there is equality between God and His creation because all existence depends on God. The is no other source of existence since the whole creation is an expression of His powers. In His personal form, however, God is different from everything created. For the sages, this is not only the proper understanding of Vedanta philosophy but an essential philosophical principle of the Vaishnava religion (Hare Krishna). The learned call this philosophy *achintya-bheda-*

abheda-tattva: God is inconceivably equal to and simultaneously different from His creation. (*achintya*=inconceivable, *bheda*=equal, nondifferent, *abheda*=different, *tattva*=category of existence). His energies are to Him what light and heat are to fire—an integral part of His essence, different aspects of the same entity.

Because of this, the Vedas tell us that, in one sense, everything that exists is divine because it emanates from the Divine Absolute. In His Bhagavad-Gita, Lord Krishna tells us that material energy is also divine since it is part of His self. However, such divinity is not evident to our eyes because we are souls covered by illusion. The human concept of "material" arises when we see things as separate from God and when we cannot perceive the connection that everything has with its divine origin. Therefore, ultimately "material" is not the substance itself but the observer's conditioned consciousness. Lord Krishna describes His spiritual potency as "superior energy" (*para-prakriti*) and the one we call material as "inferior energy" (*apara-prakriti*), and yet He also describes them both as divine (*divya*). The superior energy (which we call spiritual) is immutable, conscious, and dynamic, while the inferior one (which we call material) is mutable, unconscious, and inert. Although they have different attributes, both are divine since they originate from the Divine. It is like a person's right and left arms; we can describe them differently, but they are not different for the person who uses them as he likes. After all, the idea of right and left is human conventionalism. Similarly, the concept of superior and inferior energies is but a description of our conditioned experience.

However, when the minute individual souls (*jiva* or *atma*) come into contact with the inferior spiritual energy (which we call material), there is a condition of incompatibility that makes us forget our superior spiritual nature and, consequently, our relationship with God. Our situation is like that of water: despite having the potential to extinguish the fire, when we put a small drop into the flames, instead of extinguishing it, it evaporates. As a result of this "extinguished consciousness" or state of forgetfulness, the soul identifies with the temporary physical body of qualitatively inferior spiritual substance and calls it material. However, for the Supreme Lord, there is no such difference between His "superior spiritual" and "inferior spiritual" energy; like for an electric generator, there is no difference between the negative and positive current since both spring from itself.

As the source and master of all energies, the Supreme Lord has the sovereign potential to manifest in His entirety through any of His potencies. A well-known example is His appearance as fire in a burning bush to the prophet Moses. If the Lord can manifest Himself through the fire, what makes us think He cannot do so through some other element of nature? Therefore, though made of physical components, the *archa-vigraha,* or the adorable form of Lord Krishna, does not lose its divine nature. After all, everything emanates from Him and is part of His existence.

We should not assume that accepting the visible form of the Lord implies imposing limitations on Him, but quite the opposite. However, if we think that the Lord, who possesses inconceivable potencies, can not manifest His form through the physical elements that are aspects of Himself, for the well-being of the fallen souls, in that case, we are imposing limitations on Him. Since our spiritual vision is null due to conditioned life, it is natural that the *archa-vigraha* appears to be devoid of life. Because the Lord reciprocates according to how we approach His manifested form, only the highest mystics can appreciate the spiritual nature of the sacred form. If a person takes such sacred form for a pagan image, the Lord will reciprocate with a similar sentiment within the heart, as the Bhagavad-Gita says.

On the other hand, if we say that there is an irreconcilable and incompatible difference between God and His energies (or spirit and matter), we forget the absolute nature of God. In that case, we will be trapped by iconoclastic feelings and conclude that devotion to the *archa-vigraha* is nothing more than idolatry to a pagan idol. Consequently, no visible form is worthy of reverence since it limits and offends the divine. The fact that the personal concept of God does not constitute a limitation in the divine nature will be a topic we will deal with later in this work.

Absolute means that the Lord is not different from His energies but also that He is not different from His form, His name, His activities, etc. Therefore, they can appear within the material creation without diminishing their power. As the Absolute Truth, Lord Krishna is not different from His creative energy (which we ordinarily call material), His name, or His form. As we already mentioned, the *archa-vigraha*, or the visible form made of physical elements, is not different from Krishna Himself. The *archa-vigraha* is carved following the specific instructions given to us by the Vedic texts and sages of yore who eye-witnessed Krishna's appearance. Therefore, when the Lord's form is cut out of His energy, by dint of His absolute nature, such form is not different from the Lord himself, despite our inability to grasp it. The *archa-vigraha*, or the adorable form of Krishna composed of physical elements, is only material to our eyes and conditioned consciousness. Its purpose is to allow the fallen souls devoid of spiritual vision a chance to look at, appreciate, and meditate on the eternal form of Lord Krishna manifested through the elements that we can perceive with our physical eyes. The conclusion is that worshiping the *archa-vigraha*, rather than the idolatry of a pagan image, is an authentic means of devotion to His most merciful form.

Anthropomorphism or theomorphism?

Anthropomorphism (*anthropo*=human, *morphe*=form) is the projection of human qualities and emotions onto the divine plane—in other words, to conceive the Divine based on our human experience. For example, if, in our experience, corpulence denotes strength and power, then God, who is the strongest and must be sturdy. If longevity means old age, God, the oldest being, must be aged. Perhaps the most noticeable artistic expression of anthropomorphism is in the Sistine Chapel, where Michelangelo represents God as a sturdy older man. Anthropomorphism is a primitive form of thinking that reduces God into an amplified reflection of the human. The natural outcome when we reject this crude vision of the Divine is *God as the opposite of everything we perceive in the world*—that is to say, the impersonal concept of God: an amorphous, ineffable, inexpressible, unknowable, intangible being without its own identity and which cannot be defined or represented.

However, the Vedic texts transcend this impersonal idea by presenting a theomorphic ideal (*theos*=God, *morphe*=form). Vedic theomorphism is not limited to the concept that humans were created in the likeness of God but that even human society is a replica (albeit distorted) of His transcendental kingdom. Unlike the anthropomorphic idea that makes God a reflection of the human, the theomorphic version makes the human a reflection of God. In other words, because God possesses personal attributes, such as form and individuality, etc., these attributes are also visible in His creation and, by extension, in all living beings. Both primitive anthropomorphism and Vedic theomorphism pay tribute to a visual, physical form. However, a casual observer makes no difference between them and considers them equal despite being the opposite. They are like the two endings of a string that are hard to differentiate when joined as a circumference. Or like the surgeon and the murderer, which appear to be the same at first glance. Similarly, the *archa-vigraha*, or the adorable form of the *avataras* of Krishna, is far removed from primitive anthropomorphic idolatry. The following graph represents this evolutionary cycle of thought.

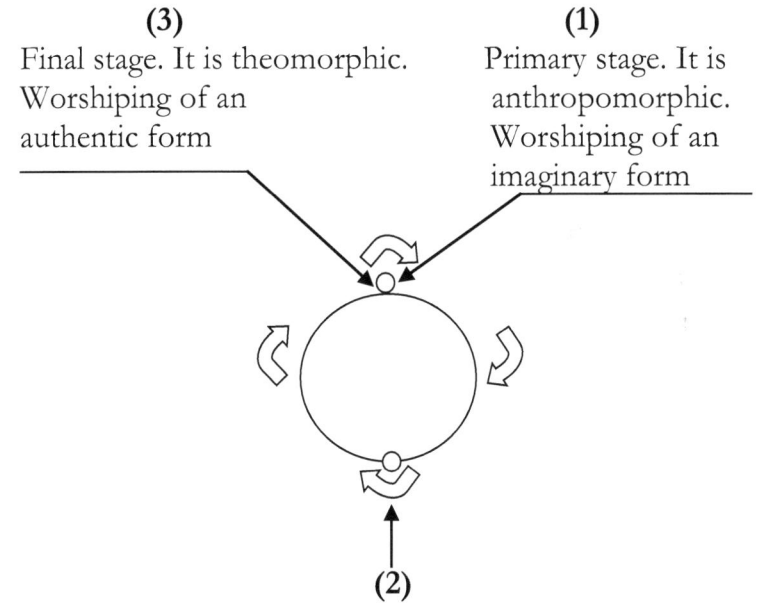

(3)
Final stage. It is theomorphic.
Worshiping of an
authentic form

(1)
Primary stage. It is
anthropomorphic.
Worshiping of an
imaginary form

(2)
Intermediate stage or casual observer. It does not distinguish between the anthropomorphic and the theomorphic. The observer sees idolatry where there is none; therefore, he condemns using icons. An impersonal concept of God prevails.

Chapter 5

The path of emancipation for each millennium

The Vedas and the sages of the tradition prescribe different forms of spiritual emancipation depending on the age and human condition. Meditation, rituals, worship, prayer, etc., in some form or another, have existed in human society since time immemorial. However, when a particular method loses its effectiveness because its proper execution is impossible for the average human being of the age, another path of spiritual emancipation takes its place.

Meditation and the Golden Age

In His Bhagavad-Gita, Lord Krishna tells us that He descends into this world in each yuga to redeem the souls who lie in the darkness of oblivion. Through these descents in His different *avataras*, He promotes the ideal religious process according to the natural characteristics of the era in question. According to the Vedic sages, in this first era of the universal cycle, Satya-yuga or the Golden Age, yogic meditation constituted the ideal method of spiritual elevation for human society. Since the regular human being of this first era possessed exceptional psychophysical qualities and the average life span reached 100,000 years, the proper practice of this rigorous yoga system was possible. However, the average person today, who lives under the demands of modern life, finds it practically impossible to fully carry out the rigor demanded by this form of meditation, which involves living in the forest, minimizing bodily demands, and tolerating cold, heat, and other inconveniences. If we add to this the poor psychophysical capacity of the human being in the age of Kali, it will not be difficult to understand why this yoga system does not fulfill its purpose in the current age.

This meditation system is also known as *astha-anga-yoga* (eightfold system). It is composed of eight levels called by the sage: *yama* (regulations), *niyama* (restrictions), *asana* (postures), *pranayama* (breathing), *pratiahara* (mental restraint), *dharana* (concentration), *dhyana* (absorption), and *samadhi* (trance). A characteristic of *astha-anga-yoga*, spiritual but mechanical, is that the accomplished *yogi* develops extraordinary powers known as *yoga-siddhis*, which defy our everyday experience. In his well-known treatise Yoga Sutra, Patanjali describes the progress and achievements that the practitioner obtains in his gradual advancement. These *siddhis* offer the *yogi* extraordinary powers, like, for example: making physical objects appear out of nowhere, transform, enlarge, or dwarf his body, stop bodily decay, prolong his life span for many, many years, be present in several places at once, make his body heavier or lighter, exercise some control over nature, control the minds of other people, etc.

However, Patanjali recognizes that these abilities are often an obstacle on the path of spiritual progress due to the facilities they bring for worldly enjoyment. Although many great saints have possessed these *siddhis*, many have used them to fraudulently claim to be incarnations of God to deceive the general mass of people.

The rituals or sacrifices

In Treta-yuga, the second era of the universal cycle, the performance of highly sophisticated rituals known as *yajña* (often called sacrifice) became the most common form of religious expression or spiritual path. During these ceremonies, the priest chanted Vedic hymns and *mantras* for the satisfaction of the Supreme. The purpose of the ritual or sacrifice is to realize that everything we possess is a gift from God that comes to us in the form of rain, the fruits of the earth, sunlight, etc., and by whose grace we can sustain our life. Through ritual or sacrifice, the faithful soul offered back to God (Vishnu) what he received from Him to express gratitude. If we act with such awareness at every moment of our life, we recognize our dependence on the divine laws that govern the universe. In this way, the faithful person creates a cycle of offering back to God what he receives from God as an act of generosity, which gradually elevates his state of spiritual consciousness. However, according to the Vedas, this system also declined over time due to an increasing inability to perform all these rituals. With the advent of the third era of the universal cycle, the adoration of the visible forms of Vishnu rose to prominence.

The adoration of the archa-vigraha

Srimad Bhagavatam mentions that when the sages perceived that members of the priestly class continually quarreled, they understood that the era of Dvapara had begun. In Dvapara-yuga the ritual centers around the *archa-vigraha* of the different *avataras* of Krishna. However, the Vedas also tell that human qualities have visibly deteriorated towards the end of the Dvapara age. For this reason, the rituals were not adequately performed even by the most gifted human beings. Lord Krishna, the original form of Vishnu, appeared in this world at the end of the Dvapara era. According to Lord Krishna himself, that form of His is so confidential that it cannot be known just by studying the Vedas.

Prayer as a means in the age of Kali

The age of Kali, the fourth of the universal eras, has a devastating effect on good human qualities. Srimad Bhagavatam tells us that humans quarrel over any insignificance in this age. We all have experienced this reality. In this age, hypocrisy and dishonesty shine brightly, which is why Kali-yuga is called the age of quarrel and hypocrisy. Memory, lifespan, and religiosity diminish to almost completely disappearing. Because of this, in the age of Kali, praying the divine names became the only effective process.

We find this emphasis on prayer in many other sacred texts of humanity. In the Old Testament (Psalm 113.3), King David affirms that the name of the Lord is to be praised from the rising of the sun to the place where it sets. In the New Testament (Romans 10.13), the Apostle Paul tells us that everyone who calls on the name of the Lord will be saved. The Prophet Muhammad advised that the name of the Highest be glorified (Quran 87.1,2). Siddharta Gautama (Buddha) is credited with saying, "All who speak my name with sincerity will come to me, and I will take them to paradise" (The vows of Amida Buddha 18).

Vedic *mantras* (*man*=mind, *tra*=emancipate, liberate) are combinations of spiritual sounds that originate in transcendence. Such *mantras* enter this world through the channels of revelation that begin with Brahma and other great sages such as Vyasa, Narada, etc. They are handed down over the millennia by successions of sages and disciples. Their proper intonation purifies our consciousness and frees us from bondage to the imaginary world because spiritual sounds are different in substance from worldly sounds. We may ask how we can murmur and hear spiritual sounds with our material tongue and ears, but the very nature of spiritual sounds makes it possible.

For example, due to his superior power and will, the king can enter the prisoners' cells; however, a condemned person cannot enter the king's chambers of his own free will. Similarly, material sounds do not have the power to penetrate divine substance, but spiritual sounds can penetrate the worldly cover and descend into this world due to their higher nature. For this reason, a *mantra* cannot be a creation of the fertile human imagination. Although the *mantras* composed with the names of God are the most sublime, the Vedic sages tell us that there are still primary and secondary names of the Godhead. Secondary names indicate His relationship with the material creation, such as the Creator, the Highest, the Almighty, etc. Primary names denote His identity, personality, forms, and attributes, such as Krishna, Rama, Govinda, etc. In principle, any name of God fulfills its purpose of spiritual emancipation. However, the Vedas promulgate that the combination of the names Hare Krishna Hare Krishna, Krishna Krishna Hare Hare/Hare Rama Hare Rama, Rama Rama Hare Hare is the greatest among all Vedic *mantras*.

For this reason, the Hare Krishna mantra is known as the *maha-mantra*, the greatest of all *mantras*. Its excellence is because its intonation can bring the soul into communion with Lord Krishna in His most intimate supreme abode, Goloka-Vrindavana, and revive a relationship that now lies dormant under the effects of illusion. In later chapters, we will dedicate a section to this topic.

The mystique behind the purifying nature of Vedic *mantras* lies in the intrinsic nature of the divine substance as different from the mundane. Material objects are other than their names; therefore, they have no identity relationship. If we are thirsty, repeating the word "water" will quench our thirst because the sound "water" is different from the substance of water. However, the spiritual substance is free from this limitation. An object and its name are identical in the divine atmosphere due to its absolute nature. The name is another aspect of the object. For this reason, the purifying action of the *mantra* is not due to a simple act of faith. It is due to the direct contact with the divine substance in its form as sound vibration. When we pronounce the name "Krishna," we touch the Supreme Lord in His form of sound vibration, which brings the purification of consciousness and the natural awakening of love for Godhead.

The holy scriptures are an example of this substantial difference. However beautiful they may be, literary works and worldly songs lose their appeal and flavor over time. It will become less and less delightful if we ask someone to read the same book repeatedly or listen to the same music. The pleasure we derive from material objects is always decadent. In contrast, the spiritual substance is diametrically the opposite. Spiritual prayers and sacred texts never go out of fashion; they never tire. Their reading and recitation never saturate the sincere seeker, who gets a deeper and more satisfying pleasure and understanding every day. Jesus' Prayer and the Hare Krishna *mantra* have existed in human society for thousands of years. Each day, they offer new light and satisfaction to the faithful and those who continually pray. Every day, whoever examines, reads, or listens sincerely to the sacred texts discovers a new pleasure and meaning because the divine substance is present as sound. The spiritual substance is not different from its names, forms, and other attributes; each is the Divinity, manifested in various aspects. As we already explained, this principle of non-difference between the Personality of Godhead and His forms, names, and activities is the foundation for worshiping the visual forms of Lord Krishna in temples all over India since time immemorial.

Chapter 6

Impersonal monism and Vedic theism

Although the Vedic universe is populated by an infinity of divinities, in the Vedas, we find an inclusive monotheism with a cosmic hierarchy in which all beings are subordinate to a Supreme Divine Person from whom everything emanates, in whom everything rests and to whom everything returns at the time of final dissolution. Vedic monotheism reaches its peak in texts like the Bhagavad-Gita and the Srimad Bhagavatam. Theism (or monotheism) is the acceptance of a personal God who rules over His creation. However, due to its similarity to primitive anthropomorphism, we naturally tend to favor the monistic philosophy or impersonal concept of God in the first stages of philosophical discernment. Hence, these two lines of thought are popularly known as personalism (God possesses personality) and impersonalism (God is an amorphous consciousness). Since time immemorial, the two have coexisted and constitute the two predominant branches of universal philosophical thought.

Monism, or the impersonal concept of God

Vedic theism states that the Personality of Godhead is the Absolute Truth—the only origin, sustenance, and resting place of all that exists. As the Supreme Person and the original cause of all causes, Lord Krishna possesses infinite attributes, such as individuality, self-consciousness, form, and activity, and is brimming with unlimited internal variety. While theism has an expansive and inclusive tendency, monism by nature is reductive and exclusive since it advocates the depersonalization of God by reducing Him to a neutral, impersonal consciousness without emotions, colors, shapes, or activities devoid of all kinds of internal attributes and distinctions.

The Rig-veda and the Upanishads speak of the brahman substance inside and outside of all beings. For the monists, brahman is an incorporeal cosmic consciousness, infinite, indefinite, indescribable, intangible, and unintelligible. It escapes all description since any quality cannot define it. Monistic thinking is not unique to India; we find it in all parts of the world since it constitutes the first step in understanding God. It is natural for the inquisitive human to prefer monistic thinking due to the tendency to think of spirit as the opposite of matter, an amorphous substance devoid of all tangible attributes. In other words, monistic logic postulates that if the material substance possesses attributes (color, shape, smell, sound, etc.), being its opposite, the spirit lacks all of them. The natural result of this logic is the impersonal concept of God because when we subtract all kinds of attributes from the spirit, what remains is a sterile consciousness incapable of creating, acting, or feeling and lacking identity and other types of distinctions. Hence, we talk about the reductionist nature of monistic thought since it reduces the Divinity to the minimum expression: nothing more than consciousness without attributes. Because of this, the monistic logic affirms that if the physical existence is personal, the spiritual one must be impersonal. The essential proposition of monistic thought is that there is only one entity, an impersonal consciousness without any attributes or varieties. For the monist, everything is ONE (mono).

To explain in detail the different aspects and variants of

monistic philosophy would unnecessarily increase the volume of this work, apart from not being its purpose; therefore, we will only mention its basic postulates. Monism denies the existence of attributes in the spiritual substance by appealing to the reductionist theology, known in the Judeo-Christian language as "the negative way," defining the Divine by what it is not. The monists of the Vedanta philosophy (the Vedas) call this process *neti neti*, "it is not this, it is not that." We mentioned that if we extract from a being all the positive attributes (form, color, individuality, will, character, tangibility, powers, acts, creativity, etc.), we end up with a sterile conscience. Just like if from a work of art we extract the colors, the lines, the aesthetic forms, the solidity of the canvas, its texture, etc., can we still call it a work of art? If we describe a person by saying that he is neither white nor black nor of any other color, not tall or short, pleasant or unpleasant, not blond or brown-haired, rich or poor, with no name, etc., can we call what is left a person? Is a king if he has no kingdom, subjects, palace, money, will, treasure, or crown? If God has no attributes, is He God? God of what? The limitation, "the negative way," is that we can spend a lifetime saying what God is not without ever getting to tell what He is.

Another of the fundamental principles of monistic philosophy is that there is no difference between individual consciousness (*atma*) and Supreme Consciousness (*paramatma*). Monism states that when the soul frees himself from material captivity, he dissolves his identity and becomes what he is, ONE with the Supreme Consciousness, just as the drop of water loses its identity when entering the sea. This is because, according to monism, the soul has no individuality. Therefore, the idea that we are individuals is an illusion, a product of ignorance (*avidya*), since there is only ONE universal consciousness without variety or distinctions. Because monistic thinking denies the categorical distinction between the individual soul and the Supersoul (God), it naturally considers that devotion to God (*bhakti*) also falls within the realm of illusion. This is a logical conclusion since if there is no supreme God who distinguishes Himself from the individual soul, an exchange of affection is impossible. To express love and service, we need at least two entities distinguished from each other. For the monistic philosophers, the form of Krishna and His different *avataras* are a temporary manifestation of that impersonal consciousness within the material illusory world. Due to such understanding, monists often engage in practices similar to *bhakti* (devotion to God).

However, it is only superficial or apparent *bhakti* since such practices aim not to love God but to become ONE with the impersonal Supreme Consciousness and thus cease to exist as an individual being. If there is no individuality, there cannot be an exchange of love. This form of apparent devotion practiced by the monists is known as *kaivalia-kama-bhakti*, "devotion with the desire to become the worshiped object;" therefore, it is not genuine devotion in the sense of what the term implies. According to monism, when we realize that each of us is that supreme, unique consciousness, that is the stage of perfection. At that time, devotional practices cease.

Another aspect of monistic philosophy is the denial of the reality of the universe; that is, the universe we perceive is an illusion. Coherently explaining the creation of the universe and the existence of souls without implying transformation in spiritual substance constitutes a challenge for every theologian since change is the fundamental characteristic of matter. Creation means not only modification but also addition. According to the monists, if God creates, He transforms because there is an increase in His existence as he goes from less to more. This would undermine His self-satisfied status since a complete and self-satisfied being would not be motivated to create anything. Therefore, for many monists, the universe's existence is simply unacceptable, which is why they relegate it to the condition of illusion, a mere appearance. This postulate is known as the doctrine of illusion (*vivarta-vada*).

For some monists, this illusion is impossible to explain, while others describe it as a dream of the brahman (the impersonal Supreme Consciousness). Those who propose that it is a dream of this Supreme Consciousness (*brahman*) recognize some internal activity within brahman and call it *lila*. The term indicates a kind of divine game or entertainment, an action performed without any end other than pleasure. The most common translation for the word *lila* is "pastime." According to this type of monist, the *brahman* (the Unique and Undivided Consciousness) dreams that he has become an endless number of tiny particles (that we call individual souls). As such, they develop a false feeling of individuality, but once they merge into the Divine Consciousness after attaining liberation from material existence, they become one with *brahman*.

Other monists reject this idea and propose that the illusion covers the brahman since they consider that dreaming implies the existence of dynamism in the *brahman*, which lacks all sorts of attributes and is passive by nature. For this monist, brahman is *nihshakti* (without creative potencies), *nirguna* (without attributes), and *nirakara* (without activity). To support this postulate (that *brahman* is the only existing reality and that the universe does not have an actual existence but is only apparent), these monists rely on various statements from the

Upanishads, which they consider to be the central message of the Vedas: 1.*Prajñam-brahman*, "*brahman* is consciousness;" 2. *ayam-atma brahman*, "the self is spirit;" 3. *tat-tuam-asit*, "you are that;" 4. *aham-brahmasmi*, "I am spirit;" 5. *so'aham*, "I am Him"; 6. *sarvam khalo idam brahma*, "everything is brahman," etc. Due to their denial of all varieties and distinctions within the spiritual substance, monists are known as *Advaitists* (non-dualists), and their school of thought is *Advaita-vedanta* since they interpret Vedic thought in the light of monism. *Advaita-vedanta* aims to dissolve one's spiritual identity by merging with the Supreme Consciousness.

Vedic theism

Unlike monists, for Vaishnavas (devotees of Vishnu/Krishna who are monotheism), the spiritual substance is not sterile—rather, quite the opposite; it is full of infinite spiritual attributes such as form, personality, variety, color, activities, emotions, etc. According to Srimad Bhagavatam, and as we have already mentioned, monism, or the impersonal concept of God, is only the first phase in understanding God. For example, when we see a mountain from a distance, we barely perceive a grayish-blue blur, but as we get a little closer, we can see all kinds of details, such as trees, waterfalls, lakes, rocks, flowers, varieties of birds, insects, caves, animals, etc. We can even appreciate different shades of the same color, like green birds perching on green trees and eating green fruits. At this moment, we have the whole experience of the mountain. Srimad Bhagavatam tells us that the perception of the Supreme Reality occurs in three aspects: *brahman* (the Impersonal Consciousness), *paramatma* (God as Supersoul in the heart), and *bhagavan* (the personality of God).

Brahman, or impersonal Supreme Consciousness, is often

compared to the rays of the sun that illuminate creation; however, the sun's rays are not the sun in its entirety. To understand the sun simply as its rays is an authentic but partial realization since beyond the solar rays is the sun globe with its shape as a luminous disk. The sages compare the solar disk to that feature of God as the Supersoul in the heart (*paramatma*). The Supersoul accompanies the individual soul (*atma*) in his wandering through the material creation, acting as a guide and witness to his thoughts and actions. It is by the grace of the Supersoul that the individual soul remembers, forgets, and acts according to his wishes in previous births. But when we perceive all the inner details of the sun, it is like understanding God as *Bhagavan*, the Supreme Personality who transcends creation. This distinction between the impersonal aspect of the divine and the Personality of Godhead is also established in the Vedas by the terms *brahman* (spirit) and *parabrahman* (supreme spirit) or *atma* (individual soul), and *paramatma* (Supreme Soul).

Bhagavan, the personal feature of God, overflows with infinite divine attributes and is identified by the Vedas as Lord Krishna/Vishnu. In comparison, the impersonal aspect of which the monists speak includes but a minute fraction of the divine attributes of Bhagavan, the Supreme Personality of Godhead. Bhagavan is the source of both the impersonal consciousness (Divine Light longed for by monists) and the Supersoul in the heart, on which the yogis meditate. The body of Bhagavan-Krishna is *sat-cit-ananda*, "eternal, all-knowing, and blissful." Bhagavan is the personification of the infinite spirit, the Vedic OM (the main sound of the Vedas). He is omniscient, omnipresent, and is not subject to birth, old age, or death. Individual souls are divine because they are minute portions of the body of Bhagavan, Lord Krishna, who is substantially divine par excellence.

Because our human experience dictates that everything personal is limited, our theistic or personal understanding of God is challenging to grasp. We easily succumb to the idea that since, as persons, we are limited beings, therefore, if God had personality, He would also be limited. However, the Personality of Godhead is subject neither to our limitations nor our experience of the world; we should not make our material experience the measuring rod of God's possibilities. Our material form is not the model for conceiving the potential of spiritual forms. Being almighty, *Bhagavan* is independent of the laws of nature. Why should His form be subordinate to the limitations imposed by worldly forms? Because Bhagavan-Krishna possesses inconceivable potencies (*achintya-shakti*), in Him, all opposites harmonize, and all contradictions coexist in perfect harmony. For the Supreme Personality of Godhead, Bhagavan-Krishna, personality is not a limitation but a display of His fullness. If God lacked the attributes that we find in the creation, such as beauty, feelings, activity, form, emotions, individual personality, etc., in that sense, He would be incomplete and inferior to us since He would be lacking something that we possess and enjoy.

Furthermore, if personality and other attributes do not exist in the Creator, where did we get them from? The Vedas describe Lord Krishna as *purnam* (the complete whole). He is everything; He lacks nothing and is the source of everything. Bhagavan-Krishna is always more, never less; He is always expansive, not reductive.

As we mentioned, a canvas or artwork embellished with artistic ines, colors, and various shapes is always *more complete* than a blank canvas. Likewise, a consciousness brimming with personality, form, beauty, colors, taste, emotions, activity, etc., is "more complete" than an impersonal consciousness devoid of attributes. Lord Krishna is not "devoid of" but is "overflowing with" infinite attributes. The impersonal consciousness or Divine Light appreciated by the monists (*Advaitis*) is nothing more than His impersonal aspect. This effulgence springs from His divine body, implying that Lord Krishna is simultaneously impersonal and personal. To know only His impersonal aspect is a partial realization of His totality. We must understand that God is personal and simultaneously infinite. However, we cannot reconcile these two aspects because the concept of personality seems contradictory and incompatible with the idea of infinity. But this does not mean that such a contradiction exists in God since His inconceivable nature makes it possible. Such a contradiction only exists within the human experience due to our limitations. We must also remember that this Vedic theism, as expounded by the Vaishnavas (Hare Krishna devotees), goes hand in hand with the realistic concept of creation, or the recognition that the material universe is real and not just an illusion.

Part Three

The Philosophical Principles

Chapter 7

Vishnu, the supreme deity of the Vedas

Vishnu is perhaps the most popular name for Lord Krishna in the Vedas, so we often hear of Krishna as the eighth incarnation of Vishnu. Even though this is not a misstatement, it is not entirely accurate either. We will delve into this subject later. Those who postulate the Aryan Invasion Theory maintain the invaders brought the Vedas to India and Vishnu with them). Therefore, He was initially a different deity from Krishna, who must have been a god of tribal origin, which the Vedas disapprove of, as we should expect. However, the Taittiriya Aranyaka (a portion of the shruti or "primary revelation") identifies both as the same entity. Others consider that, in its origin, the Vedic religion was polytheistic and centered on the worship of the sun, which, as we have already mentioned, is far from the truth.

We also mentioned that the form of expression we find in texts like the Rig-Veda, whose language hides multiple levels of meaning, results from a very different conception of the world from that of the modern human. Because of different human natures, some Vedic trends focused on the most external aspects of the Vedas (rituals, ceremonies, etc.). At the same time, the mystical traditions read in the Vedic hymns a meaning that transcends the glorification of the temporary universal creation. While for the ritualistic tradition, the purpose of a particular hymn may be the satisfaction of the solar divinity, for the mystic, it is a call to the communion of the soul with the Divine Consciousness (represented by the sun), which enlightens us, destroying ignorance just as the sun illuminates the darkness of the universe.

In the Rig-Veda, we find the seed of the mysticism of the Upanishads. Despite its many praises for different divinities, we see a gradual progression toward integrating all existence into a Universal Being that encompasses everything. For example, some of the hymns of the Rig-Veda reflect metaphysical questions about the substratum of everything that exists. From its beginning, the Rig-Veda (1.164.46) alludes to that one supreme truth which the sages call by various names (*ekam sat vipra bahuda vadanti*). This concept develops into the well-known Purusha-Shukta or Hymn of the Original Person in its tenth and last book. The word *purusha* means "person" at all levels of meaning. The translation we often find as "Hymn of the Cosmic Being" is not a standard or correct rendition of the word *purusha*. The second verse of this Hymn of the Original Person tells us: "All that exists is this *purusha* (this person) who is all that was and will be. Such is the glory of this *purusha* (this person)." The Rig-Veda recognizes that even though this *purusha* is the universe because it is different from creation, He simultaneously exists separate from it. This a postulate is the seed of the mysticism we find in the Upanishads and the theistic devotional tradition of the Vaishnavas; and, therefore, of the Hare Krishna movement. In fact, the mysticism we see in the different Vedantist traditions depends on how they interpret this quote. This tendency of the Rig-Veda towards the unification of all existence—and to see all the divinities as different aspects of a single supreme divinity—is evident in the question that we find in the Purusha-Shukta: "Who is the supreme deity to whom we should direct our offering and praises?" In other words, behind all the infinity of divinities, there exists one supreme divinity who is the monarch of the universe, whom the sages worship, and from whom the multitude of deities, as expressions of His different attributes, derive their names and powers.

However, since deities such as Agni (the ruling deity of fire), Indra (of the rain), Surya (the solar deity), etc., are the beneficiaries of much of the Vedic hymns, some postulate that they were the more prominent Vedic deities. In contrast, Vishnu, who only receives a limited number of hymns, must have been a secondary divinity. However, the fact that so many hymns are meant for Agni, Indra, etc., is precisely due to their status as minor deities who interact with humans through ritual. It is like the less prominent members of a large company's administrative body are the ones who interact the most with the public, receiving their orders and applications, and not the chief executive.

The oldest commentaries on the Rig-Veda, the Satapata Brahmana and the Aitareya Brahmana (1.1.1), written by the priestly communities of yore, whose function was to explain the Vedic hymns, is where we find clearly defined the status of these divinities. In both millennial texts, the sages of the Rig-veda state that among all the deities, Agni is the lowest and Vishnu the highest. The Purusha-Shukta identifies the *purusha* (the original person) with *yajña* (sacrifice, ritual), who in turn is identified with Vishnu as the Lord of the ritual. In the Taittiriya Samhita of Yajur-veda, this identification of the *purusha* with Vishnu is much more explicit. There is a harmonic process that begins in the Rig-veda, which speaks of one supreme truth that the sages call by different names, and, as previously mentioned, the sages identify with both the *purusha* (the original person) and *yajña* (the sacrifice) who in turn identify with Vishnu.

A well-known Rig-Veda *mantra* (1.22.20) establishes Vishnu's position above all other divinities: "As the sun's rays extend beyond vision, similarly the great sages and divinities always contemplate the supreme abode of Vishnu. Because these elevated souls can contemplate that abode, they can reveal it to others." We find a similar statement in the Katha Upanishad, which explicitly states that the destiny of the mystic who controls his passions is the supreme abode of Vishnu, to whom the Rig-Veda attributes the epithet of *gopa*, an essential characteristic that later we will find in Krishna. Some other Upanishads, such as Subala, Taittiriya, etc., use the term *brahman* in relation to Narayana, one of the best-known names for Vishnu/Krishna in the Vedas.

No other Vedic divinity is described as immortal—only Vishnu, identified with *brahman*, the eternal divine substance. The Vedas express Vishnu's unique attributes of immortality through His names: *sarva-karana*, "the cause of everything;" *sarva-niyamaka*, "the controller of everything;" *antaryami*, "who dwells in everyone's heart;" *sarvajña*, "the knower of everything;" *sarva-shakti*, "endowed with all potencies;" *sarva-tisayi*, "the greatest of all;" *yajna*, "the personification of the ritual;" *prayapati*, "the Lord of all creatures;" *visuakarma*, "the creator of the universe;" *purusha*, "the original person;" *urugaya*, "praised with select prayers;" *urukrama*, "the one that encompasses the entire universe;" *vishnu-gopah*, "protector of the universe;" *sarva-raksaka*, "protector of all;" *shipivishta*, "who possesses the splendor of all the divinities;" *sarva-devatah*, "the personification of all divinities;" *ritasya-garban*, "personification of the ritual;" *mahima*, "the greatest of all;" *sarva-vyapakatva*, "the omniscient."

Devotion to Vishnu as the supreme deity of the Vedas goes back to very remote antiquity, although not everyone could discern His supremacy. The Vedas themselves reveal stories about this. This is why the advent of Lord Krishna almost at the beginning of the age of Kali had a crucial impact in uncovering the most confidential aspect of Vishnu, the supreme deity, whose understanding is the purpose of the Vedas. However, in His Bhagavad-Gita, Lord Krishna informs us that understanding His identity as the supreme Vishnu is not possible just by studying the Vedas but by pure devotion of the soul. Lord Krishna also tells us that when this understanding disappears from human society, He descends to restore it. Since then, this doctrine of Vishnu's avataras has permeated India's religious psychology.

Chapter 8

Material nature

We already know that in the Rig-veda lies the seed of Vedic monotheism that fully germinates in texts like the Bhagavad-Gita and Srimad Bhagavatam, which contain the philosophical basis of the Hare Krishna movement or Vaishnava religion.

The personality of God as the Complete Whole

The concept of God that the Vedas reveal is not limited to an impersonal inert consciousness but quite the opposite. As we mentioned, He is *purnam* (the complete whole). As the complete whole, the Personality of Godhead contains everything to an unlimited degree: infinite forms, individuality, names, dynamism, emotions, will, mutable and immutable potencies, and all that is within and without our experience. Therefore, as the possessor of all opulence, Bhagavan-Krishna lacks nothing. Thus, existence (*sat*) and non-existence (*asat*) are part of His self. In fact, non-existence is but another aspect of His self, implying that atheism is the acceptance of the aspect of God as non-existence.

Material nature is one of the multiple potencies of Bhagavan-Krishna and is known as external potency (*bahi-ranga-shakti*). This external or material potency is the distorted reflection of the spiritual or internal potency (*antaranga-shakti*). While the external potency manifests the material creation, the internal potency manifests the divine creation with its limitless spiritual worlds called Vaikuntha (without anxiety), where Lord Krishna eternally dwells in various aspects and forms. Material creation is described as a shadow that reveals the nature of the object in a limited way. The Vedas also tell us that, being a replica of the eternal world, everything that originally exists in the spiritual creation manifests itself in this world, albeit in a distorted or perverted way. Often the sages give the example of a large tree that grows on the shore of a lake and whose reflection we see in an inverted way; that is, the highest part of the tree is reflected in the water as the lowest or deepest. In other words, this world, with its human society, geography, rivers, colors, emotions, feelings, etc., resembles (albeit distorted and pale) the spiritual society of Vaikuntha, the divine world. This spiritual society is infinitely more vibrant with emotions, feelings, colors, sounds, and endless variety. In Vaikuntha, the liberated souls live with great joy in the company of the Personality of Godhead, Lord Krishna.

The creative process

Earlier, we mentioned the monists' objection to accepting the reality of the universe since this would imply a transformation in spiritual substance, which is the distinctive quality of matter. However, for Vaishnavas, creation does not mean transforming the divine substance since material energy is only one of the limitless potencies (*shakti*) of Bhagavan-Krishna, the Supreme Person. As a spider creates a web without undergoing transformation, Lord Krishna manifests and withdraws His energies at will without modifications. This doctrine is known as the transformation of the potencies (*shakti-parinama-vada*). Creation does not imply the entry into existence of a new entity previously non-existent, nor is its creation *ex nihilo* (out of nothing) in the Judeo-Christian sense since everything exists in latent form in the infinite nature of the Supreme Person. The Vedas postulate that material nature is one of the eternal potencies of God, by whose will He manifests it over and over again. This constitutes the eternal process of creation and destruction of the material universes. Krishna is the supreme whole; therefore, the spiritual potency that manifests the eternal spiritual worlds has its counterpart in the external potency that creates the impermanent material universes.

This external energy, or material nature, consists of three distinctive modes or qualities called in Sanskrit *gunas*, literally "rope," which ties the conditioned souls. These three *gunas* are *sattva*, "lucid mode, or mode of goodness;" *raja*, "passion," and *tama*, "ignorance." When the soul comes into contact with these three *gunas*, he forgets his eternal spiritual nature and concludes that the temporary physical body is his true identity. As previously mentioned, it is due to this forgetfulness that the external potency (although spiritual) is called material since it covers the pure consciousness of the soul. The Srimad Bhagavatam, the cream among the Vedic scriptures and the favorite of Vaishnavas, offers a detailed description of the creative process of the material universes, which we present here in a simplified way.

Lord Krishna, the original personality of God (*Bhagavan*), is not directly involved in creation. His potencies and partial manifestations carry out this function. Just as from the flame of a candle, we can light many other candles with similar light and heat without exhausting the original flame; similarly, Lord Krishna expands or multiplies Himself in an infinity of forms that are simultaneously one and different from Him. If we stand in front of thousands of mirrors, we will see thousands of replicas of ourselves that move according to how we move; none of them can move independently from us. In the case of Lord Krishna, each of His manifested forms is autonomous, omniscient, and eternal. The expansions involved in the material creation have a four-armed Vishnu appearance. They are known as *purusha avataras* and are expressions of the personification of the spiritual potency of Krishna. Let us remember that the potencies of Krishna are not only metaphysical principles but also concrete personalities. Since Krishna is the origin of the personality principle, in Him, everything is personal.

The first of these manifestations involved in the material creation is Maha-Vishnu, or "the greatest Vishnu." This Vishnu rests on an ocean of spiritual waters called the Causal Ocean (*karana-samudra*), which flows from His divine perspiration, also known as the *viraja* River, which acts as a kind of border between spiritual and material creation. In this Causal Ocean are all the elements of material creation, also called *maha-tattva*. It is like a dark shadow in the corner of the spiritual sky where material creation occurs. From the divine breath and the pores of this gigantic form of Maha-Vishnu's transcendental body (the first *purusha avatara*), billions of universes manifest in the form of seeds. The Vedas call them *hiranya-garbha*, (golden eggs). Maha-Vishnu activates these seed-like universes with a touch of His divine glance. Because of this, they grow and develop. Creation is also one of Krishna's *lilas* or pastimes which we will discuss later. This Maha-Vishnu rests in a condition of apparent sleep on the waters of the Causal Ocean. This state is known as creative sleep (*yoga-nidra*). Each of these universes is like a bubble. Within them is the cosmic manifestation with millions of planets and galaxies we see in the sky. Inside each of them also lies the second *purusha avatara* that rests on the waters filling the lower half of this universal bubble. From the navel of this second form of Vishnu grows a stem crowned by a gigantic lotus flower on which Brahma, the first created being of the universe, whom we previously mentioned, manifests.

From this second *purusha avatara* emanates a third one that permeates each atom of the creation and enters the heart of every living being as the Supersoul (*paramatma*), who accompanies each living entity in his wandering through material existence as the witness to our actions. This form of Vishnu within the heart that yogis meditate on and who is also present in a Vaikuntha (spiritual) planet within each universe called *Shwetadwipa* by the sages—something like an embassy of the eternal spiritual realm within the material universe. The celestial beings approach this abode, *Shwetadwipa*, praying to Vishnu when they perceive a need for His descent as an *avatara*.

When Maha-Vishnu (the first *purusha avatara*) exhales, creation manifests, lasting for trillions of terrestrial years. When Maha-Vishnu inhales, it re-enters His divine body, the universal destruction, to exhale it again, thus beginning another creative process in this eternal cycle. Because there is an infinite number of individual souls, new souls will be conditioned by material nature; therefore, the "soul bank" is never exhausted. According to the sages, the living entity who achieved a significant accumulation of knowledge and piety during the previous creation but still harbors desires for lordship over matter is born as a Brahma within one of the manifested universes. Sitting on his great lotus within this universal bubble, Brahma engages for a long time in meditation and penance to find the cause of his origin and the purpose of his existence. Brahma receives the sound of the Vedic mantras from Lord Krishna and is enlightened with an ocean of transcendental knowledge in a perfect meditative trance. Endowed with enormous creative power, Brahma manifests the infinity of planetary systems within the universe and the prototypes of living beings, celestial and human, and other species of life that gradually populate the universe. In this way, each living entity receives a type of body according to its degree of spiritual evolution at the time of the previous universal annihilation.

Brahma is not an independent god, nor is he the god of creation as he is often portrayed. Brahma is the first created being within the material universe, a powerful celestial being or sub-creator who designs the internal structure of the universe in the service of the Supreme Lord and whose lifespan is equal to the duration of the universe. During the day of Brahma (twelve hours of universal time), a thousand cycles of the previously mentioned four universal *yugas* pass; that is, four thousand three hundred and ten million years. A similar period is the duration of his night, in which there is a partial annihilation of the universe that regenerates with the new day's arrival. This means that 24 hours of a day in Brahma's life correspond to eight thousand six hundred twenty million terrestrial years. Brahma's lifetime lasts one hundred celestial years, the equivalent of eight thousand six hundred twenty million terrestrial years multiplied by three hundred and sixty-five (days of the year) and by one hundred (the years of Brahma's life), yielding an approximate three hundred eleven thousand and forty billion years for the duration of the universe. At the end of Brahma's life comes the time for total universal annihilation. As we mentioned, the entire material creation and the conditioned souls are absorbed once more into the body of Maha-Vishnu. There, they remain in a repose state until they manifest again at the beginning of the following creative cycle. If the soul acting as a Brahma is free from worldly propensities by the time of universal annihilation, he attains spiritual emancipation and returns to the supreme abode. According to the Vaishnava sages, the purpose of material creation is to please those souls who wish to experience the separate existence of God as independent enjoyers. But how is this possible?

Chapter 9

The genesis of material existence

We mentioned earlier that, as the complete whole (*purnam*), Lord Krishna possesses all kinds of energies, including the energy we call "material," the counterpart to the divine creation. We also know that each individual soul, being part and parcel of God, possesses His divine qualities, although to a small degree. It is just like a golden pebble that possesses the same attributes that the gold mine, though in lesser quantities; —or like the drop of water from the sea, which has the same qualities as the sea but in minute quantities. This means that the living entity is qualitatively one with God but quantitatively different. Let us remember that the Vedas tell us that God is equal to all His creation and simultaneously different from it. Even though we explained it earlier, we cannot emphasize its importance enough. Because the individual soul (*jiva*) is part and parcel of the Supreme, the qualities of enjoying, controlling, and independence also exist in us, although to a limited degree.

How the living entity distances himself from his relationship with the Personality of Godhead is difficult to conceive in our conditioned state since this occurs outside of material time and space. A.C. Bhaktivedanta Swami Prabhupada, the founder of the Hare Krishna Movement, in his writings, talks, and conversations, expressed over and over that before being conditioned by material nature, the spirit soul coexisted alongside the Supreme Personality of Godhead, Lord Krishna, in His spiritual abode (Vaikuntha). However, some souls (very few if we recall that souls are infinite in number) venture to prove a separate existence away from God—as independent enjoyers, which is possible because we are gifted with free will.

Sometime after Bhaktivedanta Swami Prabhupada departed from this world (and even before), some of his disciples approached prominent members of the religious society from which Prabhupada came. As a result, they absorbed a different version of the root cause of the conditioning of the soul. According to this version, the soul never enjoyed the company of God before falling into material existence, which became a point of controversy among his disciples that persists even today.

The Vedic-Vaishnava texts describe the soul as *tatastha-shakti*, the "marginal potency" of the Personality of Godhead because, by nature, the soul can exist both under the influence of the spiritual or material nature. It is like the sand on the seashore that sometimes is under the water and others under the sun. Based on specific texts, many Vaishnavas hold that this "marginal potency" that lies beyond material time and space is permeated by an infinity of souls, like the infinity of light particles that inhabit the sun's rays. Consequently, this is the place of origin of the souls conditioned by material illusion and not Vaikuntha, the abode of the Lord. Only when their consciousness is activated can they choose to rise to the spiritual world or glance at the illusory material creation. By opting for the first, they enter the eternal kingdom of God (Vaikuntha); by opting for the second, they become conditioned to material existence. In short, according to this version, the souls in the material creation at no time in their eternal existence enjoyed the personal association of God.

As we previously expressed, Bhaktivedanta Swami (Srila

Prabhupada), the founder of the Hare Krishna movement, defended his postulate that souls come from Vaikuntha, the kingdom of God. However, in chapter 89 of his book "Krishna, the Supreme Personality of Godhead," he states that the souls belong to a "region" called *brahmajyoti*, the divine impersonal consciousness, the effulgence of Krishna's divine body. In this case, Prabhupada writes:

"The brahma-*jyotir* is a combination of the minute particles known as spiritual sparks or the living entities, known as *chit-kana*. The Vedic words so' ham, or 'I am the *brahma-jyotir*,' can also be applied to the living entities, who can also claim to belong to the *brahma-jyotir*."

Another version of the conditioned souls' origin tells us they have existed within the womb of material nature for eternity. Hence, they are known as *nitya-baddha*, eternally conditioned (*nitya*=eternal *baddh*a=conditioned). Therefore, this condition is *anadi* (beginningless). This implies that, like the previous theory, these souls never dwelled in the company of God.

Again, judging from his words—which we are about to see—Bhaktivedanta Swami disagreed with this idea. Nevertheless, despite that, in his writings, lectures, letters, and conversations, he repeatedly stated that souls fall from their original state in the kingdom of God; at times, he seems to oppose this idea. Let's see.

In his commentary on verse 7.1.35 of the Bhagavata Purana regarding the fall of Jaya and Vijaya, two inhabitants of Vaikuntha —the abode of God— Prabhupada writes:

"Otherwise, it is a fact that no one falls from Vaikuntha."

Also, in the comment to verse 3.15.48, Prabhupada asserts:

"From Vedic scriptures, it is understood that sometimes

even Brahmā and Indra fall down, but a devotee in the transcendental abode of the Lord never falls."

Again, commenting on verse 3.16.26, he also tells us:

"The conclusion is that no one falls from the spiritual world, or Vaikuntha planet, for it is the eternal abode."

Once more, in his commentary on verse 3.16.29, Prabhupada adds:

"Ordinarily, there is no possibility that the four sages could be so angry with the doorkeepers, nor could the Supreme Lord neglect His two doorkeepers, nor can one come back from Vaikuntha after once taking birth there."

However, every time his disciples inquired on the subject, Prabhupada emphasized that all souls originally dwelled in the company of God, rejecting the idea that the conditioned souls never enjoyed personal association with the Lord. In his talks, Swami Prabhupada insisted that this potential of our free will allows us to abandon the company of the Lord if so we desire; otherwise, the term "free will" would be meaningless. The soul's free will is so perfect that even in a divine world, the possibility of experiencing another form of existence if we wish is not forbidden to us. This is the whole meaning of "free will."

In other words, if the soul, as part and parcel of God, also participates in His attributes such as eternity, conscience, beauty, personality, bliss, etc.—albeit minutely— there is no reason to think that this does not include the attribute of independence. Therefore, it is not incongruous to accept that some souls may choose to exercise their free will to experience independent life at some point in their eternal existence.

According to Srila Prabhupada, we never lose this potential, as it is intrinsic to the soul. In fact, being able to decide our destiny makes us individual entities with personal emotions. Ironically, this possibility of leaving the company of God (if so, we prefer) constitutes the perfection of a free existence. Despite living in a spiritual world in a state of inconceivable happiness and satisfaction, this does not make the individual soul a programmed entity that only reacts to stimuli. Even in the divine world, the soul owns his destiny. As a limited entity, the soul is not omniscient; that is to say, he does not know everything—a quality enjoyed only by God. Therefore, the capacity for experiencing a variety of new emotions to enjoy a different reality always remains with the individual soul.

However, the opponents of this version argue that the soul cannot fall from the abode of God (Vaikuntha) because it is under the protection of the spiritual potency of the Lord. Nevertheless, Srila Prabhupada always emphasized that the capacity to choose is intrinsic to the soul. He spoke about the falling potency as part of the soul's existence, as we will read. Due to our minute and fallible nature, to fall is our inalienable right. Often, Prabhupada emphasized, as previously mentioned, that even in the company of the Supreme Person, the freedom of the soul is so complete and perfect that we have the freedom to experience another form of existence distanced from His company. Regardless of how paradisiacal existence the soul enjoys in the divine creation, the soul never loses the capacity for choosing, even though such a possibility seems inconceivable in our present condition. However, this distancing does not necessarily arise based on envy as we experience it in this world, but rather as a young son who tries to imitate his father. This tendency to become an independent enjoyer exists in us (the souls) because we are part and parcel of God, the Supreme Independent Enjoyer.

The spiritual creation is perfect, one of complete freedom. Therefore, although we do not fall due to a lack of protection from the Lord or the influence of illusory energy (since it does not have access to the spiritual realm), we still do not lose our capacity or freedom to choose. The controversial fall of the soul is not due to an accident or external influence but a choice. It is an act of free will, a power to choose, a faculty that the soul never loses. Our perfection as souls does not mean that we are programmed to act perfectly, but rather that we can choose to act perfectly. This brings total freedom to the soul because we can choose our destiny. Therefore, serving and loving are much more pleasant because they are acts of conscious will. As Prabhupada himself put it:

"The subjection of the soul to the laws of a foreign mistress [material illusion] is the result of his own deliberate choice… Whenever he chooses deliberately not to serve the Absolute, he thereby *ipso facto* loses this natural or free state and is compelled to submit to the Divine Will under pressure". (Shri Chaitanya's Teachings pp.447-448).

When we serve and love, even if we have the option of not doing it, such a decision offers greater satisfaction. But, on the other hand, when the soul chooses not to serve or is curious about experiencing a "separated" existence as an independent enjoyer, he first accepts a human body within the material creation.

> "Originally, the living entity is a spiritual being, but when he actually desires to enjoy this world, he comes down. From this verse, we can understand that the living entity first accepts a body that is human in form within the material creation, but gradually, due to his degraded activities, he falls into lower forms of life into the animal,

plant, and aquatic forms. By the gradual process of evolution, the living entity again attains the body of a human being and is given another chance to get out of the process of transmigration. If he again misses his chance in the human form to understand his position, he is again placed in the cycle of birth and death in various types of bodies." (Commentary on Srimad Bhagavatam 4.29.4)

As a human, he can exercise, through his free will, his intention to experience existence as an independent being. But, logically, once in the material creation, this feeling of independence flirts with the forgetfulness of our eternal identity as a minute soul dependent on God. In this state, we become controlled by the three modes of material nature (goodness, passion, and ignorance), a distorted reflection of the modes of spiritual nature (knowledge, eternal existence, and bliss). After all, to fully satisfy the experience of being an independent enjoyer, there is one requirement: we must forget our identity as a servant of the Personality of Godhead. In this way, dwelling within our hearts, the Lord helps us satisfy our desire to experience an independent or separate existence. This tendency toward independent enjoyment is present in us. Everyone in this world attempts to control everything around him in a spirit of enjoyment. It is a fact that everyone wishes, to a greater or lesser degree, to create his small universe with his family, society, or kingdom over which to feel control and ownership.

However, such separation of the soul from God occurs only in consciousness due to our illusion because even if we try, we can never abandon the Supreme Lord. He accompanies us in our wandering through material existence as the Supersoul within everyone's heart. In this way, the soul gradually descends to the most insignificant species of life, experiencing the most distorted and dark forms of consciousness in the forgetfulness of God. Nevertheless, as minute souls, we are so dependent that to satisfy our desire to experience an independent existence, Lord Krishna gives us this forgetfulness as an expression of His benevolence.

In His Bhagavad-Gita, Lord Krishna tells us that He rewards each soul according to his propensity by satisfying his desires. Therefore, if the individual soul wishes to experience the most intimate communion, Lord Krishna makes it possible by offering him knowledge and devotion. Still, if the soul wants to experience a separate existence, He provides forgetfulness to make such an experience possible. This choice makes the soul an individual being to the full extent of the term. Falling connotes something that occurs against our will, but choosing to experience separate existence as an independent enjoyer is an act of free will available to every free soul in a free world. In other words, Vaikuntha, the spiritual creation, is not the world of the "it is not possible" but rather a world where "everything is possible." It is a place of complete and infinite freedom.

Understanding this can be difficult, and as expected, Prabhupada's disciples often had a hard time realizing that a soul can abandon the company of God; therefore, again and again, in his writings, talks, and letters, Srila Prabhupada insisted on this point. Finally, in 1972 this controversy about whether the soul was in the company of God before falling into the material world arose among the members of his Society. To end the debate, Prabhupada sent a well-known letter to his disciples in Australia (addressed to Madhudvisa Dasa), of which we reproduce some portions.

"We never had any occasion when we were separated

from Krishna... Even with Krishna desire for sense gratification is there. There is a dormant attitude for forgetting Krishna and creating an atmosphere for enjoying independently. Just like at the edge of the beach, sometimes the water covers, sometimes there is dry sand, coming and going. Our position is like that, sometimes covered, sometimes free, just like at the edge of the tide. As soon as we forget, immediately the illusion is there. Just like as soon as we sleep, dream is there... Formerly we were with Krishna in His *lila* or sport. But this covering of *Maya* may be of very, very, very, very long duration; therefore, many creations are coming and going. Due to this long period of time it is sometimes said that we are ever conditioned... But after millions and millions of years of keeping oneself away from the *lila* of the Lord, when one comes to Krishna consciousness, this period becomes insignificant, just like dreaming. Because he falls down from *brahmasayujya* [the state of impersonal liberation sought by the monists], he thinks that may be his origin, but he does not remember that before that even he was with Krishna... *Brahmasayujya* and *Krishna lila*, both may be possible, but when you are coming down from *brahmasayujya* or when you are coming down from *Krishna lila*, that remains a mystery".

Here are some other quotes:

"Because we have also come down from Vaikuntha some millions and millions of years ago..." (Lecture on the Bhagavad-Gita, 2.6, London, August 6, 1973).

Srila Prabhupada so strongly defended the free will of the soul at all times of its existence, that even though the Bhagavad-Gita tells us that once the soul returns to the divine world he does not fall again, Prabhupada stressed that he can return to this world. The fact that this does not happen is due to his free choice—one experience is enough!

Devotee: "Well, I believe you once said that once a conditioned soul becomes perfect and gets out of the material world and goes back to Krishna-loka [Krishna's abode] there's no possibility of falling back."

Prabhupada: "¡No! There is possibility, but he does not come back" [In other words, the soul prefers not to do it]. (Lecture on the Chaitanya Caritamrita, Adi lila, 7.108, San Francisco, February 18, 1967.

Disciple: "But ultimately, if we come to Krishna, there's no return."
Prabhupada: "There is return. That is voluntary. Return there is."
Disciple: "If we want."
Prabhupada: "Yes."
Disciple: "So we can come to the spiritual world and return?
Prabhupāda: "Yes."
Disciple: "Fall down?"
Prabhupada: "Yes. As soon as we try, 'Oh, this material world is very nice,' 'Yes,' Krishna says, 'Yes, you go.' " (Conversation, Los Angeles, May 13, 1973).

Disciple: "Why he gave us independence then?"
Prabhupada: "Then… that is the distinction between you and a stone. Because you are moving, therefore He has given you the independence."
Disciple: "… They say that in the spiritual world we say that everything is very peaceful, there no birth and death, there is

no material conditions. So if the conditions in the spiritual world are so nice and everything is spiritually... everything is spiritual, how is it that one can become envious of Krishna in such conditions? This is a very..."
Disciple: "How is it that, if everything is free from envy, free from bad material elements..."
Prabhupada: "Yes"
Disciple: "How it is that..."
Prabhupada: "That is independence. That is independence. In spite of all these things, because you have a little independence, you can violate."
Disciple: "It's very difficult to understand."
Prabhupada: "No, it is not difficult. It is not difficult... Because you are part and parcel of God, God has full independence, but you have got little independence, proportionately, because you are part and parcel."
Disciple: "But in the Gita it says: 'Once coming there, he never returns.'"
Prabhupada: "But if he likes, he can return... That independence has to be accepted— little independence. We can misuse that.... That misuse is the cause of our fall down."
(Conversation, Mayapur, February 19, 1976)

Disciple: "In the Srimad Bhagavatam it says that Krishna did not want us to come to this material world. If Krishna did not want us to come, why are we here?"
Prabhupada: "Yes. You forced Krishna to allow you to come." (Lecture, Bhagavad-Gita, Melbourne, June 27, 1974).

Prabhupada: "Instead of using independence properly, when he misuses independence, he falls."
Guest: "I am sorry, he what?"

Prabhupada: "He falls down on account of his independence... Independence means you can do whatever you like...So, we sometimes commit mistake... Or we are prone to fall down because we are small... Only a few fall down... Not all the time. But there is a tendency of fall down, not for all, but because there is independence... Everyone is not liking to misuse the independence... So everyone can know that independence means one can use it properly, one can misuse it. That is independence. If you make it one way only, that you cannot become fall down, that is not independence. That is force. (Conversation, Los Angeles, June 23,1975).

Prabhupada: "This is factual evidence showing that it is possible at any time to fall from the Lord's association. One need only misuse his little independence." (Caitanya Caritamrita, Madhya, 10.65, purport).

Srimad Bhagavatan 4.28.53

Translation

The brāhmna continued: My dear friend, even though you cannot immediately recognize Me, can't you remember that in the past you had a very intimate friend? Unfortunately, you gave up My company and accepted a position as enjoyer of this material world.

Prabhupada's purport

"This is an explanation of how the living entity falls down into this material world. In the spiritual world there is no duality, nor is there hate ... When the living entities desire to enjoy themselves, they develop a consciousness of duality and come to hate the service of the Lord. In this way the living entities fall into the material world. In the Prema-vivarta it is said: "The natural position of the living entity is to serve the Lord in a transcendental loving attitude. When the living entity wants to become Krishna Himself or imitate Krishna, he falls down into the material world. ... By misusing his independence, the living entity falls down from the service of the Lord and takes a position in this material world as an enjoyer—that is to say, the living entity takes his position within a material body."

Srimad Bhagavatan 4.28.54

Translation

My dear gentle friend, both you and I are exactly like two swans. We live together in the same heart, which is just like the Mānasa Lake. Although we have been living together for many thousands of years, we are still far away from our original home.

Prabhupada's purport

"The original home of the living entity and the Supreme Personality of Godhead is the spiritual world. In the spiritual world both the Lord and the living entities live together very peacefully. Since the living entity remains engaged in the service of the Lord, they both share a blissful life in the spiritual world. However, when the living entity wants to enjoy himself, he falls down into the material world. Even while he is in that position, the Lord remains with him as the Supersoul, his intimate friend. Because of his forgetfulness, the living entity does not know that the Supreme Lord is accompanying him as the Supersoul. In this way the living entity remains conditioned in each and every millennium. Although the Lord follows him as a friend, the living entity, because of forgetful material existence, does not recognize Him."

Prabhupada: "That tendency is there [to fall]. Because we are a very small fragment of spiritual identity, that tendency is there... We are little particles. God is big fire; we are small particles. So, we are playing with the big fire very nice, but there is chance of falling down. That chance is there. The big fire does not fall. The big fire is always blazing. But the small fire, although it is possessing the same quality of fire, it may fall down... Therefore, we have got the tendency to be separated from the big fire." (Tehran Conversation, August 10, 1976).

Prabhupada: "...God has created you perfectly. He has given you independence. You fall down... He has created you already perfect. Because you are perfect, therefore, you have got the independence to misuse. You are not a dead stone. That is perfection." (Conversation, Los Angeles, December 6, 1973)

Prabhupada: "... I mean to say, potency of falling down is always there, potency... And because we are part and parcel of God and because we are now in the material world, it is understood that we have fallen down. ... At any moment we can fall, the tendency is there." (Lecture, Bhagavad-Gita 2.62-72, Los Angeles, December 19, 1968)

"There is a bona fide method for achieving spiritual perfection by the spiritual spark soul and if he is properly guided then he is very easily sent back to home, back to Godhead from where he originally fell. (Letter to Dr. Bigelow, January

20, 1971).

Similar quotes abound everywhere in the work of Srila Prabhupada, who always referred to the process of devotion as going "back home, back to Godhead," not only in the moral sense as some nowadays propose, but in the sense of returning to our original home.

However, based on the first given quotes, many consider that Prabhupada advocated for the theory that souls do not fall from the kingdom of God. They also add that whenever Prabhupada postulated the opposite theory (the fall of the soul from the kingdom of God), it was only due to extrinsic circumstances, a necessity of the moment. Others propose something more reasonable; when an author's words seem ambiguous, the best way to clarify doubts is to ask the author himself. We have just seen this.

Perhaps the term "fall" could be part of the cause of such controversy. However, these quotes from Bhaktivedanta Swami clarify that the "fall of the soul" is not an accident caused by external forces; instead, it is a free choice of the soul itself. Hence, sometimes Prabhupada says that the soul falls, and sometimes it does not. This implies that, rather than "falling" from the kingdom of God, the soul can choose to "abandon it" if we are allowed to use such a term. Logically, in the moral or existential sense, this "abandonment" is a "fall." However, it is not a fall in the physical or geographical sense, as the word seems to indicate, but a fall in consciousness.

However, as the Supreme Enjoyer, Krishna also enjoys redeeming the souls from their state of forgetfulness or fallen condition through His descents into the material world in the different *avataras*. In his desire to become an independent enjoyer, the soul remains trapped within the material creation for millions of births. When the end of the life of Brahma—that is, the time of the dissolution of the material creation comes—those souls who are still bound by illusion enter the body of Maha Vishnu (the first *purusha avatara*) just to be born again during the next creation.

Ultimately, as we mentioned, this "separation," "abandonment," or "distancing" from God is like a dream. When we sleep at home, we are close to our relatives. However, we forget everything around us in our sleep and experience life as if we were in another place. Even if our father sits next to us, we will feel we are one and away from him due to our dreaming condition. Similarly, in his state of forgetfulness, the soul believes that he is separated from God and dreams that he is a king, a president, a soldier, a successful merchant, or an enjoyer within this world. Due to continuous rebirth, the accumulated experiences in the subconscious gradually bring the soul to the point of frustration, a moment in which he begins to inquire about his eternal spiritual nature. Nevertheless, what the soul experiences as millions of births in material existence is a fleeting instant in our eternal existence in Vaikuntha, the spiritual world.

Once under the influence of material energy, our consciousness becomes covered. In this condition of forgetfulness—that we call "to fall"—it is impossible for the individual soul to revive his original spiritual consciousness on his own. Submerged in an ocean of forgetfulness within material existence, we need Krishna's grace to return to our original home. If, after experiencing material existence through millions of births, the sincere desire to return home, back to Godhead, awakens in our heart, we receive the grace of the Lord in the form of the company of holy people, under whose guidance we revive our potential for *bhakti* (devotion).

Then, what is the illusion?

The influence of the illusory energy *(maya)* on the soul is not eternal, but as one of the potencies of Krishna, the illusion is not false either. However, it is nothing more than our state of forgetfulness of God. When we forget that everything that exists is part of God or fail to see everything in its correct perspective, we consider ourselves independent enjoyers. At that moment, we come under the jurisdiction of the external potency of God. The sages call it material due to its illusory effect on our consciousness, thus causing our forgetfulness. For this reason, it is known as *maya* (what appears to be real). Ultimately, *maya* or illusion is nothing else than our desire to enjoy separate or independent from God. However, despite being in the material world, the enlightened soul does not suffer from such forgetfulness, so he does not fall into illusion.

Although the pure soul recognizes the reality of the universe, maya does not exist for him, for he sees everything in relation to its original creator and not for his independent enjoyment. Material energy is another of Krishna's many potencies, and only when we desire to experience independent pleasure does it cause our illusion. Therefore, to the Vedas, no Devil opposes the will of God and snatches the souls away, causing the suffering that we see in the world. The sages tell us that the soul creates its illusion in his attempt to experience a separate existence of Krishna (the complete whole), who offers us the freedom to experience a separate reality. Ultimately, all the suffering the soul experiences in his wandering through material existence is like the suffering we experience in a nightmare, which, although annoying, is nothing more than an illusion and ends on awakening. The Bhagavad-Gita clarifies that once the soul awakens from this dream and returns to the spiritual creation, he never again experiences material existence—for as Prabhupada tells us, he prefers not to do it again!

Chapter 10

The individual soul

We already know that each spiritual soul has its eternal identity, and despite being infinite, not one is a replica of the other —each one has its characteristics. If we are all different in this world, aesthetically, emotionally, and psychologically, we can imagine how much psychospiritual and aesthetic variety exists in divine creation (Vaikuntha)! This is Krishna's inconceivable creative ability. According to the Vedas, neither this world nor human beings are the pinnacle of divine creation, but a world substantially different that lies beyond worldly time and space.

Each soul eternally coexists in a love relationship with the Supreme Lord in this spiritual realm. The Bhagavad-Gita tells us that there was no moment when the soul began to exist. The concept that the soul was never created may be difficult to conceive because existence without creation contradicts our everyday experience. The Upanishads describe the soul in its conditioned state as a tiny spark of pure consciousness compared to one ten-thousandth of the tip of a hair. However, the soul has its own spiritual body in its liberated condition, personality, and identity. In this tangible, palpable, eternal spiritual body, we relate to the Supreme Personality of Godhead, Lord Krishna, in a tangible, eternal, spiritual world.

The spiritual substance is tangible

The difficulty in understanding the tangible nature of spiritual substance is our misconception that spiritual means impalpable, intangible, incorporeal, and by definition, the opposite of material substance. However, the Vedas inform us that spiritual substance is not just the opposite of matter but also has its own characteristics. The attributes we perceive in the matter are but a pale reflection of the intrinsic attributes of spirit, just as the cloudy reflection of the moon in a lake vaguely expresses its qualities. The relationship between the material and spiritual substance is like that of an object and its shadow. The shadow of a beautiful person is also beautiful; however, the shadow only gives us a glimpse of the person's beauty. The silhouette's dark contour cannot reveal colors, aromas, internal varieties, states of consciousness, emotions, etc., that exist in the original. Similarly, gross matter shows only a slight trace of the attributes that exist in spiritual substance.

Although we cannot touch or see the spiritual substance in the present condition, this does not mean that it is intrinsically impalpable and intangible. On the contrary, just as there are sounds we cannot hear because their decibels are above or below those picked up by our physical ears, spirit substance exists in a different dimension than the physical space. Because of this, in our present condition of existence, we cannot touch the divine substance, but this does not presuppose that the spiritual entities within their spiritual dimension lack their own tangible and concrete spiritual form in an equally tangible and concrete spiritual world.

Unlike the physical body, which is different from the soul, the spiritual body is the very form of the soul. Like the physical body comprises material elements, the spiritual body is of the same divine substance as the spiritual abode, Vaikuntha. The form of the soul's eternal body varies according to each soul's specific relationship with the Supreme Personhood of God. The Sanskrit word used to describe this relationship is *rasa*, which denotes a type of delight or taste. By *rasa*, we mean a particular loving exchange in transcendence between souls and Krishna, characterized by each soul's specific feeling towards Him. The sages call this loving exchange *rasa* or mellow. The *rasa* principle constitutes the backbone of all Vaishnava philosophy. Without fully understanding what *rasa* is, it is impossible to understand the nature of Krishna and His transcendental activities (*lilas*).

When the modes of nature trap the spirit soul, he forgets his original constitution, which is required to experience what is to exist independent from God. We then develop the erroneous concept of being a product of material creation. Being covered by a physical body composed of subtle and gross elements (false ego, mind, intelligence, ether, air, fire, water, earth), the spiritual body of the soul is reduced to the divine and tiny spark that the Upanishads describe. This divine spark gradually revives his eternal form through spiritual practice, and according to the degree his consciousness develops, his spiritual identity gradually flourishes. It is like the blossoming of a rose, whose beautiful shape exists latently within the bud. Little by little, it develops until it manifests the fullness of its shape, its color, and its aroma, with all its petals fully open. In this way, when the practitioner revives his original consciousness, he returns to the abode of Krishna, thus recovering his eternal body and his constitutional position in one of the different *rasas* (relationships spiritual mellows) between the soul and Krishna.

Chapter 11

Krishna: The Supreme Divine Person and source of all pleasure

The mere idea of a supreme being generally entails the conclusion of an entity that, by definition, must be inconceivable, indescribable, and, therefore, unknowable. In principle, this assumption is not wrong. Even the Upanishads also describe the supreme as a being from whom the mind and words cannot approach. However, this inconceivable nature is but one of the many qualities of Krishna, the Personality of Godhead.

In His Bhagavad-Gita, Lord Krishna describes Himself as inconceivable. Nevertheless, paradoxically, He also tells us that He can be known as He is by pure devotion of the soul. One of the most amazing excellences of the inconceivable Krishna is His ability to be conceived. If we understand that *inconceivable* carries a different connotation when viewed in the light of Krishna's nature, we can reconcile this apparent paradox. It is precisely due to His inconceivable nature that in Krishna, all contradictions coexist in perfect harmony.

The Vedas recognize that what is not possible through human effort is possible through the descent of divine grace. Lord Krishna is like the sun. Although we cannot conceive of the immense potential of His unlimited rays, we can understand His appearance, form, nature, and character. Knowing these features of God makes possible the expression of the most intimate form of love because when two entities love each other, they naturally want to know each other more intimately. Krishna is not the God who hides His face from us, but one that looks for an opportunity to show it to us.

On the other hand, if the personality of Godhead, Lord Krishna, were indescribable in the absolute sense, the descriptions that the Vedas give us of His divine figure would be meaningless. So also, the words of the Bhagavad-Gita would be wrong when the Lord tells us that those who meditate on Him with devotion can know Him as He is. The truth is that the word inconceivable acquires a different dimension in connection with God. Not being able to conceive the Inconceivable is perfectly conceivable, but if the Inconceivable can be conceived, this is actually inconceivable. This is the true meaning of the word inconceivable when applied to Lord Krishna since, by His will, we can conceive Him, the Inconceivable, by His inconceivable powers.

Lord Krishna exists in another plane of logic, time, and space, free from all worldly conditioning; therefore, Lord Krishna's form, although defined and concrete, is simultaneously expansive and infinite. Lord Krishna encompasses the entire universe and the infinity of existence through His expansive nature. At the same time, in His concrete aspect, He manifests His personal form, free from limitations. This implies that Lord Krishna is simultaneously infinite and concrete, conceivable and inconceivable. He is infinity personified; therefore, He can perform all kinds of activities—however contradictory they seem to us. Krishna's form is simultaneously transcendent (existing beyond creation) and immanent (permeating creation).

In His aspect as the *purusha avataras* that manifest the creation, Krishna is so gigantic that millions of universes in seed form emanate from His body—and inconceivably so small that He enters each atom to the point of experiencing it as if it were a universe in itself. The Vedas tell us that Lord Krishna simultaneously walks and does not walk; He is far and near, outside everything, and within everything. His eyes, ears, legs, and hands are everywhere, and unlike the physical senses of ordinary beings, each of His divine senses can perform the function of any of the other senses. The Vedas also tell us that Krishna sets material nature in motion by impregnating it with spirit souls just with His gaze. Considering all this, we should ask ourselves, what is the limitation in possessing such a form and personality? There is none—quite the opposite. To be infinite and simultaneously personal is to be truly inconceivable. In contrast, the opposite, being infinite but not personal, constitutes a limitation since something is lacking—and where there is a lack, there is a limitation. God lacks nothing; He is always more, never less.

Judeo-Christian theology tells us that we are *imago Dei*, made in the image and likeness of God; this principle finds its apex in the Vaishnava religion. We must remember that Vaishnava theology is not anthropomorphic but theomorphic. It is not that the form of Krishna is similar to the human, but rather the other way around: it is the human form that is made in the image and likeness of the form of Lord Krishna, who is the archetype of all existence. We may wonder why the Lord has a body with senses (eyes, mouth, arms, and legs), something that, being God, obviously He does not need. The answer is that Krishna's bodily attributes are not the product of necessity but His freedom and infinite fullness. Necessity is the characteristic of dependent souls, while fullness is the essence of Krishna. Therefore, we should not try to understand Krishna's bodily attributes in the light of our human experience. Just as a king possesses an immense variety of attire, not out of necessity but out of opulence, Lord Krishna's divine body similarly overflows with infinite attributes resulting from His fullness. Indeed, the Lord does not need eyes to see, arms for holding, nor legs to move; however, this does not presuppose that He lacks them. Not needing does not imply lacking; in the same way, having does not imply needing. Lord Krishna is the opposite of the reductionist idea of the impersonal God with no form, attributes, or name. Being the Supreme Divine Person, Lord Krishna possesses infinite names, infinite forms, and infinite attributes. Let us remember that Krishna is always more, never less.

While in His impersonal aspect, Lord Krishna permeates the entire universe, in His personal form, He embraces His devotee and offers him His company. Although He sees the whole universe with His omniscience, He also looks lovingly at His devotee with His beautiful eyes and smiling face. Just as the rays of light from a bulb spread in all directions, the supra-sensory body of Lord Krishna can see, feel, smell, create, maintain, destroy, and perform an infinite number of functions with any of His senses. Krishna's senses are molded to His will; therefore, they do not exist in Him as a necessity but for the pleasure of possessing and rejoicing in them. Although He permeates the hearts of all beings, He is simultaneously present before His devotees in a concrete way to offer them His company. He can bless all creation simply with His will and embrace His devotees with His divine arms. Although he is the original person, He possesses exuberant and eternal youth. The difference between divine personality and the impersonal concept of God lies in the possibility of personal, loving exchanges. Having divine attributes (and not the lack of them) is a sign of fulfillment. Consciousness personified and full of beauty is "more complete" and inclusive than the intangible, impersonal and sterile consciousness. God is always more, never less. Krishna is overflowing with all kinds of variety, which increases His fullness and beauty, just as a colorful work of art on a canvas is more beautiful and complete than a sterile white canvas.

Krishna is simultaneously ineffable and concrete, incomprehensible and comprehensible, inexplicable and expressible, inconceivable and conceivable. This is not a contradiction but a logical derivative of His divine condition. Although the Vedas tell us that He defies the understanding of human reason, they also tell us that through His inconceivable potencies, Krishna can make Himself understood by the individual soul. At the time of His advent, a little over five thousand years ago, Lord Krishna bore witness to His divinity, and His enlightening words were compiled in the sacred scripture that we know today as the Bhagavad-Gita. As the personality of God (*Bhagavan*), Lord Krishna has unlimited opulence that makes him supremely attractive, though six of them are most prominent to human perception: wealth, strength, fame, beauty, knowledge, and renunciation. He who possesses all these qualities, and each of them to an unlimited degree, is understood to be supremely attractive. The word Krishna comes from the Sanskrit root *krish* (attraction), while the syllable *na* denotes *ananda* (pleasure). Therefore, the name Krishna means infinite attraction and pleasure.

Krishna: the personification of pleasure

Unlike the inert and impassive God of impersonal monism, Lord Krishna is, by nature, a dynamic and pleasure-filled entity. As His parts and parcels, we are also dynamic and pleasure seekers beings. The Vaishnava sages tell us that if the tiny soul is so active despite being trapped in a material body, we must intuit how active the soul must be when free from material entanglement. Furthermore, if so much activity is possible for the tiny soul, we can hardly imagine how active the Supersoul must be. The sages call this is spiritual dynamism of Krishna, *lila*, activities of divine pleasure, or eternal pastimes, which are expressions of this unlimited joyful dynamism.

Krishna's intrinsic character is boundless bliss; therefore, He always enjoys an infinity of *lilas* by which He expands His bliss. By "expand," we do not mean that Krishna is an entity that grows from a lesser to a greater condition like ordinary objects. On the contrary, there is an expansive dynamism in Lord Krishna that transcends worldly logic. His bliss and pleasure are infinite, yet simultaneously and inconceivably, they increase more and more without ever having been less. Everything in Krishna increases permanently without going from less to more like ordinary entities. It is the expansion of infinity within infinity. At every moment, Krishna is more in all respects without previously having been less. However, this is just a little indication of His inconceivable nature.

Our experience dictates that desire arises as a product of dissatisfaction; therefore, if the Supreme Personality of Godhead wishes to expand His pleasure, this should not lead us to think He is an imperfect or incomplete entity. Krishna's desire is not like that of ordinary souls but the expression of His perfection and fullness. In this way, He also enjoys the act of desiring. Krishna is not deprived of any experience. We can say *He desires when He wishes to desire*—that's His perfection. Such desires are an expression of His pleasure potency and are, therefore, categorically different from ours. Desire in Krishna is an expression of His dynamic pleasure; He satisfies His unlimited desires with His unlimited potencies. The bliss generated by this spiritual dynamism in Krishna surpasses the spiritual pleasure of inactive impersonal consciousness postulated by the monists, for it is a dynamic state of divine bliss. Even in human beings, desiring is not always a symptom of dissatisfaction since desiring is the nature of the soul. The spiritually self-satisfied sages also desire, but their desires are pure. A self-satisfied sage is free from desires, yet he desires to do good to others because of his spiritual purity. Desire also exists in the state of spiritual perfection, but it is not worldly desire. The desires that ordinary beings harbor are due to the lack of something. However, we have the experience that sometimes we perform exclusive activities to expand our pleasure.

Although analogies and material examples always have imperfections, they help us understand what we mean if we take their essence. For example, when we go to the beach, we often invite several friends because their company increases our pleasure. The pleasure will increase even more if we listen to pleasant music or engage in beach games with them because, as the sages say, variety is the mother of enjoyment. As parts and parcels of Krishna, we also can increase our pleasure. Lord Krishna is the original source of this tendency for pleasure; it exists in Him perpetually and naturally and, by extension, in each one of us. Through His *lilas* (divine pleasure activities), Krishna and the souls around Him obtain endless pleasure. This tendency in Krishna to perform new *lilas* at every moment is as natural in Him as is the action of burning for fire—that the more fuel we add to it, the more its flames grow, and the more its flames grow, the more fuel it demands. Similarly, Krishna''s dynamism and divine yearning continually increase and can consume the unlimited amount of pleasure His potencies provide Him. Just as the sun constantly bursts the explosive potential found within itself, Lord

Krishna incessantly rejoices in the limitless capacity for pleasure and dynamism in the infinity of His being.

Krishna is the personification of *ananda*, the transcendental bliss that all transcendentalists seek. Therefore, the Vedas describe Him as the supreme enjoyer since no other entity can enjoy at the same level—nor with the same intensity and variety as Krishna. Therefore, the Vedas describe Him as *rasika-shekara* (the enjoyer of all kinds of emotions and activities) and *rasa* (the personification of the enjoyable). As a *rasa*, Krishna is the supreme entity to be enjoyed, and as *rasika*, He is the greatest enjoyer. The sages tell us that this combination makes Him *akhila-rasa-murti*, the personification of whatever form of enjoyment we can conceive.

Chapter 12

Radha and Krishna: The Original Divine Couple

Krishna's spiritual potency (*para-shakti*) consists of three aspects that Vaishnava sages call *sandhini*, *samvit*, and *hladini*. Let's explain. *Sandhini* is the aspect through which Lord Krishna maintains His eternal existence and everything that exists. Hence, we could call it existential potency. *Samvit* is His cognitive potency through which Krishna manifests His omniscience; He knows everything that exists and makes Himself known, and *hladhini* is His pleasure-giving potency, which supplies Him with infinite bliss. Each of these three aspects is an intrinsic part of Krishna's spiritual body in the form of eternity (*sat*), knowledge (*chit*), and bliss (*ananda*), respectively.

Radha: the pleasure potency

These properties make Krishna *ananda-murti*: "the personification of pleasure." Therefore, Krishna's *lilas* or pastimes are *purna-ananda*: "overflowing with divine bliss." His pleasure potency (*hladini*) supplies Him with as much bliss as His infinite being demands. In other words, Krishna's potencies satisfy His endless desires for pleasure. These divine potencies of Krishna are not just metaphysical principles or impersonal energies but concrete personalities like Krishna Himself. His potencies satisfy His infinite impetus for undying pleasure by serving Him just like the arms serve the body. As the complete whole, Krishna is never alone; His potencies always surround Him and assist Him just like the subjects serve a king. Krishna is always in the company of His pleasure potency (*hladini-shakti*), personified as Radha, the young girl we often see in works of art alongside Krishna. As His pleasure potency, Radha embodies the highest love for Krishna. Radha is the feminine counterpart of God.

Through Radha, His pleasure potency, Lord Krishna delights in His self; on the other hand, Radha receives infinite pleasure from Her loving service to Krishna. The difference between Radha and Krishna is that of water and the stream of water. The stream of water is nothing other than water, but when it is in motion, we call it a stream of water. There is no difference between Radha and Krishna—both are the same entity, the same being. Krishna is the energetic enjoyer, and Radha is the enjoyed energy that gives Him pleasure. Both are simultaneously one and different. Radha and Krishna are the potent and the potency—a single being eternally manifested in two bodies to enjoy the original conjugal loving feeling the sages call *adi-rasa* (*adi*=first, *rasa*=mellow).

As His pleasure potency, Radha's body is the transformation of love for Krishna, whose essence is *maha-bhava*: "the highest ecstasy of love for Krishna." Radha is the supreme spiritual gem; Her only occupation is to fulfill all of Krishna's desires. Being unlimited, Krishna continually manifests unlimited desires that He satisfies by His unlimited pleasure potency in a perpetual dynamism. Radha is as spiritual, infinite, and divine as Krishna Himself. Her body is also *sat-chit-ananda* (knowledge, eternity, and bliss). Her divine attributes are endless since Radha is the other face of Krishna, His counterpart, His harmonic opposite, the feminine aspect of Krishna. While impersonal consciousness is the neutral aspect of divine substance, Radha and Krishna complement each other as divinity's male and female aspects. This complement permeates even material nature. These concepts may be difficult to grasp because we generally have a very abstract idea of God; however, Radha and Krishna are the archetypes of the human way of life and everything that exists. They are the Original Divine Couple.

The Original Couple

For centuries, the nature of sexual psychology in human beings has been a topic of interest to theologians, sociologists, psychologists, etc. While some exploit sexuality in the name of spirituality, others have gone to the extreme of considering it the devil's work. Even Saint Augustine, a great pillar of Christianity whose influence dominated the Church for almost a thousand years, was a great detractor of human sexuality. For Augustine, Adam transmitted his sin to humanity through procreation. But on the other hand, there is no shortage of mystics who consider that the seed of romantic feelings originates in the divine. They tell us that the Lord and the liberated souls exchange such sentiments in His eternal abode in their original pure state.

In one way or another, all beings feel attraction to God, even if they do not realize it. We have all experienced the pleasure of being attracted to some attractive object or person. But, as the origin of everything, is Krishna deprived of the experience of feeling attraction to something beautiful? No. Krishna is *purnam* (the complete whole). Therefore, he is not deprived of any experience. On the contrary, Krishna is attracted by all the beauty and pleasure of His infinite self, personified in the form of Radha, His feminine counterpart, who captivates Krishna Himself. In this way, Krishna also enjoys the pleasure and the attraction experience.

The relationship between Krishna and Radha (His female counterpart) is the origin of the romantic, loving feelings between a man and a woman we see in this world. However, it is distorted because its motivation is sexual attraction, which is the basis for worldly passions. The female form we see in this world is so attractive to us because it reflects Radha, Krishna's pleasure potency; similarly, the human male form reflects the original form of Krishna. In other words, the human forms that we call man and woman are nothing more than a distorted reflection of the eternal spiritual forms of Radha and Krishna, who are the origin of the masculine and feminine principle that becomes visible in creation. Radha and Krishna are the original couple from whom all existence comes and the source of romantic love. The beauty of Radha reveals the infinite artistic potential of Krishna by which Krishna captivates Himself. Just as an artist creates a beautiful work of art and then delights in contemplating it, Krishna delights in His counterpart Radha, the most exquisite expression of His aesthetic and creative potential. As Her pleasure potency, Radha has the power to captivate Krishna, who enjoys being the Supreme Captivator and the Supreme Captivated. While His potencies enjoy Krishna, Krishna enjoys His potencies.

In both enjoying and being enjoyed by Radha, Krishna enjoys Himself; therefore, Krishna is simultaneously the enjoyable object and the enjoyable subject—the attractor and the attracted. Radha and Krishna experience the original romantic conjugal feeling that permeates creation through this eternal loving dynamism. However, Krishna is not only the creator of the world but also the creator of the feeling we call love and its different flavors. He created brotherly, paternal, and romantic love to enjoy them for eternity. Because of this, we can participate in such feelings as His parts and parcels. Therefore, the Vedas describe Lord Krishna as *adi-purusha*, the original person or enjoyer. Such loving exchanges in transcendence *(rasa)* constitute the central theme of Vaishnava theology.

Chapter 13

Krishna: the origin of spiritual mellows

Existence has a purpose: to enjoy. Because the soul's intrinsic nature *sat-chit-ananda* (eternity, knowledge, and bliss), the tendency to enjoy is natural. In the state of conditioned existence, this tendency of the soul towards pleasure manifests itself distorted under the modes of nature, which is why worldly pleasure culminates in suffering. However, in its liberated state, each soul expresses its blissful nature in an affective relationship towards the Supreme Person, which, as we have said, the sages call *rasa*. The word rasa means flavor, but there is no equivalent translation for its philosophical denotation in modern languages. As we previously said, *rasa* is a sort of loving exchange between two or more entities.

We live by and for the rasa

The variety of sentiments and affections we perceive in our relationships is a distorted reflection of the multiple ways Krishna relates to liberated souls. For example, we all experience different aspects of our personalities in our daily relationships. For someone, we may be the master, and for someone else, a mere servant or a friend; for our children, the father or mother; for our parents, their child; and to our spouse, the lover. In all these relationships, we manifest different aspects of our person; therefore, each experiences us differently. From all these exchanges of affection, we derive a specific "flavor;" in other words, we savor a particular type of feeling that goes from the most formal protocol to the most informal intimacy.

By nature, the more formal the relationship, the less spontaneous the affection and the more prudent the exchanges will be. The opposite is also true because as formality decreases, spontaneity increases. For example, the relationship between a king and his servant by nature lacks intimacy; the king orders, and the servant serves. The affection that characterizes this relationship is formal since it is tinted by respect and obedience that limits intimacy, leaving little room for informality. However, the king also has close friends who treat him informally, or as we might say, as equals. They call him by his name or nickname, and they may even laugh at him without him taking it disrespectfully because informal affection is spontaneous and candid. In this atmosphere of intimate affection, the king is seen more as a friend than a king because, in the face of the informality of love, his status as king is irrelevant since when love is spontaneous, a feeling of equality prevails. The same person who orders the death of an inmate, whom the subjects respect and the adversaries fear, can be the object of laughter from his friends if he loses a game or trips and falls. This type of relationship is more pleasant than the strictly formal one since it allows the open expression of affective emotions without the restrictions imposed by formalities. We all prefer a good friend more than a good servant.

Leaving the realm of brotherly love, we find the *rasa* or "flavor" of paternal affection, also characterized by spontaneous love. No matter how powerful the king is, his parents will always see him as their beloved son, admonish him if they think it necessary, and always treat him with fatherly affection. His prestigious and influential status is irrelevant to them since the spontaneity of parental love transcends all formality. Before his parents, the king ceases to be the king and is simply their son.

Similarly, the king's sons will climb on his shoulders, pull his hair, eat from his plate, etc., regardless of his exalted position. The fact that his father is the much-feared king does not restrict his informal and spontaneous love for him. In other words, in the privacy of the home, the king is not the king, but another family member, since spontaneous and intimate love by nature overshadows all formalities. So what about conjugal love? Even more than any other form of affection, conjugal love does not recognize barriers or protocol. Lovers can touch any part of their bodies at will, taunt each other, blame each other for their conduct, and even treat each other with disdain naturally. In their home environment, the relationship between the two is so intimate that the queen is nothing more than a wife and the king is simply her husband. Out of love for her, the mighty king, speaking words of repentance, begs her forgiveness after a conjugal quarrel. Intimate love is so pleasant that we discard the sense of superiority to preserve it. The truth is that each affective relationship offers a different flavor. Like ice cream with its varieties of flavors, love offers us different tastes by combining the various affection that expresses other aspects of our personality.

We already mentioned that these various forms of affection (*rasa*) originate in transcendence, where they are shared between liberated souls and Lord Krishna. Because Krishna is the origin of all variety of feelings, each soul experiences Him according to their particular relationship. As the original enjoyer of all forms of love, there is no emotion that Krishna is unaware of and has not already enjoyed before we experience it. However, unlike the divine world where Krishna is the center of everything, each of us tries to be the center of the existential orbit surrounding us in this material world. In the divine world, Vaikuntha, Lord Krishna (as the original enjoyer), is the center of that transcendental society of which this world is but a pale reflection. In Vaikuntha, each soul has a specific affective relationship with Him, while in the case of souls trapped by material existence, this relationship lies in oblivion. In such a condition, we seek satisfaction in enjoying a variety of *rasas* or distorted affective relationships in a temporary world. Our search for the many forms of pleasure reveals our longing to enjoy rasa. The joy that we derive from the exchanges of these affections gives meaning to our lives. For this purpose, we devise a great variety of activities, designs, fashions, music, etc. If these "flavors" did not exist, we would not be interested in anything. They give meaning to our life. Ultimately, we live by and for pleasure. Our life is a continuous search for different varieties of rasa or pleasures that we derive from the affective exchanges with the world around us.

The temporary reflection of the original *rasa* cannot bring us permanent satisfaction since the pleasure we derive from worldly relationships gradually wanes and loses its appeal. If we repeatedly read the same literary work or listen to the same song, the pleasure will decay; that is the nature of this world. The mundane *rasa* causes saturation and is ever-decreasing. It often ends in significant disagreements since it is not a *rasa* in the real sense of the word but only a distorted reflection of it—a shadow of the original *rasa* that each soul shares with the Lord. However, the spiritual *rasa* continuously increases since the more refined feelings are the longer-lasting ones. Mental pleasures are more extensive and exquisite than corporal ones; intellectual pleasures are superior to mental ones, and spiritual pleasures surpass all in quality since they maintain their freshness and are ever-increasing. The more we cultivate the soul's activities, the higher the taste or pleasure we develop. Faithful persons can read sacred texts throughout their lives, and instead of being satiated, their pleasure and understanding increase with time.

Chapter 14

The form of Krishna invites us to spontaneous love

Although Lord Krishna is one, He manifests Himself in an infinity of forms that are qualitatively equal to the original form. His form as Vishnu, mentioned in the Rig-veda and venerated by certain Vaishnavas as their supreme deity, is easily distinguished by His four-armed appearance, holding a disk, a mallet, a lotus flower, and a conch. The different *avataras* of Krishna descend into this world through His Vishnu feature; hence, we often hear that Krishna is the eighth incarnation of Vishnu. However, in the Srimad Bhagavatam, Lord Krishna is described as the original Vishnu, and the sages confirm Him as *avatari* (the source of *avataras*).

According to Bhagavad-Gita, the original form of Krishna is confidential even to the four Vedas. Because Lord Krishna is the archetype of the human form, His form is similar to the human (although, as we explained above, it is the human form that resembles the form of Krishna). While His appearance as Vishnu (which is Krishna's formal and solemn mood) by nature inspires obedience to the Almighty God, the human-like form of Krishna naturally invites us to spontaneous love.

What do we mean when we say that Vishnu is the formal aspect of Krishna? A.C. Bhaktivedanta Swami, the founder of the Hare Krishna Movement, gave the analogy of the president in his home and the president in his office to help us understand the intrinsic difference between the original form

(Krishna) and His manifestations as the four-armed Vishnu. Most of us have a distant and unfamiliar experience with the person who occupies the position of president. Our relationship with him is so remote and formal that we can hardly say it is a relationship. His presidential sash and entourage of ministers, ambassadors, and cabinet inspire power and solemnity. Undoubtedly, this image of the president in his office is the most common and the one that we all immediately recognize.

Nevertheless, the president has another aspect of his personality that is more intimate and rarely seen by most people: the president in his home, an aspect known only to his closest confidants. As we already explained, this confidential environment has no solemnity or protocol. Here the president is one more member among his relatives and friends. Following this analogy, we can say that the form of Krishna is His aspect of "God at home," where an intimate atmosphere of spontaneous love reigns, while His aspect as Vishnu is "God in his office," that of the Almighty God, creator of the universe.

Krishna: the intimate aspect of God

The example of the king we previously mentioned helps us understand that no matter how powerful and revered a person may be in the eyes of the world, in his environment of relatives and close friends, he will always be treated with informality. However, his subjects rarely perceive such exchanges. Therefore, the Bhagavad-Gita tells us that the form of Krishna is difficult to see even for celestial beings, what to speak of human sages!

The concept of God as a powerful being engaged in the creation and maintenance of the world is but a minute description of Krishna's character, for He is by nature cheerful, dynamic, and humorous, and His human-like form inspires feelings of spontaneity. In Krishna, we also find specific attributes unique to His person. The sages describe them as *rupa-madhuri*, His lovely form; *venu-madhuri*, His lovely flute; *lila-madhuri*, the sweetness of His pastimes; and *guna-madhuri*, the sweetness of His divine attributes. More than with His immeasurable power, Krishna enchants His devotees with His unique qualities that awake spontaneous love. After leaving this world, the souls who attain such spontaneous love enjoy Krishna's company in His supreme abode, Goloka-Vrindavanad. Those whose devotion is still tinged with reverential sentiment generally ascend to the abodes of Vishnu called Vaikuntha.

Krishna's abode

Beyond the divine effulgence on which monists meditate is the eternal abode of the personality of God, Lord Krishna, in which He perpetually dwells in the company of the perfect souls. The Bhagavad-Gita gives us the analogy of a tree whose roots extend upward and its branches downward, indicating that the material creation is a distorted or inverted reflection of the original spiritual creation. As we have already explained, the spiritual substance has attributes, but its dimension of existence lies outside material time and space. Therefore, the spiritual world is not intangible or ethereal but a pure, palpable, and concrete spirit. It is a world of eternal bliss, vibrant and brimming with infinite shapes, colors, smells, solidity, emotions, etc. In fact, practically everything we see in this world, in its essence, has its original counterpart in the spiritual world. The spiritual world (Krishna's abode) is a mystical realm challenging to understand because it defies our worldly experience and defeats the imagination of the most creative minds. The laws and logic governing Krishna's abode differ from those governing material creation.

The supreme abode of Krishna (Goloka-Vrindavana) is also known as Gokula, Goloka, Vrindavana, etc. It is a divine pastoral realm that inspires sentiments of spontaneous and informal relationships. Goloka-Vrindavana is the pinnacle of spiritual creation and reigns supreme among the infinite Vaikuntha spiritual abodes where the different four-armed Vishnu forms dwell. Unlike this world which is a temporary creation of material potency, Vrindavana is a creation of the spiritual or internal potency of Krishna. Everything there is pure consciousness; therefore, the trees, the land, the rivers, the grass, etc., are conscious entities. The inhabitants of this spiritual world are liberated souls who eternally exist in their divine bodies brimming with eternity, knowledge, and bliss. Even Vrindavana's animals are not ordinary beings. Their consciousness is not covered by profound ignorance as we see it in this world. They are pure souls who have assumed such forms at will to give pleasure to Lord Krishna as pets or objects of His affection according to their innate spiritual *rasa* or mellow. The only similarity that the animals of Goloka-Vrindavana share with those of this world is their external appearance since everything that exists there is pure consciousness. Regardless of its outward appearance, in Goloka-Vrindavana, everything speaks, feels, and vibrates with life so that all entities can express and share sublime feelings. In Vrindavana, each tree is a wish tree. The ground is divine spiritual gems. The water is like nectar. Each word is a song, each step a dance, and the atmosphere overflows with divine bliss, and all entities are highly delightful. Worldly time is conspicuous by its absence, so there is no past or future as experienced in this world since existence is a continuous present. We are sentient beings because we are a fraction of the substance that makes up that divine world.

While Vaikuntha, Vishnu's abode, is attained by following the regulated practices of devotion (*bhakti*), Vrindavana, the supreme abode of Krishna, is reached only by spontaneous devotion (*raganuga-bhakti*)—that is, by souls who develop a type of love and devotion that goes beyond conventional religion. In Vrindavana, Lord Krishna eternally manifests as a divine cowherd boy whose beauty defies human imagination. Srimad Bhagavatam tells us that His body's hue is like blue sapphire, blue lotus, or dark clouds laden with water. His eyes are like the petals of the lotus, and His eternal appearance is that of an ever-fresh young teenager whose beauty invites romantic love. In this idyllic pastoral setting, Krishna likes to decorate His head with peacock feathers and bunches of wildflowers from the forests of Vrindavana for the pleasure of His associates. His lips have the hue of a ruby. His teeth are like a row of pearls, and His curly jet-black hair falls on His cheeks, decorating His ever-smiling face. The fingers of His pink-palmed hands, softer than rose petals, are decorated with divine gems and hold a flute. All articles related to Krishna, be it His jewels, garments, name, etc., are of the same divine substance as His self since they are manifestations of His spiritual potency. As a young cowherd boy in the divine forests of Vrindavana, this aspect of Krishna invites informal and spontaneous love, specifically romantic conjugal love. However, we can appreciate Krishna's beauty depending on our degree of love and devotion. That's a mystery!

Yoga-maya: the spiritual illusion

In that pastoral environment of Goloka-Vrindavana's forests,

Lord Krishna freely expresses Himself as the ideal son, friend, and lover to the souls who have attained a spontaneous love relationship with Him. In this exchange of love, such souls do not perceive him as Almighty God in the same way that the king's friends and relatives do not perceive him as such in their home. In turn, Krishna reciprocates this spontaneous love with the same taste (*rasa*) with which each soul approaches Him. But how can a soul in communion with Krishna ever forget His status as Almighty God? This is possible by an aspect of Krishna's internal potency known as *yoga-maya*, the illusory spiritual potency which governs the spiritual realm.

The illusory energy (*maya*) that causes the soul's forgetfulness and separation from God is the mundane counterpart of *yoga-maya*, the illusory spiritual potency whose function is to unite the soul more intimately with Krishna (*yoga*=union, *maya*=illusion). If knowledge of Krishna as the Supreme God prevails, the feelings of awe and reverence restrain the natural flow of spontaneous love. However, under the influence of *yoga-maya*, Krishna's identity as the Almighty God is either unknown or irrelevant to the liberated soul. Thus sprouts the spontaneous love for Krishna free from awe and reverence. Only selected enlightened souls touched by the Divine Grace can attain this state of forgetfulness or "divine ignorance." *Yoga-maya* links the soul so intimately with Krishna that it blinds the perception of His infinite power and opulence. It is like the eyelid; it is so close to the pupil that it cannot see it.

Although during their life in this world, the souls who attained the abode of Vrindavana were sages in full knowledge of the position of Krishna as the Almighty God, under the effect of *yoga-maya* in the spiritual world, they are not aware of His supremacy. Hence, in Goloka-Vrindavana, Krishna does not express as the Supreme God but simply as the most beautiful of the cowherd boys, the most attractive adolescent, the best of friends, the most beloved son, and the best of lovers, in a natural, divine and rural environment ideal for love free of formalities. In that inner realm of Vrindavana, Krishna is also known as Govinda, for He gives infinite pleasure to the divine senses of the soul. Govinda-Krishna is the life of the inhabitants of Vrindavana, who love Him without any trace of awe and reverence. This pastoral setting of Vrindavana and Krishna's appearance as the eternally divine playful cowherd boy provides the appropriate psychological background for spontaneous affectionate relationships.

Chapter 15

Krishna: the source of the varieties of affections

We already mentioned that the various sentiments and affections we experience in this world originate in transcendence as an exchange of love between the liberated souls and the Personality of Godhead, Lord Krishna. Lord Krishna lies at the center of these loving exchanges as the axis around which all existence revolves. As such, He relates with the pure souls expressing different aspects of His personality according to the specific *rasa* (loving affection) in which each soul manifests attraction for Him.

The most prominent of these love exchanges in transcendence *(rasa)*, which the sages call spiritual mellows, are *santa-rasa* (neutrality), *dasya-rasa* (servitude), *sakhya-rasa* (brotherly love), *vatsalya-rasa* (paternal love) and *sringara-rasa* (conjugal love). The perfect souls experience each one with greater or lesser intensity. These five *rasas* are known as primary *rasas* because seven other *rasas* considered secondary are subordinate to the five primary ones. As part of its eternal essence, each soul participates in one of these five *rasas* with the Personality of Godhead—one that is natural to them according to their unique constitution and from which we derive infinite pleasure. It is natural for us to long for the ideal friend, parent, lover, servant, etc., because Krishna is the perfect friend, father, son, and lover of each soul. We all have a particular *rasa* (relationship of affection) with Lord Krishna that is intrinsic to our existence.

All these different relationships with God (*rasa*) are possible since Lord Krishna is not only the personification and the enjoyer of *rasa*, but He reciprocates with a similar sentiment in which each soul feels attraction for Him. Moreover, the Bhagavad-Gita tells us that this reciprocity extends to all souls in their measure. Therefore, even those who approach Him within another religious model and atheists who attempt to deny His existence, to satisfy them, Krishna offers them forgetfulness.

Krishna is *rasa-murti* (the personification of affective exchanges). The essence of these loving exchanges is *prema*, pure love; therefore, Krishna is also *prema-murti* (the personification of love). Krishna enjoys different kinds of prema through different *rasas*. *Rasa* and *prema* always go hand in hand. Due to His intense desire to enjoy *rasa*, when Krishna deposits this *prema* in the devotee's heart, *prema* acquires such a peculiar flavor that it is mysteriously much more attractive to Krishna Himself. A great Vaishnava sage has given us the example of the flute and the flute player. The flute player can whistle by expelling air; however, when it passes through the inside of the flute and comes out through its holes, it emits a much more pleasing sound even to the flute player himself. Similarly, when *prema* springs up in the devotee's heart, it is much more enjoyable to Krishna Himself.

Since material creation is an inverted or distorted reflection of the eternal world, we experience these *rasas* in a distorted way; at its center lies not the Personality of Godhead but each of us. Because we temporarily assume the position of master, father, friend, lover, etc., *rasa* takes on a selfish character. In this world, we try to enjoy such *rasas* imitating the Personality of Godhead, the creator of the different flavors of love and the original enjoyer. In other words, we falsely assume the position of the enjoyer.

Santa-rasa: neutral affection

Santa-rasa is a mild feeling of love for God, so it is called neutral. The Sanskrit word *santa* means "calm, equanimous, peaceful," etc. Rather than a dynamic relationship with a flow of affective exchanges with the Personality of Godhead, *santa-rasa* is a feeling of admiration for His glory, power, greatness, and majesty. Although a type of *rasa*, it is hardly *rasa* in the term's complete sense. The simile of *santa-rasa* in ordinary life is the admiration we feel when seeing a powerful or famous person with whom we do not have a personal relationship. Even if we occasionally talk to the person, this is not an actual relationship since it does not go beyond the admiration of his qualities. Because Vrindavana, the supreme abode of Krishna, is the realm of spontaneous love, there is hardly any room for this type of *rasa*, at least in its pure state; however, this does not imply that *santa-rasa* is ordinary.

Most human beings, and even great thinkers and pious souls, have little knowledge of the personal attributes of God, much less are they aware of their specific relationship or *rasa* with Krishna. Therefore, such admiration for the divine, while worthy, is generally limited to the impersonal concept of God. This understanding is undoubtedly remarkable, but it is still only a hint of *santa-rasa* in its fullness. It is when we become more aware of the personal aspect of God that *santa-rasa* matures and a feeling of admiration for His identity and personal attributes arises. Because *santa-rasa* lacks dynamism (*santa*=calm, peaceful), it is not what we may call a relationship as such, but rather an admiration of the infinite glory of the Supreme Person. In its most embryonic state, *santa-rasa* is the foundation of spiritual consciousness.

Dasya-rasa: the affection in servitude

By becoming aware of the greatness of the Personality of Godhead, it is natural for the tiny soul to develop a feeling of servitude that matures through spiritual practice. The souls who identify with this *rasa* attain the Lord's company as personal servants in one of His eternal abodes after leaving this world. Like the other *rasas*, this relationship of servitude can be of a lesser or greater intimacy. In the case of the inhabitants of the Vaikuntha worlds (the abodes of Vishnu), this sentiment is characterized by a sort of formality since, although they live immersed in an ocean of bliss, they are aware that Lord Vishnu is the Almighty God. This naturally restrains the spontaneous affection since Vaikuntha is the abode of reverential love for God.

Although the term Vaikuntha is often used to indicate spiritual worlds in general; however, it explicitly denotes the spiritual abodes where Krishna's forms, as the four-armed Vishnu, predominate. Therefore, Vaikuntha is also called Vishnu-loka (*loka*=planet, abode). The most prominent characteristic of Vaikuntha (or Vishnu-*loka*) is *aishvarya* (divine opulence). There, Lord Vishnu reigns as the Almighty Supreme God, surrounded by immeasurable opulence. Vaikuntha is a paradise. It is the supreme destination of emancipated souls. In this divine realm, the perfect souls live eternally in perfect bliss in an idyllic spiritual society. Human society is nothing more than a distorted and corrupted reflection. The English word paradise is a cognate of the Sanskrit term *paradesha* (*para*=supreme, *desha*=place), the supreme destiny of souls. The Srimad Bhagavatam (2.9.11,12) gives us a description of the inhabitants of Vaikuntha that defies worldly imagination:

> "The inhabitants of the Vaikuntha planets are described as having a glowing sky-bluish complexion. Their eyes resemble lotus flowers, their dress is of yellowish color, and their bodily features are very attractive. They are just the age of growing youths. They all have four hands. They are all nicely decorated with pearl necklaces with ornamental medallions, and they all appear to be effulgent. Some are effulgent like coral and diamonds in complexion and have garlands on their heads, blooming like lotus flowers, and some wear earrings."

Those who achieve a great cumulus of religious piety or devotion to Vishnu are promoted to the kingdom of Vaikuntha after abandoning material existence. The joy and bliss of the paradisiacal life in Vaikuntha are impossible to describe. The fact that Vaikuntha is eternally free from the calamities that plague us in material existence is only a speck of its glory. The sages tell us that if we imagine an ideal living condition in this world or the celestial world and multiply it an infinity of times, we still cannot conceive the bliss of the inhabitants of Vaikuntha in the company of Vishnu, the Supreme Divine Person and Laxmi-devi, His pleasure potency and female counterpart. Vishnu, the formal and majestic aspect of Krishna, is also known as Narayana (the resting place of all beings); similarly, Laxmi-devi is the formal and opulent aspect of Radha in Vaikuntha. Laxmi-Narayana is the form of Radha and Krishna that eternally dwell in the Vaikuntha worlds, whose spiritual society is infinitely more vibrant, perfect, and colorful than a human society with its countless imperfections. The mere fact of perpetual life in the divine atmosphere of Vaikuntha, contemplating the glory of Laxmi-Narayana, where everything is a manifestation of Vishnu's internal spiritual potency and, therefore, a conscious entity—it is a joy that goes beyond the ingenuity of human imagination. Each time Laxmi-Narayana cast their glance on the inhabitants of Vaikuntha, it plunges them into an ocean of transcendental bliss.

Because *dasya-rasa* (the mood servitude) is the essence of every soul, it does exist in Goloka-Vrindavana, the abode of Krishna (the supreme Vaikuntha), but not as we find it in Vaikuntha. In Goloka-Vrindavana, *dasya-rasa* exists as a support or background since everyone is engaged in Krishna's service, although with different moods or *rasas*. Nevertheless, in that supreme realm, the mood of servitude is overshadowed by the spontaneous love that springs from the forgetfulness of Krishna's position as the Supreme Divinity caused by the action of *yoga-maya*. Laxmi-Narayana associates in Vaikuntha are their blissful servants in every sense of the word; however, in Goloka-Vrindavana, many of Krishna's servants, like His intimate friends, serve Him in a childlike mood.

Sakhya-rasa: friendly love

Sakhya-rasa, brotherly or friendly affection (*sakhya*=friend), is another of the five main *rasas*. In this type of love, we find a more intimate affection than in the mood of pure servitude because it implies an informal relationship between friends. Informal or casual dealing with Krishna arises from what the sages call spontaneous devotion (*raganuga-bhakti*) in conjunction with the effect of *yoga-maya*'s action on the consciousness of the individual soul (*jiva*). In addition, Krishna's exuberant qualities (His beauty, charm, appearance, etc.) awaken in the soul an intense desire to obtain Him. With the blessings of

Radha (Krishna's pleasure potency) and under the influence of *yoga-maya* (which covers the knowledge of Krishna as the Almighty God), a spontaneous and dynamic love arises in the soul that transcends conventional spirituality. Such a fortunate soul is attracted only by the enchantment of Krishna's sweetness (*madhurya*). This is what distinguishes the inhabitants of Vaikuntha from those of Goloka-Vrindavana. Whereas the formers feel attraction to Vishnu's majesty or opulence (*aishvarya*), the latter are attracted to the sweetness (*madhurya*) of Krishna, the supreme Vishnu, even though both opulence and sweetness are two aspects of His self.

The magical effect of *yoga-maya* on the consciousness is so profound that the soul experiences Krishna exclusively as the best and most charming of friends, thus facilitating the expression of love without any protocol barrier. To the inhabitants of Vrindavana, Krishna is *bala-gopal*, the most charming shepherd boy in all creation. In such an environment, Krishna is simply the dearest friend, so no one imagines He is the Almighty Personality of Godhead. For them, Krishna is one of the inhabitants of Vrindavana, whom everyone loves with all their heart. No power in all creation can make them think any other way. Although the opulence of Vrindavana knows no limits, the pastoral atmosphere of its divine forests and Krishna's appearance as a simple cowherd boy favors the informality of love. With the bodily appearance of children between seven and eight years old, Krishna and His cowherd friends eternally frolic in childish games with the same informality as ordinary children of this world. As *rasika-shekara* (the enjoyer of all kinds of exchange of affection), Krishna responds to their innocent and childish love with the same mood that He receives from them. Needless to say, these cowherd boys are either eternally liberated souls (never conditioned by illusion) or conditioned souls that, by means of their devotion, reached the friendship *rasa* of Vrindavana after abandoning this world.

Like the ordinary children of this world, in Vrindavana, Krishna plays as a frolicsome child and wrestles with the cowherd boys as the perfect friend. Even on occasions, Krishna is defeated (or allows Himself to be defeated) by one of His cowherd friends and has to carry out the punishment imposed on Him, like carrying one of the cowherd boys on His shoulders. Sometimes His cowherd friends offer Krishna treats that they keep in their bags and which they have previously bitten, something that no soul in knowledge of Krishna's opulence as the Supreme God would ever do. But these liberated souls eternally relate to Krishna in this way in the pastoral environment of the magical and divine village of Vrindavana, where the beauty of spontaneous love reigns without restrictions or limits. Because they are under the influence of *yoga-maya*, the cowherd boys feel equality towards Krishna. They think that despite His possessing exceptional qualities and being the dearest of them all, Krishna is just another cowherd boy. Due to His unmatched qualities, the cowherd boys admire Him as the highest among them and love Him more than their life itself. *Yoga-maya* covers the perfect souls, and by Krishna's will, it occasionally makes Him "forget" His own divinity so that Krishna can fully enjoy the intensity of the childish mood. It is not that Krishna acts as if He were a child, but rather that under the effect of *yoga-maya*, Krishna actually experiences being a child playing with His friends. This "forgetfulness" that *yoga-maya* exercises upon Krishna's condition as the Almighty God comes to an end also by the will of Krishna Himself. In this way, Krishna plays with His infinite energies in infinite ways.

Absorbed in this mellow, Krishna enjoys the pleasure of original youthful psychology, experiencing Himself not as Almighty God but as the friend of His friends. This kind of informal love brings more pleasure to Krishna than the Vedic rituals and hymns sung by the sages and the formality of the solemn love of Vaikuntha. In Vrindavana, Krishna expresses His entire being in full, beyond simply being the God of material creation—just as a magistrate does in his home, indifferent to his respectable social status. We could say that in Vrindavana, Krishna is not God but simple Krishna.

Krishna's associates are also of various categories and types; some are manifestations of His self, and others are individual souls. The most prominent among Krishna's cowherd friends is Balarama, who is often depicted by His side in works of art representative of Vrindavana's *lilas* (pastimes). Balarama is not an ordinary cowherd boy but the personification of Krishna's internal or spiritual potency (*chit-shakti*) that manifests the spiritual creation. In essence, Balarama is not different from Krishna. Balarama is another aspect of Krishna Himself. Just as He does with Radha (the pleasure potency), Krishna also personifies His spiritual potency in the form of Balarama and thus expands the pleasure of *rasa*. In Goloka-Vrindavana and Krishna's pastimes in this world, Balarama acts as Krishna's older brother. In this way, Krishna also enjoys having an "older brother." In fact, as His spiritual potency, Balarama serves Krishna in all types of *rasas*. The only difference between the two is aesthetic; for Krishna is like a sapphire or blue lotus, His garments are yellow, and He carries a peacock feather on His head. For his part, Balarama's divine complexion is white as snow, His garments are blue, and He decorates His head with a white peacock feather. Eternally, both are the most charming cowherd boys and the very life of the infinity of inhabitants of Goloka-Vrindavana. Many other cowherd boys are also personifications of different aspects of Krishna, such as Shridama (Krishna's intelligence), Sudama (Krishna's pure ego), Vasudama (Krishna's heart), Kinkini (Krishna's mind), etc.

As for the individual souls who enjoy the company of Krishna in Vrindavana, there are generally two types: *nitya-siddhas* and *sadhana-siddhas*. The first (*nitya-siddhas*) are eternally liberated and perfect souls (*nitya*=eternal, *siddha*=perfect) or souls never conditioned by material nature. The second (*sadhana-siddhas*) are souls who were conditioned by illusion at some moment in their existence but attained the company of Krishna in Vrindavana through the force of spiritual practice. These two types of associates exist in all *rasas* or relationships with Krishna.

These cowherd boys who always surround Krishna in a childish mood are of four types. The ones called *sakhas* (friends) have an eternal appearance slightly younger than Krishna. Still, because their loving affection towards Him—although very informal—has traces of *dasya* (servitude), they naturally tend to serve Him. Then there are the *suhrit-sakhas* (well-wisher friends) who are cowherd boys whose eternal appearance is slightly older than Krishna. Therefore, their affection is also slightly tinged with a feeling of protection. These two types of friendly love are an example of mixed sentiments (*sankhula-rasa*).

Another category of cowherd boys is the *priya-sakha* (confidential friends), also called *krishna-prana* since Krishna is like their life itself—to the point that if they do not see Him for an instant, they feel that they are going to die. These cowherd boys are the same age as Krishna, and their feeling is not mixed with another *rasa*; it is pure friendship without a trace of protection or servitude (*kevala-rasa*). They play with Krishna just like children of the same age. They are innumerable, and some are *yukteshvara* or group leaders (*yukta*=group, *ishvara*=controller). The previously mentioned cowherd boys (Sridama, Sudama, Vasudama, and Kinkini) are some of the *yukteshvara*.

Then there are the *priya-narma-sakha* or Krishna's eight most intimate cowherd boyfriends. Although they are slightly younger than Krishna, their feelings towards Him are similar to what Radha's cowherd girlfriends feel towards Her. Because these cowherd boys know the secrets of Krishna's loving affairs with Radha (His pleasure potency) and the rest of the Vrindavana cowherd girls (*vraja-gopis*), they also serve Krishna intimately whenever these pastimes take place. These eight cowherd boys are also group leaders (*yukteshvara*); they are Subala, Arjuna (not the prince of Bhagavad-Gita), Gandharva, Vasanta, Ujjuala, Kokila, Sanandana, and Vidadgdha. Like Krishna, Balarama also has His group of cowherd boys who are part of His entourage of personal associates.

There are other cowherd boys known as *vidushaka-sakha* (jester or buffoon friends), of whom Madhu-mangala is generally the most mentioned. They are experts in the art of making Krishna laugh. Other cowherd boys very close to Krishna are the *vita-sakha* (artistic, sensual friends), who are experts in dressing Him attractively to captivate the hearts of the cowherd girls of Vrindavana. Many other cowherd boys are called *sadharana* (ordinary friends) since they number in the thousands of millions and always surround Krishna serving Him in many ways. Let us remember that none of these cowherd boys are ordinary souls. They are sages who attained a high degree of spontaneous devotion (*raganuga-bhakti*) in childlike friendly love for Krishna rarely seen in this world.

While the physical bodies of this world are dull and limited to pale or dark complexions, the bodily appearance of the cowherd boys is very bright and attractive. Some of their bodies are like sparkling sapphires; others are silver, emerald green, crystal white, ruby red, etc. In this colorful and luminous environment, Krishna eternally enjoys childhood pastimes in the company of His friends in Goloka-Vrindavana. Occasionally Krishna manifests His pastimes in this world. The sages tell us that Krishna reveals His *lilas* on the human plane every day of Brahma—that is, once every eight thousand six hundred twenty million earth years. As expected, to properly understand the transcendental nature of these *lilas*, or divine pastimes of Krishna, we need to know what we call *tattva* (or categories of existence, philosophical concepts, etc.). If not, we will see His *lilas* in the light of religious immaturity and relegate them to the status of comics, fables, mythology, etc. As the original cause of all causes, Krishna has no origin; therefore, he has no mother, father, brothers, etc. By understanding the philosophical concepts that support the Vaishnava philosophy, we know that when we hear that Radha is Krishna's eternal consort and that Balarama is His elder brother, we speak in terms of their role in Krishna's eternal pastimes (*lilas*). In other words, understanding Krishna-*tattva* (the philosophical principles) is the only way to understand *krishna-lila* (the activities of eternal enjoyment or divine pastimes).

Vatsalya-rasa: parental afection

Just as Krishna has His servants, His close friends, and even His older brother (Balarama), He also has His eternal parents,

Nanda and Yashoda. Like many of Krishna's associates, Nanda and Yashoda are not ordinary spirit souls but specific manifestations of the *svarupa-shakti*, the supreme potency of Krishna, by whose will they are eternally endowed with paternal and maternal affection towards Him. These associates are known as *parikaras*. No superhuman power can convince Nanda and Yashoda of Krishna's divinity. If so, their pure paternal feeling would be tinged with solemn affection and veneration for the Supreme God, breaking the flow of spontaneous paternalism love. In turn, Krishna reciprocates the pure love of Nanda and Yashoda as the perfect son, and with His childish pranks at every moment, He immerses them in an ocean of infinite bliss. At the same time, simultaneously, He enjoys the paternal and maternal love that He receives from them, just as if He were an ordinary child. The bliss that mother Yashoda experiences in having the personality of Godhead—the personification of all beauty and bliss—sitting on her lap, babbling unintelligible words just like an ordinary baby, is unimaginable even to the inhabitants of Vaikuntha. Although Nanda and Yashoda are the perfections of parental love and the eternal parents of Krishna, souls who cultivate this kind of love are also allowed to serve Him with similar affection.

Krishna's abode, Goloka-Vrindavana, is the original transcendental society where the Supreme Personality of Godhead resides with His eternal associates and His transcendental family, which He manifests through His internal potency. Nanda and Yashoda also have their parents, brothers, sisters, nephews, cousins, etc., who act like Krishna's grandparents, uncles, cousins , and other relatives. In turn, all the inhabitants of Vrindavana also have their parents, cousins, uncles, etc., for whom Krishna is like life itself. Moreover, the eternal fathers and mothers of Krishna's friends in Vrindavana love Krishna more than they love their children and other family members. On Krishna's planet, everyone is a liberated soul endowed by *yoga-maya* with psychology suitable to perfectly play its corresponding role in Krishna's *lila*. After all, everything in the spiritual world is a manifestation of Krishna's divine potency and, therefore, is meant for His pleasure.

The Vedas describe the abode of Krishna as a thousand-petaled lotus, at the center of which lies the divine village of Vrindavana, the most intimate portion of that supreme spiritual world. Its opulence manifest as a magical village brimming with *prema* (pure love). Both the parents of Krishna (Nanda and Yashoda) and those of Radha (Vrisabhanu and Kirtida) live in grand palaces of cowherd kings that intermingle with the forest environment of the place. The tales and fantasy stories that we find in this world, generated by the fertile human imagination, are but a pale hint of the magic of the rural environment in Goloka-Vrindavana with its magical palaces and forests. Goloka is so-named because, besides its being a pastoral kingdom, on this supreme spiritual planet (*loka*), there is an infinity of divine cows (*go*) called Surabhi that Krishna herds with His shepherd friends. Like everything in Goloka-Vrindavana, the Surabhi cows are perfect souls whose *rasa* is to give pleasure to Krishna as His pets or objects of His love; thus, they are endowed with beauty and attributes that far surpass the best of human fantasy. The name Vrindavana is due to the abundance in this abode of forests (*vana*) of Vrinda plants, also called Tulasi. The glory of the Surabhi cows and the *vrinda* plants in the abode of Krishna is so evident that this spiritual world is also known as Goloka-Vrindavana, the world of the Surabhi cows and Vrinda forests (*go*=cows, *loka*=world, *vrinda*=tulasi plants, *vana*=forest). The

Tulasi plant is a manifestation of Krishna's pleasure potency (Radha), who is pleased to serve Him in that way.

As cowherd kings, the eternal parents of Radha and Krishna possess infinities of these divine Surabhi cows, which Krishna herds on the banks of the Yamuna River in the company of Balarama and thousands of millions of cowherd boyfriends. As they do so, Krishna enjoys original youthful psychology, indulging in childish games and mischief of all kinds just as if they were ordinary children. After all, the childlike joy of the conditioned souls of this world is but an imitative and distorted replica of this aspect of Krishna. Let us remember that Krishna is the origin of all exchanges and relationships. However, even though Krishna and Balarama are surrounded by millions of cowherd boys, by the effect of *yoga-maya,* each one of them experiences that Krishna and Balarama are exclusively by their side, so they feel infinitely fortunate.

Srimad Bhagavatam describes how Krishna and Balarama often decorate their heads splendidly with forest flowers while singing and dancing for the pleasure of their friends, the cowherd boys. While doing so, they look like the best actors in a theatrical play. Even though the cowherd boys spend all day playing with Krishna and Balarama, their love is so intense that during Goloka-Vrindavana's divine night, they dream that they are still playing with them in the forests on the banks of the Yamuna River. The *lilas* or pastimes of the cowherd boys with Krishna are pleasant to hear.

Sringara-rasa: romantic conjugal love

We mentioned earlier that just as Radha and Krishna are the eternal prototypes of the masculine and feminine principle that permeates all creation, similarly, their love exchanges are the origin of the romantic conjugal feeling. Of all the types of loving exchanges, the romantic or conjugal relationship is the most intimate, intense, and pleasant. By nature, in the marital romantic relationship, all other forms of love are present somehow since a lover can also be an admirer, a servant, a friend, and a protector. This conjugal feeling is so complete that though we may have a wondrous kingdom, fortune, friends, parents, servants, etc., the heart will not be satisfied until it is complemented by a romantic partner. It is a fact that the whole world revolves around romantic love. Throughout the ages, poets, singers, writers, dramatic artists, painters, sculptors, etc., have glorified this sentiment.

Because in the Vaikuntha worlds, Laxmi-Narayana is the reverential form of Radha-Krishna in Vrindavana, in Vaikuntha, only Laxmi-devi shares romantic love with Vishnu (Narayana). But Vrindavana, the abode of Radha and Krishna, is characterized by spontaneous love; there, Krishna is the personification of conjugal love and the perfect lover of millions of souls who have achieved such a relationship with Him. Everything in Krishna, His charming beauty, His attractive and smiling face, ways of dressing, speaking, His pastoral kingdom, etc., awakens the longing for romantic union in the hearts of the cowherd girls Vrindavana (*gopis*). Some among them were great sages that reached the highest degree of love and devotion in a previous life

The soul whose intrinsic nature partakes in the conjugal *rasa* is naturally drawn to Krishna's beauty with a desire for romantic union, the most intimate form of love and the one that most captivates Krishna's heart. These souls who have reached such a high degree of perfection as we find in the conjugal love of Vrindavana assume spiritual bodies of feminine appearance with the appropriate innate psychology to eternally relate to Krishna in this *rasa* of romantic love. Although these transcendental affairs of Krishna with the cowherd girls may resemble the romances of the men and women of this world, in reality, they are quite the opposite. The former is the product of the highest pure love for God, while the latter results from lust arising from our forgetfulness of God. The difference between the two is similar to that between gold and iron; the first is always pure, while the second oxidizes.

Nevertheless, those who do not understand their divine essence look at these pure spiritual affairs in the light of worldly experience. Therefore, saintly people are usually cautious in discussing these topics in front of an unfamiliar audience. Since the material creation is an inverted or distorted reflection of Goloka-Vrindavana, we perceive this highest form of divine love in this world in a distorted way because its foundation is the sensual pleasures arising from worldly lust. It is like the highest part of a large tree whose reflection we perceive as the lowest in a river.

As His pleasure potency, Radha is the supreme among all Krishna's transcendental lovers. Yet, because the spiritual *rasa* is eternally increasing, as Krishna expands or duplicates in different ways, so Radha also multiplies in an infinity of forms to satisfy Krishna's infinite ways of enjoyment. Therefore, just as their cowherd friends (*gopas*) always surround Krishna and Balarama, Radha's girlfriends (the *gopis*), counted by the millions, always surround Her. Some of these cowherd girls are eternally perfect souls (*nitya-siddha*), while others are souls who reached such perfection in this world through spiritual practice (*sadhana-siddha*). Just like the cowherd boys, the cowherd girls are also grouped into various categories known as *sakhis* (friends), *nitya-sakhis* (constant friends), *priya-sakhis* (very dear friends), *prana-sakhis* (close friends who are like life itself) and *parama-prestha-sakhis* (the most beloved among Radha's close friends). The latter ones are known as *astha-sakhis* (*astha*=eight, *sakhi*=female friend), and they always surround Radha at all times. Radha's *astha-sakhis*, or eight main friends, are 1. Lalita, 2. Vishaka, 3. Chitra, 3. Champakalata, 5. Tungavidya, 6. Induleka, 7. Rangadevi and 8. Sudevi. All of them are extensions of Radha's body; in other words, they do not belong to the category of individual souls (*jiva*). The complexion of their spiritual bodies is gorgeous, and as manifestations or duplications of Radha, they overflow with endless divine attributes from which Krishna derives infinite pleasure. Apart from Radha's eight confidential gopis friends, there are other *gopis* of great prominence in Vrindavana who are leaders of groups consisting of millions of *gopis*. There are also older *gopis* who are friends of Yashoda and serve as Krishna's nurses.

In this way, Radha surrounds Krishna with endless extensions of Her form and individual souls (*jiva*) who have achieved the same conjugal *rasa*. To increase Krishna's pleasure, the cowherd girls are of various emotional natures. They can be *mridui* (delicate), *prakara* (severe), *madhya* (in between delicate to severe), *prabhalga* (mature and resourceful to the point that they know how to control Krishna with their tricks), *dhira* (gentle and sober), *adhira* (uneasy and jealous) *mudha* (or credulous and innocent). All this brings variety to Krishna's conjugal *rasa*. For Krishna to savor the different dimensions of conjugal love, *yoga-maya* endows the cowherd girls with different tendencies. Some cowherd girls favor Radha; they love Her above everything else. Others are neutral, indicating that they love Radha and Krishna with the same intensity, while others compete with Radha for the love of

Krishna. Each cowherd girl personifies at least one attribute of Radha, who possesses an infinity of them and manifests them at will for the pleasure of Krishna according to the place and the specific circumstances of the *lila*. For this reason, Krishna's love for Radha, and vice versa, reigns supreme in Goloka-Vrindavana. No other cowherd girl subjugates Krishna with Her love as much as Radha does.

The most prominent among Radha's rivals is Chandravali. She is a duplication of Radha Herself, another aspect of Her being acting as Her cousin and rival in the eternal *lila*. Just as Radha has Her confidential friends who favor her, Chandravali has Her *gopis* friends who favor her and are therefore partial towards her. By competing for the love of Krishna, the divine *lila* takes on an intense dynamism that lends an unequaled beauty to the love pastimes of Krishna, who is the Supreme Enjoyer and the most handsome and gallant cowherd boy in Vrindavana. This transcendental rivalry between Radha, Chandravali, and many other prominent *gopis* for the love of Krishna gives Him great pleasure. It serves as the background for myriad love pastimes between Radha and Krishna. Sometimes, because of Her picaresque character, love disputes arise between Radha and Krishna, which leads Radha to express a feeling of anger and reproach towards Krishna. Still, due to the nature of divine feelings, this "anger" of Radha is the source of great pleasure for both Herself and Krishna, although externally, it appears to be the opposite. When this happens, Radha's confidential friends take sides in Her favor and reproach Krishna for His inappropriate behavior. These amorous quarrels, anger, and reproaches of the *gopis* towards Krishna overflow in such pure and spontaneous conjugal love that it transcends the barriers of our imagination. In their rapture of divine anger, Radha and Her *gopis* friends reproach Krishna, the Supreme Personality of Godhead, who the pure souls worship and the radiance of whose feet the greatest sages and celestial beings long to see in their meditations. So is the inconceivable love of Vrindavana!

We must never forget that the bodies of the liberated souls that inhabit Krishna's abode are not like material bodies, but rather the soul itself assumes a particular form according to the *rasa* in which it participates. The spiritual bodies are pure consciousness—the essence of the self; therefore, the love of the cowherd girls for Krishna is entirely free from selfishness. Knowing that Krishna derives pleasure in their company, the cowherd girls adorn and embellish themselves solely to please Krishna with their *prema* (love). At the same time, Krishna reciprocates their love, and in doing so, He enjoys the divine bliss of the original romantic sentiment (*adi-rasa*). This feeling is so delightful and profound that to serve Krishna in this way, even Balarama (Krishna's internal potency, which acts as His elder brother in the eternal *lila*) manifests Himself as a cowherd girl to taste the sweetness of His conjugal love. Balarama's identity as a cowherd girl in the *lila* is Ananga Manjari, Radha's younger sister. We must not forget that only the exalted souls, on account of their eternal constitution and intense love for Krishna, attain this conjugal *rasa*. Upon abandoning this world, they assume a female spiritual body endowed with the appropriate psychology for this kind of *rasa* in Goloka-Vrindavana. The proper understanding of Krishna's loving affairs with the *gopis* of Vrindavana constitutes the most confidential and highest part of Vaishnava philosophy.

Like the rest of the inhabitants of Vrindavana, the bodily nuances of the *gopis* defy material experience. The Vaishnava saints reveal that Radha is the color of molten gold. Her eyes are blue; Her jet-black hair spills black curls that adorn Her face, whose incomparable beauty defeats the splendor of the full moon. Her smile enhances the brilliance of Her red lips, revealing pearl-like teeth. The charm of Her infinite attributes knows no limits, for She is the supreme creation of Krishna. The bodily appearance of the other *gopis* is also quite varied. The hue of their divine bodies can be white, lotus blue, crystal, gold, tan, gray, pink, blackish like the bee, sparkling like lightning, like a peacock feather, or similar to wildflowers, etc. A beautiful combination of textures and characters embellishes them. They satisfy Krishna by decorating their lovely countenances with divine gems, with the beauty of their divine garments, and by displaying their artistic abilities.

The *manjaris* (flower buds, sprouts) stand out among the cowherd girls. They are called *manjaris* because they are young girls just at the onset of puberty (twelve or thirteen years). The *manjaris* are Radha's most intimate servants, so they are always by Her side. The love of the *manjaris* for Radha is so deep that they do not accept any romantic exchange with Krishna; their feeling is that Krishna belongs only to Radha and no one else. Their love for Krishna manifests itself as an unequaled love for Radha. Since Radha is Krishna's supreme love object, the manjaris are more faithful and attached to Radha than Krishna Himself. This identification with Radha's happiness is so deep and selfless that when Radha and Krishna engage in their transcendental affairs, the *manjaris* enjoy such a deep pleasure that it surpasses the one experienced by other cowherd girls when they have romantic exchanges with Krishna. Such is the supreme nature of their love for Krishna, utterly free of self-interest. This feeling of love for Radha and Krishna (which tends to lean more towards Radha than towards Krishna) is the highest form of love for Krishna; because of this, the love of the *manjaris* reigns supreme in Vaishnava theology. Vaishnava saints have written extensively on these topics for centuries, but here we present only a pale hint of the dimension of Radha and Krishna's loving *lila*. In this way, Krishna, the Supreme Enjoyer, reciprocates our love as master, servant, father, son, friend, or ideal lover.

The form of Vishnu is distinguished from Krishna by His four arms, in which He carries a lotus, a conch shell, a disc, and a club.

From the divine body of Maha Vishnu, the material universes emanate like bubbles, to be again absorbed at the moment of universal annihilation in an eternal creative cycle.

The human forms that we call man and woman are in the image and likeness of Radha-Krishna, the Divine Couple, the origin of the romantic conjugal feeling that permeates creation.

Hare Krishna

Goloka is like a thousand-petalled lotus, at the center of which lies Vrindavana, the most intimate abode of Radha and Krishna. In the spiritual sky surrounding it, there is an infinity of planets Vaikuntha where Radha and Krishna dwell in their forms as Laxmi-Narayana and other avatars that come to this world. At one end lies *mahat-tattva*, the material creation.

Krishna with Balarama (to Krishna's left), His first expansion. Balarama personifies the spiritual potency (*chit-shakti*) that manifests the spiritual world.

He acts as Krishna's brother in childhood pastimes, and both are always in the company of their cowherd boys friends (*gopas*).

To enjoy maternal *rasa*, Krishna expresses Himself as the eternal son of mother Yashoda.

Radha-Krishna in the company of their most confidential friends, the cowherd girls (*gopis*).

Chapter 16

Other aspects of the spiritual mellows (rasa)

However, not all individual souls who develop spontaneous affection for Krishna (be it as a well-wisher, friend, father, mother, or conjugal lover) possess the same degree of spontaneity in their love. Let us remember that the flow of spontaneous love is proportional to the attraction to Krishna's personal qualities, which overshadow His condition of Almighty God. Suppose the affection for Krishna is not of the highest degree but exceeds the reverential affection of Vaikuntha. In that case, Vaikuntha is not the destiny of this particular emancipated soul since this is not the goal of his devotion. On the other hand, even when such affection is very high, it may also not reach the intimacy that characterizes Vrindavana; therefore, the destiny of such an emancipated soul lies somewhere between these two abodes.

The mystical kingdom of Krishna (Krishna-loka or Goloka-Vrindavana) resembles a thousand-petaled lotus flower. At its center lies His most intimate abode, the pastoral kingdom of Vrindavana, where Radha and Krishna eternally delight in pastimes of love in the company of their most intimate divine associates. Because the divine village of Vrindavana lies at the center of Goloka, this abode of Krishna—the supreme spiritual world—is known as Goloka-Vrindavana. However, Goloka is not limited to the pastoral portion of the Vrindavana forests. In the divine realm of Goloka, there are cities such as Dvaraka and Mathura, which are also the destiny of those whose love for Krishna exceeds the reverential affection of Vaikuntha but still lacks the spontaneity that characterizes the inhabitants of the most intimate abode of Vrindavana. In Dvaraka and Mathura, Krishna and Balarama do not wear the garb of cowherd boys, nor do they manifest themselves as such but as great kings served by a large entourage in an urban environment of infinite opulence. There, Krishna's associates are not the cowherd boys but friends and subjects that make up that divine society whose palaces contrast with the natural and rural environment of Vrindavana, with its forests, rivers, etc.

In Dvaraka and Mathura, Krishna and Balarama manifest their natural sweetness partially since they are adolescents surrounded by princely formality and not playful cowherd boys. The love of the inhabitants of Dvaraka and Mathura is very advanced; however, because they are aware of Krishna's divine opulence (*aishvarya*), such love lacks the sort of informal intimacy that we see in the divine village of Vrindavana, which lies at the center of Goloka.

Under the effect of *yoga-maya*, the inhabitants of Vrindavana are unaware of Krishna's divinity; therefore, they are engrossed only in His sweetness (*madhurya*). The nature of love for Krishna of the inhabitants of Dvaraka and Mathura is halfway between Vaikuntha and Vrindavana. In Dvaraka, Krishna is surrounded by millions of subjects, friends, and servants. While in Dvaraka, Krishna multiplies Himself thousands of forms similar to the original and simultaneously dwells in thousands of palaces in the company of His thousands of queens. This is an example of His mystical opulence. The most prominent among Krishna's queens in Dvaraka are expansions of Radha, His pleasure potency. However, many of His queens are individual souls who, although situated in the conjugal *rasa*, do not possess the highest degree of spontaneous love that characterizes the cowherd girls (*gopis*) of Vrindavana.

Nevertheless, these manifestations of Radha, acting as the queens of Krishna in Dvaraka, possess the necessary psychology to enjoy the conjugal *rasa* as Krishna's formal wives. Among the hundreds of thousands of queens, the most prominent are Rukmini, Satyabhama, Jambavati, Kalindi, Mitravinda, Nagnajiti, Bhadra, and Laxmana. In this way, in Goloka-Vrindavana, Radha and Krishna enjoy the informality of furtive love in the forest environment and the formalities of love between spouses in a palatial urban setting. In Dvaraka and Mathura, Krishna has His "father and mother," named Vasudeva and Devaki. However, because they know the divinity of "their son," their love does not flow with the same spontaneity as Nanda and Yashoda's, "Krishna's parents" in Vrindavana. Under the effect of *yoga-maya*, Nanda and Yashoda think that Krishna is their little son needing their care and protection.

According to the eminent Vaishnava sages Rupa Goswami and Jiva Goswami, the Goloka portion of Goloka-Vrindavana is the majestic manifestation of the divine village of Vrindavana—a kind of "outer edge" that surrounds the divine and simple rural environment of Vrindavana, the most intimate abode of Krishna, which lies at the center of Goloka-Vrindavana or Krishna-loka. In this portion that surrounds the divine village of Vrindavana (Goloka), the sweetness (*madhurya*) of spontaneous love for Krishna also predominates, but not to the same level of spontaneity that we find in Vrindavana, the central and most intimate portion of Goloka. However, we should not assume that Vaikuntha, Dvaraka, and the other kingdoms of the divine world are more opulent than Vrindavana due to their majestic nature. In fact, Vrindavana surpasses them all in opulence; the difference is that its opulence manifests as a magical pastoral kingdom where the sweetness of Krishna and spontaneous exchanges predominate. The sages tell us that if we add a small portion of salt to a glass of water, the salty taste will be prominent, but adding a bucket of salt to a large lake will not be noticed. Similarly, the opulence (*aishvarya*) of Vrindavana surpasses that of any other kingdom of Krishna. Still, unlike Dvaraka, Mathura, and the infinity of Vaikuntha worlds, such opulence is eclipsed by the infinity of its sweetness (*madhurya*).

Those whose devotion to Radha and Krishna surpasses the intimacy we find in Dvaraka and Mathura but do not have the spontaneity required to achieve their company in Vrindavana do not reach this intimate portion of Goloka where Radha and Krishna dwell with their more confidential entourage. Nor do they enter the abodes of Dvaraka or Mathura that lie on the "outskirts" of Vrindavana since these are not the goal of their devotional practice. Hence, these souls attain the association of Radha and Krishna in Goloka, the area bordering Vrindavana. According to some Vaishnava sages, this portion of the supreme abode (Goloka) is attainable by faithfully following the guidelines and regulations of devotional practice (*vaidhi-bhakti*). In contrast, the most intimate portion of Goloka, Vrindavana, is only reached by the highest spontaneous love (*raganuga-bhakti*) free from all vestige of reverential affection.

Goloka-Vrindavana's luminosity is known as *brahmajyotir* (*brahma*=spirit, *jyotir*=effulgence), the divine effulgence or impersonal consciousness—what the monists and *yogis*, who discard the path of devotion (*bhakti*), long to attain by endeavoring to dissolve their individual identity. According to the intensity of their devotion and their eternal rasa with Krishna or Vishnu, different types of Vaishnavas achieve the different abodes of the spiritual world, such as Vaikuntha Dvaraka, Mathura, Goloka, Vrindavana, etc. It is worth remembering another vital aspect of Vaishnava philosophy: Krishna, in His original form (*svayan-bhagavan*), never sets even one foot outside of Vrindavana (the most intimate portion of Goloka, His supreme abode). The forms of Krishna and Balarama as kings in the kingdoms of Dvaraka and Mathura, known as Vaasudeva and Sankarsana, respectively, are replicas of their original forms in Vrindavana. When Krishna and Balarama abandon Vrindavana in their pastimes in our world, they do so as Vaasudeva and Sankarsana, while their original forms in Vrindavana assume an unmanifested state; however, due to the introductory nature of this book, we will not delve into this topic.

The intensity of romantic conjugal love

Another topic of prominence about Krishna's transcendental loving affairs with the cowherd girls of Vrindavana is that, unlike in Dvaraka, this love is not solemnized by the formality of marriage. Due to its complexity and philosophical subtlety, this subject can lead to misperception; therefore, the sages have pondered it for our benefit. However, it is worth remembering that both the queens of Dvaraka and the cowherd girls of Vrindavana are not ordinary beings but direct expansions of Radha (Krishna's pleasure potency) or liberated individual souls who have reached the conjugal *rasa*.

In His pastimes in Dvaraka, Krishna formally accepts the souls who have reached the conjugal *rasa* as His divine wives, and with them, He enjoys the romantic love solemnized by the marriage rules. However, although this relationship with

Krishna demands great affective spontaneity, both the queens (*mahishis*) and most of His friends of Dvaraka never treat Krishna with the informality and even the reproach with which the cowherd girls (*gopis*) and cowherd boys (*gopas*) of Vrindavana often do. The urban social atmosphere of the large cities of Dvaraka and Mathura is ideal for the flow of this *rasa* (semi-formal, semi-informal). There we find neither the formality of the reverential love of Vaikuntha nor the necessary elements for the expression of spontaneous love in all its splendor, something which naturally encompasses the charm of the forests of Vrindavana. As the Supreme Enjoyer, Krishna enjoys all forms of *rasa* and flavors of love: formal, informal, semi-formal, semi-formal, very informal, and a combination of all.

This type of conjugal *rasa* in the divine kingdom of Dvaraka, sacralized by the formality of marriage ties, is known as *suakiya-rasa* (married love). But since in Vrindavana, the love union of the cowherd girls with Krishna is not sacralized by matrimonial ties, love takes on a more furtive and intense dimension that increases with each encounter. This is because the cowherd girls have their husbands; that is, they are formally married—or at least that is what it appears to be for the psychology of the *lila*.

The supreme and forbidden love of Vrindavana

However, this union between the *gopis* and their husbands is only apparent as it is a magical effect created by *yoga-maya*. Its purpose is to intensify the emotion of the secret meeting of the cowherd girls with Krishna by providing the psychology of forbidden love, which makes the union more intense and delightful. In Vaishnava philosophy, this type of love is called *parakiya-rasa*, a conjugal feeling for God that is of such intensity that it does not require or consider social formalities. This feeling of *parakiya-rasa* (paramour love or love between lovers) for Krishna, although it seems immoral from the worldly point of view, is the exclusive privilege of highly elevated souls and the most spontaneous expression of love of Godhead. However, as we already mentioned, to understand Krishna's *lila* (pastimes), one must adequately understand the *tattva* (its philosophical background). Lacking adequate understanding and its similarity to worldly immorality, it is no wonder that worldly commentators and mundane moralists have historically misunderstood Krishna's *parakiya-rasa*.

Everything that exists is a manifestation of Krishna's potencies; therefore, everything belongs to Him, everything is Him, and there is nothing alien to Him. Radha (Krishna's pleasure potency) and Her millions of manifestations as cowherd girls are Krishna's eternal beloveds. Their so-called husbands are partial manifestations of the different potencies of Krishna. However, for the ideal flow of the *lila, yoga-maya* endows them with the sentiment that the cowherd girls are their wives. *Yoga-maya*, the supreme potency of Krishna, is so wonderful that it creates the appropriate psychology at all times in each of Krishna's *lilas*. To lead these *lilas* to perfection, we could say that *yoga-maya* always moves one step ahead of Krishna in preparing the environment for the next pastime and creating the ideal emotions and conditions for its perfection. Although the *gopis* live in their homes with their husbands and other family members, under the effect of *yoga-maya*, they are never intimately related to their husbands. Yet, this in no way obscures their feeling of being an actual spouse. The *gopis* are the eternal lovers of Krishna, His parts and portions. Therefore, no one can touch them, and there is no risk of it happening. The relationship of the *gopis* with their supposed husbands is simply psychological; it is the action of *yoga-maya* to increase the intensity of love making the *gopis* feel that they must hide their love for Krishna and secretly love him—behind the back of society. The conjugal *rasa* is the supreme essence of all *rasas*, and in turn, the essence of the conjugal *rasa* is *parakiya-rasa* (furtive love). The beauty of *parakiya-rasa* is that it assumes the appearance of forbidden and adulterous love, adding a newer and fresher dimension to the conjugal *rasa* that increases its intensity due to the impediments that stand in the way of achieving the long-awaited union with Krishna.

This type of secret union behind the back of society transcends the norms of human morality and exceeds the intensity of the formalized conjugal union. The fact that the *gopis* are "engaged" creates a giant barrier they must cross—the barrier of hidden love, of "what they will say," and the risk of being exposed. But, of course, in Krishna's *parakiya-rasa,* the possibility of immoral action does not exist. The *gopis* are expressions of Krishna's potencies; as such, Krishna interacts and plays with His potencies at will, just as a child will touch any part of his body without committing an immoral act. Therefore, the Vedic sages chant the glories of *parakiya-rasa*, the forbidden conjugal love of the Vrindavana *gopis* for Krishna, a subject of great depth in Vaishnava (*Hare Krishna*) philosophy.

Because this world is an inverted and distorted reflection of the spiritual world, it causes the *parakiya-rasa*—the climax of love for God—to manifest itself distorted as adulterous love, the most perverted and degrading form of conjugal love. Because *parakiya-rasa* can misunderstand as one of the degrading activities of the world, Vaishnava sages rarely bring up the subject due to the lack of a proper audience.

It is worth noting that the concept of the conjugal love of the perfect souls with God is not exclusive to the Vaishnava religion. However, in the scriptures of the Vaishnava tradition, we find a more explicit and detailed explanation. The prominent Christian mystics Saint Teresa of Avila and Saint Jonh of the Cross also commented on conjugal love, the pinnacle of spiritual understanding, something scarce to find in human society since it transcends the barriers even of conventional mysticism. When reading about this subject in the works of Saint Teresa and amazed by the greatness of this love, Fray Luis de Leon, in his letter to the Discalced Carmelites of the Madrid Monastery, wrote:

> "What I have read I admire, and hardly the flesh believes it, ... that brushing aside everything that is not God and offered only to the arms of their Divine Husband, embraced by Him, with the spirit of strong males in the tender and delicate arms of women, they set into motion the highest and most generous philosophy that men ever imagined—and they act in ways that the sages never imagined despite living a perfect life and heroic virtue." [Author translation]

Chapter 17

The nature of bhakti

According to Bhagavad-Gita, Srimad Bhagavatam, and other Vedic texts, *bhakti* (devotion and love of God) is the only way to obtain Krishna. *Bhakti* is not only the essence of the Vedas but of all forms of religion, for it is the intrinsic function of the soul; hence, its pleasant nature. Unlike other paths of *yoga* that cease when they reach the goal of impersonal liberation, *bhakti* continues even after liberation, for its purpose is *prema*, pure love for God, whose nature is eternal and dynamic. No matter how degraded a person's conscience may be, every human being has a natural propensity to love and serve. Any normal person loves and serves their family, nation, children, parents, friends, etc. Even if he is a rich person surrounded by servants and has no one to serve, we often see that he loves and serves his pets. People elect a politician as president when he convinces the voters that he will be the best servant. No living being is free from this propensity to serve. However, to a greater or lesser degree, all these service forms revolve around some personal benefit or satisfaction in material existence. In all the exchanges of affection in this world, we expect to receive something in return; otherwise, the relationship will end. A person will never accept a spouse knowing that they will not provide love or support, that they will not take care of their children, or if they do not meet the other's many needs. A student leaves his teacher when he has finished his education, a priest leaves a person when he is paid for a ritual, birds leave a tree when its fruits are exhausted, and a guest leaves the house after he has eaten. Similarly, a friendship ends when one's purpose is fulfilled, and a business relationship disappears when the common interest is lost.

Contrary to this, bhakti's pure form implies loving devotion to the Supreme Being without personal interest. In this exchange of love, the devotee serves Krishna solely for Krishna's pleasure without expecting anything in return. Yet, the nature of *bhakti* is such that this disinterest in personal pleasure reverts to a deep satisfaction that comes to him in return. But if this pleasure becomes an obstacle in the devotee's service to his Lord, he also disdains it. In *bhakti*, the happiness we receive is proportional to the pleasure offered by the object of love (God); therefore, anything that contributes to the pleasure of the Lord contributes to one's happiness. In essence, *bhakti* is the complete surrender of the soul to Krishna. Hence, if while practicing *bhakti*, there are still worldly desires in the heart, this will prevent us from savoring the *rasa* or mellow of pure love.

Bhakti is not a sentiment of the material world; neither are the *bhakta* (the devout soul) and *bhagavan* (the personality of God). *Bhakti, bhakta,* and *bhagavan* belong to the eternal spiritual creation. *Bhagavan* (the personality of Godhead) and *bhakta* (or the liberated soul) bring *bhakti* with them when they descend to this world to redeem fallen souls. *Bhakti* is a transcendental sentiment; it is a reciprocal force that pulls Krishna towards the devotee and the devotee towards Krishna. This is most evident in Vrindavana *bhakti*, which exerts a natural charm on Krishna Himself. In Vrindavana, Krishna derives more pleasure from being controlled by His devotees than acting as Master and Lord of creation. Hence, He forgets His opulence and serves His devotees in many ways. Krishna controls everything, but *bhakti* (the love of His devotees) controls Him. It is due to His inherent nature as an enjoyer of *rasa* (loving mellows) that the pure love of His devotees causes Him to forget His opulence and act in such a way. The power of *bhakti* is such that it controls the Supreme Controller. The love of the pure souls controls Krishna. More than His being the Almighty God, creator of the universe, Krishna is the servant of His devotees, the ever-fresh youth, affectionate and playful, sweet and loving, mischievous and obedient, sober and picaresque, modest and heroic, daring and contrite, bold and shy. But above all else, Krishna is the personification of romantic love. This—and many other qualities—are more prominent in Him than just being the God of material creation.

In this world, *bhakti* in its pure state (*shuddha-bhakti*) is rare since, generally, the practitioner's consciousness (*sadhaka*) is influenced by the modes of nature. This devotion, mixed with mundane desires, is known as *mishra-bhakti* (*bhakti*=devotion, *mishra*=mixed) and can manifest itself in various ways. According to the desire in the heart, *bhakti* can be 1. tinted with desire for material gain (*karma-mishra-bhakti*), 2. tinted with speculative knowledge (*jñana-mishra-bhakti*), and 3. tinted with desire for impersonal liberation (*kaivalia-kama-bhakti*), the latter common among monists, who often follow the regulations of *bhakti* in search of impersonal liberation. All these forms of *bhakti* (devotion) are nothing more than shadows of *bhakti* (*bhakti-abhasa*); only pure *bhakti* (*shuddha-bhakti*) has the power to attract Krishna and even subjugate Him to the will of His devotee.

Bhakti has the unique quality of harmonizing the traditional discrepancy between psychophysical demands and those of the spirit. Since in *bhakti* all that we possess is used in the service of God (thought, word, action, etc.), psychophysical demands take on a new spiritual dimension. This exclusive quality of *bhakti* makes it superior to the simple renunciation (*vairagya*) of the world's goods. *Bhakti* is the means to achieve love for Krishna (*sadhana*) and the goal (*sadhya*), which is love for Krishna. Because it is the intrinsic nature of the soul, *bhakti* does not cease after communion with Krishna but continues growing. This pure love for Krishna (*prema*) lies dormant in the heart of every living being, yet the simple regulated practice of *bhakti* does not awaken it. *Prema*, the pure love that lies dormant in each soul, must be vitalized by the touch of Krishna's pleasure potency (Radha), which enlivens not only Krishna Himself but also the individual soul when it descends upon him on account of his sincere longing to lead a life of devotion (*bhakti*).

Sadhana-bhakti (regulated practice) is the primary stage on the path; its purpose is to regulate our psycho-physical activities to keep the senses under control and purify our consciousness of the attractions to the illusory world. This primary stage is also known as *vaidhi-bhakti*, whose purpose is strictly following the scriptures' rules and regulations (*viddhi*). In the neophyte stage, the practice tends to be formal and mechanical; however, through these regulations, the practitioner gradually reaches a more advanced stage in which his devotion matures and sprouts spontaneously (*raganuga-bhakti*). Thus, his love for Krishna flows naturally without being restricted by (or limited to) the regulations of the scriptures. However, even when natural affection for Krishna springs up in his heart, the devotee does not abandon the rules of *bhakti* but continues his practice just like an ordinary devotee. The appearance of this natural affection does not imply that he has established his eternal personal relationship with Krishna. At this stage of *raganuga-bhakti*, the devotee emulates or follows (*anuga*) the example of one of Krishna's eternal associates (*parikaras*) in Vrindavana according to his *rasa*. As part of his practice, the devotee visualizes himself in his spiritual body serving Krishna in Vrindavana according to the *rasa* that draws his heart. Over time and practice, this visualization becomes more apparent, and the visualized body assumes a transcendental reality since it is the eternal sleeping identity of the soul. This visualization of one's spiritual body is not a simple imagination but a meditation (albeit imperfect at the beginning of the meditation practice) on the replica of the eternal spiritual body (*siddha-deha*).

Although *raganuga-bhakti* surpasses *vaidhi-bhakti* because it is natural and spontaneous, it is still within the practice of regulated devotion (*sadhana-bhakti*). The candidate attains the fruit of *raganuga-bhakti* when he leaves his mortal body and assumes the eternal form he meditated upon. In this stage of perfection, he obtains the association of the personality of God in the company of His eternal associates (*ragatmikas*), whether in His aspect as Vishnu in Vaikuntha, Krishna in Goloka-Vrindavana, or some of His many forms in the spiritual world. This direct loving service to the personality of God in the divine world is known as *raga-bhakti* and is only possible in an eternal spiritual body (*vastu-siddhi*). These are very advanced stages of spiritual evolution. However, the sincere practitioner who has given his heart to Krishna, even if he does not practice visualization of his divine body, on account of his pure devotion, revives his eternal identity once he reaches the supreme abode.

None of this happens overnight. It is a long process that

goes through several stages. Like all human effort, *bhakti* begins with an act of faith (*shraddha*) that springs from our hope of reaching the object of our love. This faith leads the candidate to seek the company of equally inclined persons engaged in the practice of *bhakti* (*sadhu-sanga*). Under this guidance, the candidate engages in proper spiritual practices (*bhajana-kriya*) so that gradually he cleanses his heart of impurities (*anartha-nivritti*), and step by step, his practice matures and solidifies (*nistha*). This determination leads him to experience a very intense taste (*ruchi*) for devotional activities such as hearing, talking about, and remembering Krishna's activities and pastimes. Gradually this taste is transformed into an intense attachment (*ashakti*) to the personality of Krishna and everything related to Him. When the practitioner attains such devotion, intense emotions (*bhava*) emerge as the first rays of the highest love for God (*prema*).

The experts in the science of *bhakti* tell us that there are several symptoms (*anubhavas*) that are prominent in the practitioner who has attained *bhava-bhakti* (love for Krishna with profound emotions): 1. he is naturally tolerant, 2. he does not waste his time in activities other than *bhakti*, 3. he feels a natural disinterest in the attractions of the world, 4. his heart is free from pride and desire to be recognized or respected by others, 5. he has a deep conviction of that he will receive Krishna's grace, 6. he has a burning desire for pure love (*krishna-prema*), 7. he has a natural taste for praying the names of Krishna, 8. he is attached to describing the transcendental qualities of Krishna, and 9. he likes to live in a place where Krishna manifested His pastimes.

In the stage of *bhava-bhakti*, the devotee serves the Lord with a heart brimming with a continuous flow of sublime feelings. When such feelings intensify in the heart, the practitioner achieves pure love for Godhead (*prema-bhakti*). This is the goal of *bhakti*. This pure love for Krishna (*prema*) is transcendent bliss; it is a mellow emanating from the world of pure loving exchanges (*prema-rasa*) and is rarely seen in this world. Prema is so typical of Krishna that the sages tell us that intrinsically He does not see Himself as the God of creation but as the enjoyer of *prema* (pure love), especially *prema-rasa* (pure loving exchanges) and, in particular, the *prema-rasa* of Vrindavana. The sages tell us that Krishna lives intoxicated by *vrindavana-prema-rasa*. Krishna is like an unquenchable fire that continually wants to try new forms of *prema-rasa* (love exchanges); therefore, when the first vestiges of *prema* sprout in a soul, this activates in Krishna a reciprocal feeling for delighting in the *prema* that His devotee offers Him. Although this *prema-rasa* exists within Krishna's internal potency (*svarupa-shakti*) under the effect of His pleasure potency (Radha), it acquires a very delightful effect (*prema-ananda*) for Krishna Himself.

As a reciprocal sentiment, this *prema-ananda* manifests itself in two flavors; the first lies within Krishna Himself (*svarupa-ananda*). The second is in the devotee's heart (*svarupa-shakti-ananda*). But, mysteriously, the *prema-ananda* emanating from the devotee's heart is more attractive and pleasant to Krishna than the *prema-ananda* within Krishna Himself. The analogy the great Vaishnava sage Jiva Goswami offer will help us to understand the reason for this. For example, a flute player can whistle, exhaling air through his mouth—but when this same air passes through the flute's holes, it generates a melody more attractive and charming to the flute player himself.

Similarly, when Radha (Krishna's pleasure potency) deposits Her grace in a devotee's heart, it acts as a lamp whose light reveals both the lamp itself and the objects around it. In the same way, when the light of love for Krishna (*krishna-priti*) emanates from the devotee's heart, its taste enchants Krishna in such a way that it acts as a force pulling in both directions simultaneously. This force draws Krishna towards His devotee and His devotee toward Krishna. When this attraction reaches its maximum degree, both become prisoners of mutual love. At this stage, the devotee serves Krishna with unlimited pleasure; consequently, Krishna is drawn towards the devotee to such an extent that He is subjugated to becoming the prisoner of his love.

Those who have captured Krishna with the *prema* of their heart are known as *premika-bhaktas*. The love of the *premika-bhakta* can be of two kinds. The devotee may feel attraction to Krishna's opulence (*aishuarya*) or His sweetness (*madhurya*). If his *prema* is entirely dominated by Krishna's opulence (*aishuarya*), it is known as *vaikuntha-prema*, reverential love for God. On the other hand, if his *prema* is for Krishna's sweetness (*madhurya*) but is still tinged by vestiges of His opulence (*aishuarya*), he will be attracted by the love that predominates in the abodes of Krishna known as Dvaraka, Mathura, Ayodhya, etc. But if his heart is overwhelmed exclusively by Krishna's *madhurya* (sweetness), his *prema* will be *vrindavana-prema*. Therefore, after leaving his mortal body, he becomes an associate of Radha and Krishna in Vrindavana according to his eternal *rasa*.

Chapter 18

The dynamism of love and spiritual emotions

The purpose of existence is transcendental enjoyment, and to enjoy *prema* is the essence of Krishna. The more intense *prema* is, the more intense the divine pleasure is since *prema* is an ecstatic feeling that grows and intensifies. *Prema* unites the soul with Krishna; however, it is not a union in identity but of love. It is like the union of iron and fire, in which iron acquires the heat and light of fire without losing its identity as iron. The dynamism of *prema* becomes visible in the form of a variety of sentiments or emotions (*bhavas*), which are the constituents of *rasa*—which the sages call special ecstasy (*vibhava*), subordinate ecstasy (*anubhava*), natural ecstasy (*sattvika*), and transitory ecstasy (*vyabhichari*).

The ingredients of rasa

Through *bhakti*, the practitioner develops a permanent emotion (*sthayi-bhava*) of love for Krishna in one of the five *rasas* that we already know (neutrality, servitude, friendship, paternal, conjugal, etc.). These emotions act as the ingredients that supply the distinctive aromas to the different flavors of *prema* and set in motion the loving exchanges in transcendence (*bhakti-rasa*).

What the sages call special ecstasy (*vibhava*) is that which awakens a feeling for Krishna and has a dual nature. The first is the root cause (*alambana*) of that love or what causes our attraction—Krishna himself. The second is Krishna's attributes (*uddipana*), such as His smile, His fragrance, His hair, His form, and other items such as His clothes, His flute, His peacock feather, etc. By perceiving these attributes, feelings of love for Krishna awaken in the devotee's heart, just as the feeling of love awakens in a lover's heart when she sees the belongings of her beloved. However, since the soul in the stage of *prema* is also a source of attraction for Krishna, the root cause (*alambana*) can also be dual. The first is known as the entity that enjoys (*vishaya*), and the second is where this attraction rests or the receptacle of love (*ashraya*). Therefore, as the root cause of attraction, Krishna is the enjoyer of all the beauty in the soul, while the soul is the receptacle of love for Krishna (*ashraya*), the cherished one. However, since this attraction is mutual, by being attracted to His devotee, Krishna also becomes the receptacle of love (*ashraya*), making the devotee the entity who enjoys Krishna's beauty (*vishaya*). Here is how it looks in graphic form.

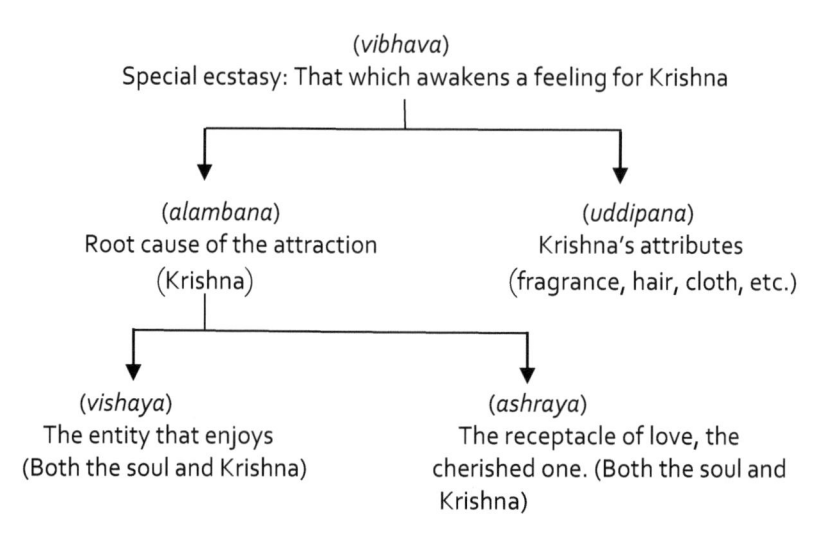

```
                        (vibhava)
       Special ecstasy: That which awakens a feeling for Krishna
                    ┌───────────┴───────────┐
                    ▼                       ▼
              (alambana)                (uddipana)
        Root cause of the attraction   Krishna's attributes
              (Krishna)            (fragrance, hair, cloth, etc.)
           ┌──────┴──────┐
           ▼             ▼
       (vishaya)                  (ashraya)
   The entity that enjoys     The receptacle of love, the
 (Both the soul and Krishna)  cherished one. (Both the soul and
                              Krishna)
```

From this dynamic of mutual attraction arise the subordinate ecstasies (*anubhava*), or thirteen spontaneous gestures that reveal the emotions that spring from the heart (such as singing, dancing, rolling on the ground, crying aloud, breathing panting, laughing out loud, etc.), regardless of the presence of others. When these sentiments increase in intensity, the natural ecstasy (*sattvika-bhava*) arises, which are intense emotions that produce eight types of physical transformations (*astha-sattvika-vikara*) such as tears, shuddering, hair standing on end, perspiration, paleness, stuttering, dizziness, and fainting. Although such emotions appear disturbing externally, they reveal the intensity of the highest divine ecstasy. Beyond these eight symptoms, the sages describe thirty-three types of transitory emotions (*vyabhichari*). They are so intense that they compete with each other to dominate the heart of the devotee, expressing sentiments that can be contradictory, like indifference and jealousy, anxiety and joy, humility and pride, confidence and disappointment, etc.

The progressive states of prema

Prema, pure love for God, can be achieved in this world; however, some of its highest symptoms can only be expressed in the soul's eternal spiritual body (*vastu-siddhi*). As a dynamic and ever-growing sentiment, *prema* varies in intensity and emotions depending on how the liberated soul experiences Krishna. The sages call these states *sneha*, *mana*, *pranaya*, *raga*, *anuraga*, *bhava*, and *maha-bhava*.

The feeling a saint experiences when his heart seems to melt due to his love for Krishna is called *sneha*. This state gives the impression that the devotee's eyes are always on the verge of shedding tears out of love for God. At that time, he cannot tolerate separation from Krishna even for an instant; his thirst for Krishna grows more and more and is never quenched. This *prema-sneha* has a dual component since, according to the nature of the devotee, it may manifest as a feeling of surrender or possession concerning the loved object. An example of this feeling of surrender is Chandravali, the manifestation of Radha, who acts as Her rival to increase the dynamism of the *lila*. The characteristic of Chandravali's love for Krishna is a feeling of "I am all yours." In contrast, Radha's love for Krishna is possessive. Radha's love for Krishna is marked by the attitude of "You are all mine." This mood is much more pleasant to Krishna since, as the possessor of everything, He feels great pleasure to be possessed by Radha, whose love surpasses all ordinary considerations of appropriateness and inappropriateness.

After *sneha,* there is an emotion known as *mana,* a kind of transcendental jealousy or anger. The exchanges between Radha, Krishna, and their cowherd friends overflow with intricacies that spring from youthful affairs. Sometimes Radha or Her friends pretend to have an unfavorable and angry attitude towards Krishna by hiding their real feeling, "Krishna will come, appease me, and try again to win my love." When this occurs, loving reconciliation arises within the divine *lila* between Krishna and His many divine lovers. However, when Radha or some other *gopi* rejects Him instead of hurting Krishna's feelings, this further increases the beauty of the *lila,* as it leads to the expression of romantic emotions in a divine reconciliation. These intimate dealings create a natural informality because the devotee feels that he and Krishna are equal. This feeling of equality is known as *pranaya* and is typical of the cowherd boys (*gopas*) of Vrindavana. They play with Krishna, absorbed in childish psychology without regard for His divinity. Due to the informality that springs from this feeling of equality, the cowherd boys roll with Krishna on the grass during His childhood games, climb on His shoulders, laugh at Him, steal food from His plate, or offer Him some candy that they have previously bitten. In the intensity of this love, the desire to please Krishna is so strong that the devotee feels that he will die if he cannot please Him. The sages describe this emotion as *raga* (very intense attraction). *Raga* is such an intense attachment to Krishna that if the devotees do not see Him for an instant, it is like their oxygen is lacking. Therefore, the devotee does whatever it takes to meet Him. In this *raga-bhava* (feeling of intense attraction), the greatest suffering is experienced as happiness if it leads to a meeting with Krishna, and the most painful happiness as pain if it does not lead to communion with Him. We have seen throughout history many saints sacrifice their lives with great pleasure for the service of God.

However, when *raga* becomes even more intense, it is called *anuraga*. Its characteristic is that each time the devotee sees Krishna, he experiences Him as younger, fresher, and more beautiful, just as if it were the first time he saw Him. His attachment to Krishna is so intense that even in His presence, the devotee experiences divine anxiety called *prema-vaichitya* that arises from the fear of just imagining being separated from Him again. A characteristic of *prema-vaichitya* is that the cowherd girls (*gopis*) often wish to be an inanimate object (such as Krishna's flute) to never separate from Him. *Prema-vaichitya* makes an instant of separation from Krishna feel like several millennia and several millennia in His company as an instant. In separation from Krishna, the cowherd boys (*gopas*) lose consciousness, while the cowherd girls (*gopis*) see Him so vividly in everything around them that they do not doubt Krishna is present. In this condition, the devotee experiences such deep emotions that the previously mentioned eight symptoms known as *astha-sattvika-vikara* manifest: tears, tremors, the hair standing on end, etc. This type of intense emotion (*bhava*) is a very advanced state of *prema* known as *mahabhava*, the highest expression of love of Godhead in which these eight symptoms manifest themselves in a much more exalted, radiant, and continuous way. *Mahabhava* (supreme emotions) is a sentiment unique to souls who have attained the position of eternal lovers of Krishna and can be experienced in separation from Krishna (*vipralambha*) and in union (*sambhoga*). Conjugal affection for Krishna also varies in intensity (reserved in Dvaraka and informal in Vrindavana), which is why *mahabhava* is of two types, *rudha* (advanced) and *adhirudha* (very advanced).

Rudha-mahabhava (or advanced *mahabhava*) manifests among Krishna's consorts, the queens in the divine abode of Dvaraka. Although this kind of conjugal love is so advanced that separation from Krishna cannot be tolerated, not even for an instant, it is nevertheless a love that is still tinged with a slight dose of reverential affection. It is a love touched with a dose of knowledge of Krishna's opulence as the Almighty God. In other words, because these queens (liberated souls who have attained the conjugal *rasa*) are aware of Krishna's divinity, in their romantic exchanges, the spontaneity of love does not manifest with the fullness or flow with the same sweetness as the one we find in Vrindavana. On the other hand, *adhiruda-mahabhava* (or very advanced *mahabhava*) is found only among the cowherd girls of Vrindavana (*gopis*) and no one else. It is called very advanced because it manifests the thirteen symptoms of *anubhava* (singing, dancing, rolling on the ground, etc.) even more intensely. Vaishnava sages tell us that *adhiruda-mahabhava* is so intense that if all the afflictions of this world and the bliss of Vaikuntha combine and pile up like a great mountain, it would not be equal to a drop of the bliss and pain of Radha's love for Krishna.

When *mahabhava* is experienced in separation from Krishna, it is known as *modana*, and when it is experienced in the union, it is called *madana*. *Modana-mahabhava* (very advanced love in separation from Krishna) is so intense that not all the cowherd girls of Vrindavana experience it, but only those who belong to Radha's group. In this rapture of love for Krishna's absence, the eight *sattvika-bhavas* (tears, tremors, the standing of the hair on end, etc.) are visible in Radha with such a unique charm that resembles a feeling of pain. Thus, it creates a divine illusion (*mohana*) so intense that only Radha is capable of experiencing it. Trapped in this divine illusion, just as if she were an ordinary mortal, Radha wishes to die so that the elements of Her body merge with the elements of the environment around Krishna to give Him pleasure. In this divine illusion (*mohana*), Radha wishes Her vital air to escape from Her body to brush Krishna's body. She longs for the water from Her body to flow into the Yamuna River to bathe Krishna's body when He enters her waters, etc. Even the animals of Vrindavana shed tears when they hear Radha's cry due to Krishna's absence, whom She wishes to make happy even if it requires tolerating the sharp pain of separation. This sentiments of Radha and Her *gopis* for Krishna is another pinnacle of the Vaishnava philosophy. It is a delightful subject to hear since it is the highest pinnacle of the feeling of love for Godhead. The beauty of Krishna's *lilas* is that, despite being the most joyous expression of the divinity in eternal spiritual bodies, such feelings resemble human frailties, adding a touch of real drama to divine *lila*. Such divine sentiments are the archetype of our similar human emotions.

This love for Krishna in His absence is known as feelings of separation (*vipralambha-bhava*) and is the most desired goal of every practitioner. Although its outward appearance resembles intense pain, due to the absolute nature of Krishna, this sentiment is a profound communion with Him that generates an indescribable bliss. Amid this divine illusion (*mohana*), Radha enters a state of divine madness (*divya-unmada*) and imagines that Krishna has returned to Vrindavana, and She gets ready to meet Him. But, not seeing Him, She again sinks into the melancholy of the pain of separation and expresses Her *mana* (anger or transcendental discontent) with words of resentment, rebuking Krishna for the ingratitude of abandoning Her. This *mana*, or anger of Radha, is a source of pleasure for both Radha and Krishna, who, like the perfect lover, offers Her words of reconciliation, setting in motion the *adi-rasa*—the original romantic, loving feeling which the individual souls imitate in this world. We spoke about this previously.

Finally, with the subsequent reencounter and union (*sambhoga*) of Radha and Krishna after having experienced intense separation (*vipralambha*), *mahabhava* reaches its climax (*madana*), which the sages also call *madanakhya-mahabhava* (whole experience of Krishna in the conjugal union). Although loving union with Krishna is available to all souls attracted to this *rasa*, the experience of *madanakhya-mahabhava* is unique to Radha, Krishna's pleasure potency, as it includes all states of *prema*. Since Radha is Krishna's innermost essence, the two never really separate in the ordinary sense. This is all part of the *lila*. A divine pastime by which Krishna savors the experience of longing for the lost love and other dimensions of His Self through Radha. In *Madanakhya-mahabhava,* one experiences Krishna in remembrance, union, separation, and thousands of different ways. Since Radha and Krishna are a single being— a single identity that has eternally manifested in two bodies to enjoy the conjugal loving *rasa*—naturally, the feeling of *madana* (supreme emotions in the union) is always present in Radha, even when both are apparently separated (*vipralambha*). Still, it manifests only when there is a union (*sambhoga*). When such a union reaches its peak, both Radha and Krishna lose consciousness of being a loving object or a beloved subject and experience only union without losing their eternal identities. This subject of the loving *rasa* between Radha and Krishna is elucidated with great clarity by the *premika-bhaktas*, devotees who relish these transcendental mellows in their hearts.

The grace of Shri guru

Achieving such a high degree of love for Godhead as that of Krishna's associates in Vrindavana (*vrajavasis*) may seem too far off for our present condition, but as a wise saying goes, "a long walk begins with a small step." This small step is the acceptance of a Vaishnava *guru*, an authentic spiritual master under whose guidance the candidate engages in devotional activities. This is the most crucial decision in a person's life. Without the blessing of a Vaishnava *guru*, the path back to Krishna becomes impossible since it is through the *guru* that Krishna's blessings come to us. The fallen souls receive Krishna's grace through holy persons who are themselves recipients of His Divine Grace and who transmit it to us in exchange for our sincere dedication.

The *guru* is the confidential servant of the Lord; therefore, devotion to the *guru* is essential to *bhakti*. To get closer to a prominent person in this world, we must first get closer to his representatives and secretaries. The science of *bhakti* comes to us through a succession of spiritual teachers (*guru-parampara*) from time immemorial, originating with Lord

Krishna Himself. Under the guidance of such a succession of spiritual teachers, the current spiritual preceptor (*guru*) receives this knowledge. In the Bhagavad-Gita, Lord Krishna endorses this system. The Vedas tell us that service to the *guru* is even more important than service to Krishna. The *guru* reconnects the fallen soul with Krishna at the moment of initiation. More than a ceremonial formality is the surrender of the heart to the Lord through His representative in disciplic succession. Without the guidance and blessing of the *guru*, we are blind on the path of *bhakti*, for progress on the way to Krishna is proportional to how much the *guru* is satisfied with the disciple's sincerity.

Through the instructions of the Vaishnava *guru*, the sincere practitioner removes from his heart all obstacles to his advancement (*anartha*) and receives the grace of Radha (Krishna's pleasure potency), which vitalizes the spiritual potential that lies dormant in his heart. *Guru* is not simply a person but a principle of eternal existence and knowledge personified by Balarama, the internal potency of Krishna, who manifests the limitless spiritual creation. Although in the more advanced stages of *bhakti*, the practitioner can perceive the guru's presence in all things, this principle of eternal existence and knowledge is also present in the world in the form of the Vaishnavas in a state of pure devotion. The quintessential Vaishnava *guru* is a liberated soul (*nitya-siddha*), an eternal associate of Radha and Krishna in Vrindavana who descends into this world to bring the fallen souls back home, back to Godhead.

Chapter 19

Krishna's lila in the spiritual and material world

Krishna's supreme spiritual realm, Goloka-Vrindavana, is a manifestation of Balarama, the personification of His spiritual potency, also called internal potency (*chit-shakti*). Although time is experienced as a perpetual present in this mystical realm, on account of Krishna's inconceivable potencies (*achintya-shakti*), His day lasts for eight periods of approximately three hours, ranging from dawn to dusk. During this period of 24 divine hours, Krishna performs different pastimes that follow one after the other without interruption for eternity. Because they occur in eight three-hour periods, the sages call them eightfold pastimes (*astha-kaliya-lila*).

At dawn, the cowherd boys, Krishna's close friends, the cowherd boys, rush to His house to wake Him up from His conscious sleep. They bring treats their mothers prepared to eat as they spend the day in the forest, herding the cows alongside Krishna and "His older brother" Balarama. Mother Yashoda also prepares sweets for Krishna and Balarama, who go to the forest, leaving the inhabitants of Vrindavana in an ocean of longing to see them again (*vipralambha-bhava*). The goal of the process of *krishna-bhakti* is to develop this feeling of separation from Krishna (*vipralambha*=separataion, *bhava*=emotion), which is an intense longing to obtain His perpetual association. Krishna sometimes seems momentarily absent from Vrindavana to increase this hankering for Him due to the separation (*vipralambha*). Such separation makes the reunion (*sambhoga*) even more delightful. This eternal swing between *vipralamabha* and *sambhoga* (separation and reunion) nurtures the relationship between Krishna and the liberated souls, perpetually enhancing the taste of *rasa*.

While Krishna and Balarama play in the forest with their friends, cowherd boys, each sees Krishna by his side, although there are millions of boys. Meanwhile, in His transcendental village, Nanda, Yashoda, the cowherd girls, and the rest of the endless inhabitants of Vrindavana spend their days engaged in their chores, absorbed in feelings of separation. Their longing to see Krishna increases more and more at every moment. Finally, with the arrival of sunset, Krishna and Balarama, along with their countless cowherd boys friends, return to the magical and divine village of Vrindavana. With their loving glances, they enliven the hearts of its inhabitants. The cowherd boys, endowed with eternal childish psychology, tell their parents all the mischief they did with Krishna and Balarama during the day in the forest on the banks of the Yamuna River. The love (*prema*) of the cowherd boys for Krishna is such that in the conscious dream of the divine night of Goloka, they dream that they are still in the forest in the company of Krishna and Balarama.

Upon His return, Krishna dines in the palace of His father Nanda in the company of His cousins, uncles, cowherd boys friends, and other associates, delighting in different subjects and activities. Well into the night, while everyone sleeps under the influence of *yoga-maya*, the spiritual dream of Goloka-Vrindavana, Krishna escapes from His father's palace and returns to the forests on the banks of the Yamuna. With the enchanting sound of His flute, He awakens in the hearts of the *gopis* the longing for conjugal union. Eager to see Him again, the *gopis* sneak out of their homes and run into the forest to meet Krishna, the original beloved of the soul. In this communion between Krishna and the most elevated souls, there is an exchange of glances, words, laughter, flirting, and loving games expressing the original conjugal feeling (*adi-rasa*) imitated by the conditioned souls in this world. Amid this eternal exhilaration, Krishna, Radha, and His millions of *gopis* engage in flirtations typical of young romantic love. In this environment, Krishna performs His well-known *rasa* dance, or dance of divine love. When Krishna manifests this captivating divine dance in His pastimes in this world, it lasts for a single night of Brahma (four thousand six hundred and twenty million earth years) that—through His mystical potency—He inserts into an ordinary human night. Whereas for Nanda and Yashoda, Krishna is the most charming son, and for the cowherd boys, He is the best of friends; for Radha and Her millions of cowherd girlfriends, Krishna is the freshest, most handsome young man, the best of lovers, the original cupid, and the personification of romantic love. As in the case of the cowherd boys, during the *rasa* dance, each *gopi* experiences that Krishna is at her side offering His love so that each one of them feels they are the most fortunate. When this divine night comes to an end, everyone returns to their homes. At dawn, the cowherd boys run to Nanda and Yashoda's palace to meet their little friend Krishna to return to the forest to herd the *surabhi* cows (also known as *kama-dhenu* because they satisfy all desires) and play childlike games, thus beginning a new day in eternity.

Simultaneously, in the endless spiritual Vaikuntha planets and other portions of Goloka-Vrindavana (such as Dvaraka, Mathura, etc.), Krishna performs an infinity of pastimes. However, this is a pale and reduced description of what Vaishnava sages have revealed to us in their writings.

Vrindavana in this world

Krishna-lila (the eternal pastimes of Krishna) also manifest in the material creation whenever Krishna descends into this world; however, when this occurs, they acquire distinctive characteristics of their own because Krishna interacts with (and sometimes imitates) human customs for our pleasure. For example, even though Krishna is not subject to the laws of material nature, in His *lilas* in this world, He is born and grows up, thus giving a dramatic touch to His earthly pastimes. Because of this, the sages call these *lilas* of Krishna, *nara-lila*, or human-like pastimes. The fact that the participants in *krishna-lila* in this world seem to suffer from human frailties gives it an unparalleled appeal.

When Lord Krishna descends into material creation, He does not do so alone but brings His potencies, associates, eternal abodes, etc. The Vedas tell us that the sacred sites where Krishna appears and performs His pastimes in this world (Vrindavana, Mathura, Dvaraka, etc.) are replicas of the spiritual abodes of Goloka-Vrindavana within the material creation. As the embassy of a foreign country, it is a sovereign territory; these sacred places are spiritual abodes. Yet, despite replicas of their spiritual counterparts, they appear to be ordinary places only because of our conditioned vision. The ability to perceive the spiritual nature of these holy places is the exclusive privilege of perfect souls. Even in their physical bodies, their high degree of *prema* enables them to see the eternal pastimes of Krishna (*nitya-lila*) in Vrindavana in the company of His associates, for they have attained supreme perfection (*siddha-avastha*). However, when Krishna manifests in human society, these pastimes become visible to everyone present without distinction. The sages call these pastimes *pra-*

kata-lila (manifested pastimes). However, when this divine play comes to an end, and Krishna's *lila* is no longer visible to the eyes of the world, the sages call it *aprakata-lila* (unmanifested pastimes). The *lilas* or eternal pastimes of Krishna in His spiritual abodes are also called *aprakata* (unmanifested) as they are not visible to the eyes of the conditioned souls.

About 100 miles southeast of New Delhi, the present capital of India, is the city of the earthly Mathura, which lies within an area that the sages call Vraja-mandala, which is about 1,453 square miles. Within this area of Vraja-mandala or district of Mathura, the divine Vrindavana touches the earth and manifests the earthly Vrindavana visible to our eyes, which is not different in substance from Goloka-Vrindavana, although imperceptible for physical eyes. However, the great Vaishnava saints tell us that in the highest state of consciousness, the vision of the divine nature of earthly Vrindavana is possible even while living in the physical body. Therefore, as in the Goloka-Vrindavana of the spiritual world, the earthly Vrindavana is the spiritual core of Vraja-mandala. The sages refer to Bhauma-Vrindavana by various names to distinguish it from the Vrindavana of the spiritual world, such as Vraja-bhumi, Gokula, or simply Bhauma-Vrindavana (earthly Vrindavana). Bhauma-Vrindavana only seems to be a product of physical nature because of the worldly covering that envelops our consciousness. In Bhauma-Vrindavana, the *lilas* of Krishna are also eternal, though sometimes they become visible or manifested (*prakata*) and other times invisible or not manifested (*aprakata*) to the eyes of the world.

Behind the illusory veil that covers our vision lies the divinity of Bhauma-Vrindavana, where, as an extension of the Vrindavana of the divine world, Radha and Krishna eternally dwell with their infinity of eternal associates. Only the most exalted devotees have access to this reality. It is in the Vrindavana of this world that Lord Krishna is born, grows up, and performs His extraordinary childhood *lilas* just as if He were an ordinary child. When Krishna's pastimes are visible in this world (*prakata-lila*), there is a kind of fusion or hypostatic union between the divine and earthly elements. However, it is not a mixture in the ordinary sense since the touch of divine Vrindavana turns divine the physical nature where it manifests.

The Krishna lila in this world

The sages tell us that Krishna descends into this world in His original form on each day of Brahma, just before the beginning of the age of Kali—that is, every eight thousand six hundred twenty million earthly years. However, Krishna executes His *lilas* in Bhauma-Vrindavana (the earthly Vrindavana) or any other manifestation of His abodes in material creation without being absent from Goloka-Vrindavana (the Vrindavana of the spiritual world). Krishna's birth (*janma-lila*) in this world is wrapped in a mystical veil since it is the work of *yoga-maya*, the illusory spiritual potency of Krishna.

As the original person, Krishna is unborn (*aja*); however, as the complete whole, possessor of infinite opulence, and Supreme Enjoyer of an infinity of pastimes, nothing prevents Him from being born if He pleases. However, as the origin of all, Krishna is also *the original or first born*. Unlike the conditioned souls who are born covered by ignorance and under the force of material nature, Krishna's birth is a *lila*, a pastime carried out by His will, with complete control and knowledge of His divine potencies—an expression of His eternal enjoyment. Because Krishna experiences birth as part of His divine *lila*, we can experience it in this world. However, Krishna is born for the pleasure of His devotees, specifically for the pleasure of mother Yashoda; however, His birth is not the result of the seminal injection. Krishna's eternal body is a divine substance; therefore, it does not develop within a mother's womb when He performs His *prakata-lila* (pastimes in this world). Thus, both Krishna's "birth" and His "conception" are alien to the biological laws of nature.

The visible pastimes (*prakata-lila*) "begin" before Krishna's advent with the birth of His eternal parents, Nanda, Yashoda, His various potencies, and other eternal associates who act as His elders. All this is carried out through His internal *yoga-maya* potency, which creates the atmosphere and psychology necessary for the perfection of Krishna's *lila*. *Yoga-maya* is like a great theater director. When Krishna manifested His *lilas* in this world about 5,100 years ago, He appeared simultaneously in the city of Mathura and the divine village of Vrindavana. In Mathura, Krishna appeared as the son of Vasudeva and Devaki, two exalted souls who practiced penances in previous lives to obtain Krishna as their son.

In contrast, Krishna is Nanda and Yashoda's eternal son in Vrindavana, the abode of spontaneous love. They are unaware of Krishna's divinity as the Supreme Lord. Both Devaki and Yashoda's pregnancy and Krishna's birth are unusual. According to Srimad Bhagavatam, the supreme text among the Vedic scriptures, by His omnipresence, first Krishna stood in the heart and mind of "His father" Vasudeva, in the city of Mathura. This is not surprising since, in His aspect as the oversoul, He is situated in the heart of every living being and within every atom of creation. However, His standing in Vasudeva's heart implies that He does so in His personal aspect as *Bhagavan* with all His opulence. Srimad Bhagavatam describes that His father Vasudeva acquired such a divine effulgence that it was difficult to look at him. From the heart of Vasudeva, Krishna transferred Himself to the womb of Devaki.

The presence of Krishna in Devaki's womb is not like that of an ordinary child compressed in the darkness of ignorance and covered by a bloody bag. Even in Devaki's womb, Krishna is always free from contact with worldly nature and has complete knowledge of His identity. He dwells in His mother's womb as He does in the hearts of all beings. Just as an ambassador from a rich country to a poor one lives in a grand mansion surrounded by luxury like that of the country he represents, similarly for Krishna, there is no difference between Vasudeva's heart, Devaki's womb, and His abode in Goloka-Vrindavana. The Srimad Bhagavatam also describes that Devaki's body acquired an indescribable radiance during her divine pregnancy. Because the personality of God situated Himself within her, the heavenly entities offered her prayers. When finally, by the action of *yoga-maya,* the pregnancy ceased, the majestic form of the four-armed Vishnu—adorned with all His divine assets—appeared before Devaki, dazzling her with His presence. Devaki, whose heart longed for maternal *rasa* with Krishna, prayed to this form of Vishnu, expressing her desire to have Him as a son. Because Krishna repays the love of His devotees according to the way they wish to love Him, He manifested the captivating form of a divine baby at once. As we have already mentioned, this form that Krishna showed before Devaki in Mathura, either as a baby or later on in His youthful appearance, is not the original form of Krishna (*svayam-bhagavan*) from which all other forms spring. Such form is a manifestation known as Vaasudeva (notice the two As, not to be confused with Vasudeva, Krishna's father, in the city of Mathura). Devaki's brother (the cruel King Kamsa) knew of a prophecy that he would die because of his sister's eighth child, so he hoped to kill the child. Therefore, Vasudeva (Krishna's father) took the baby Krishna-Vaasudeva from the great city of Mathura to the village of Vrindavana to protect Him from Kamsa, where, unknown to him, a similar event had occurred.

Vrindavana is the eternal abode of Krishna, from which He is not absent even for a fraction of an instant. Due to the nature of Vrindavana's love, Krishna does not appear before Yashoda as the mighty four-armed Vishnu to whom Devaki offered prayers. In Vrindavana, Krishna is actually born of Yashoda, although, as we have already said, this birth is not like that of an ordinary soul. Krishna dwells in the divine womb of Yashoda just as He dwells in the hearts of all beings. Through His *yoga-maya* potency, in earthly Vrindavana, Krishna performs the *lila* of being born to such perfection that both His mother, Yashoda, and His father, Nanda, actually believe that Krishna was born from them; therefore, He is their son. Because Krishna likes to enjoy the spontaneous love from the motherly *rasa*, *yoga-maya* ingrains this fatherly feeling towards Krishna in Nanda and Yashoda. They do not know that Krishna is the personality of God. This divine "ignorance" is the highest state of enlightenment.

Tired of the effort of bringing a child into the world (a sensation also caused by *yoga-maya*), Yashoda lies soundly asleep with her divine son. He was born along with His *yoga-maya* potency in the form of a girl—without Yashoda being aware of it. Vasudeva enters the room with the Krishna born in Mathura (Vaasudeva-Krishna) and deposits Him right where the original Krishna (*svayam-bhagavan*) lies, who—by the action of *yoga-maya*—is not visible to Vasudeva. At that moment, Vaasudeva-Krishna (the Krishna who appeared in Mathura) enters the body of *suayam-bhagavan* (the original Krishna born in Vrindavana), and only one Krishna is visible. In return, Vasudeva takes *yoga-maya* as a girl and returns to Mathura. When Yashoda awakens, she realizes that "her son" Krishna has been born. Once Vasudeva is back in the city of Mathura, the evil Kamsa tries to kill the girl, believing Her to be the daughter of Vasudeva and Devaki. However, the *yoga-maya* girl assumes a form as the personification of material nature (Durga), announcing to Kamsa that the child at whose hands he will die was born somewhere else. Then, she disappears. Let us remember that the birth of Krishna is a display of His mystical potency and not under the laws of material nature; His entering or leaving the heart of living beings is something like a king passing through the different rooms of his palace.

Krishna performs His childhood pastimes for the next ten years—the most attractive of all His *lilas*—in Bhauma-Vrindavana (the earthly Vrindavana). The Vaishnava sages reveal that although these *lilas* of Bhauma-Vrindavana are a metaphysical continuity of the *lilas* in Goloka-Vrindavana (the spiritual world), there are still specific differences between the two. In Goloka-Vrindavana, Krishna always has the appearance of a fresh young man just at the ideal age for relishing the flirtation of romantic love. Yet, under the influence of *yoga-maya*, the cowherd boys perceive Him as a friend of their age, while in the eyes of Nanda, Yashoda, and adult relatives, He is perceived as their son or most beloved child. However, because of His *yoga-maya* mystical potency, in Gokula or Bhauma-Vrindavana (the earthly Vrindavana), Krishna is actually born, grows, etc.—apparently just as if He were an ordinary child—to give the perfect human touch to His earthly *lilas* while enjoying the varieties of *rasa*. This is the reason why the sages tell us that Krishna's *nara-lilas* (the human-like pastimes) in Gokula or Bhauma-Vrindavana (the earthly Vrindavana) are even more attractive and complete than in Goloka-Vrindavana (the Vrindavana of the spiritual world) since they resemble the fragility of human nature. However, we must remember that since this world is a distorted version of divine creation, ultimately, our human activities resemble Krishna's activities.

Another distinctive aspect of the *lilas* in Bhauma-Vrindavana is that Krishna, even as a cowherd boy, satisfies His friends and other inhabitants by fighting with great demons who threaten to create chaos in Vrindavana. These demons of *krishna-lila* are not ordinary people but souls who, in previous births, performed severe penances to achieve worldly achievements, on account of which they developed great power. However, due to their desire to lord over material nature, they developed a mentality adverse to Krishna. Whereas death comes to ordinary beings by the effect of the laws of material nature (old age, disease, calamities, etc.), these souls—although of perverse conscience—are fortunate. As a result of meritorious acts or their many penances, when Krishna personally kills them by touching their physical body, their consciousness is purified. Thus, they achieve either impersonal liberation (the goal of the monists) or are promoted to Vaikuntha, or even in Goloka-Vrindavana.

Another fundamental characteristic of *vrindavana-lila* concerns Krishna and His cowherd girl lovers (*gopis*). According to the Vaishnava sages, in Goloka-Vrindavana (the spiritual world), the feeling (*bhava*) of the *gopis* for Krishna is naturally that of a lover (*parakiya-bhava*) without the need for marriage. This is possible since, in the spiritual world, both the relationships with Krishna and the feelings are eternal; that is, they do not have a beginning (*anadi*). We previously mentioned that this is only because of *yoga-maya*'s effect, to increase the intensity of the *lila* and makes the cowherd girls appear to someone else's wives when actually they are the eternal beloved of Krishna. However, in Bhauma-Vrindavana (the earthly Vrindavana), to give the human dimension to the *lila*, the *gopis* do marry, although their supposed husbands never touch their bodies. According to the sages, *yoga-maya* substitutes the *gopis* for their illusory forms at the time of their wedding, thus creating the illusion of marriage.

Another notable distinction is that not all the souls who participate in the Vrindavana of this world are eternal associates who descend with Krishna from the spiritual world. However, some are souls who achieve a high state of perfection and reenter the eternal *lila*. When a soul makes sufficient progress on the path of *bhakti* and realizes his eternal relationship with Krishna, upon leaving his body, he is born somewhere in the material universe where Lord Krishna will manifest His pastimes. In other words, he attains Krishna's association in one of the manifestations of Vrindavana within the material creation, where he participates in His pastimes even in his physical body. In the company of Krishna and His eternal associates who have a similar feeling (*bhava*) to his own, his love for Krishna increases. From them, he receives the necessary virtue to perfect his eternal service. Then, leaving his physical form, his association with Krishna continues without interruption in his spiritual body in the divine world, for the *krishna-lila* in this world is a continuity of the eternal *lila* in the spiritual world. For example, about 5,100 years ago, during *krishna-lila* in earthly Vrindavana, some of the *gopis* were great sages who previously awakened the attraction for the conjugal *rasa* in their hearts. Therefore, they were born in

Bhauma-Vrindavana as cowherd girls and attained the company of Krishna.

In this regard, Srila Prabhupada comments in chapter 28 of his book "Krishna, the Supreme Personality of Godhead." "Just as the sun globe is passing over many places across this earthly planet, so *krishna-lila,* or the transcendental advent and pastimes of Krishna, are also going on continuously, either in this or another universe. The mature devotees, who have completely executed Krishna consciousness, are immediately transferred to the universe where Krishna appears. In that universe, the devotees get their first opportunity to associate with Krishna personally and directly. The training goes on, as we see in the *vrndāvana-līlā* of Krishna within this planet. Krishna, therefore, revealed the actual features of the Vaikuntha planets so that the inhabitants of Vrindavana could know their destination."

However, in chapter 46, "Uddhava visits Vrindana," Prabhupada makes a different comment. "This is the result of Krishna conscious practice. If we practice Krishna consciousness in this present body while in a healthy condition and in good mind, simply by chanting the holy *mahā-mantra,* Hare Krishna, we will have every possibility of fixing the mind upon Krishna at the time of death. If we do this, then our lives become successful without any doubt… Therefore, to remain always absorbed in Krishna consciousness was the standard of the inhabitants of Vrindavana, as exhibited by Maharaja Nanda, Yashoda, and the *gopis*. If we can simply follow in their footsteps, even to a minute proportion, our lives will surely become successful, and we shall enter the spiritual kingdom, Vaikuntha."

The apparent discrepancy can be adjusted if we consider that both cases are possible depending on each soul and his ultimate destiny according to his *rasa*. In his writings, Prabhupada often uses the term Vaikuntha not only to refer to Vishnu's abode but generically to indicate the spiritual creation in general, which includes Goloka-Vrindavan. As in the previous case, he often uses Krishna instead of Vishnu concerning Vaikuntha.

Srimad Bhagavatam also describes that some of the cowherd girls who had just entered *vrindavana-lila* did not have the necessary qualifications to participate in Krishna's most intimate *lilas* because they still had traces of material conditioning. Despite the intensity of their sentiments of conjugal love for Krishna, they still had vestiges of feeling that they belonged to someone else and not exclusively to Krishna. These cowherd girls did get married and had children. Because of this, they were not graced from the very beginning with the intimate association of Krishna. Therefore, when Krishna sounded the irresistible melody of His flute, inviting the gopis to participate in His attractive dance of love in the middle of the night, these *gopis* could not participate since their relatives prevented them. However, due to the burning fire of love for Krishna in their hearts and the blessings of the most prominent *gopis*, they gradually purified the last vestiges of conditioning. Thus, they attained the loving company of Krishna in their spiritual bodies while their physical bodies slept in their homes with their husbands, children, and other relatives.

Since Krishna's relationship with the *gopis*, either as wives (*svakiya-rasa*) or secret lovers (*parakiya-rasa*), is a topic of subtle complexity, the great Vaishnava sages have thoroughly elucidated this issue in our favor in different ways. For example, preventing others from looking at the relationship as a secret lover (*parakiya-rasa*) in the light of ordinary adulterous behavior, the sage Jiva Goswami often emphasizes the relationship of Krishna with the *gopis* as formally married (*suakiya-rasa*). In this way, he satisfies those who fail to appreciate the pure divine essence of the secret lover (*parakiya-rasa*) relationship between Krishna and His *gopis*. According to Jiva Goswami, since the *gopis* are an intrinsic part of Krishna and belong only to Him, this must be the eternal relationship between them. At the same time, Jiva Goswami also emphasizes the temporary and illusory character of the marriage of the *gopis* to their husbands during the *lila* of this world. However, avoiding denying the eternal reality of the relationship of secret lovers (*parakiya-rasa*), Jiva Goswami tells us that, although illusory, the marriage of the *gopis* with their spouses is also real because it is an action of *yoga-maya*, the magic potency of Krishna. Jiva Goswami adds that this relationship of the *gopis* with Krishna in the unmanifested pastimes (*aprakata-lila*) of the Vrindavana of the spiritual sky is like formally married couples (*svakiya*) without the slightest trace of marital union with others. It is a natural conjugal relationship without a beginning through marriage since eternal relationships have neither a beginning nor an end (*anadi*). Since this relationship of secret lovers between Krishna and His *gopis* is a natural sentiment, it does not demand the existence of husbands. Therefore, it is understood that its foundation is simply the pleasure that this eternal attraction generates in Krishna and His cowherd girl lovers (*gopis*). It is a natural sentiment that they manifest toward each other.

Another great Vaishnava sage, Visvanatha Chakravarti, offers us a slight variant of the same eternal principle. Visvanatha maintains that love as a secret lover is present not only in Krishna's pastimes in this material world (*prakata-lila*) but also in the unmanifested pastimes of Vrindavana in the spiritual world (*aprakata-lila*). For Visvanatha, the gopis or cowherd girls, being personifications of Krishna's pleasure potency, are fundamentally His eternal wives. Their relationship as secret lovers, whether in the Vrindavana of the spiritual world or the earthly Vrindavana, is simply the distinguishing feature of their eternal sentiment for Krishna. Such a feeling is like Nanda and Yashoda's feeling of parental love for Krishna, which is eternal and does not depend on Krishna's birth. Visvanatha considers that the marriage of the *gopis* in the *lila* of this world is carried out by *maha-maya* (the external energy) and not by *yoga-maya* (the spiritual illusion or internal energy). Therefore, although it is real, it is not absolutely real. Therefore, according to both sages, obeying the inconceivable nature of *krishna-lila*, the marriage of Krishna's eternal associate *gopis* with their husbands in this world is a magical unfolding of *maya* (the illusory potency) that enlivens the *lila*.

Some Vaishnava sages see this apparent difference between the two explanations more in terms of their modes of expression than in the character of the relationship itself. Both agree that the relationship between Krishna and His *gopis* is as eternally betrothed (*suakiya-rasa*). However, *yoga-maya* superimposes the feeling of secret lovers (*parakiya-rasa*) to increase the pleasure of the union so that both can savor the most intense and intimate form of conjugal love, which requires transcending the barriers of the illicit. Although one relationship appears to be transitory and the other permanent, both are eternal *rasas* since the *lilas* of Krishna, both in the Vrindavana of the spiritual world and those manifested to human eyes in the Vrindavana of this world, are eternal.

In turn, other great Vaishnava sages clarify this apparent complexity by telling us that the excellence of Krishna's pastimes in earthly Vrindavana is not because the relationship of secret lovers is exclusive to the pastimes in this world but because in this world, they manifest with greater intensity. Since *parakiya-rasa* resembles illicit love, this provides the ideal background for fully expressing the emotions of conjugal love—the act of transgressing social norms by total and unreserved surrender to Krishna, the eternal lover of all souls. Ultimately, for the *gopis*, who are direct extensions of Radha's body (the pleasure potency of Krishna) or individual souls who have attained the conjugal rasa, their relationship with Krishna is neither as wives (*svakiya-rasa*) nor as secret lovers (*parakiya-rasa*). These are nothing more than concepts of human morality that do not apply to love relationships in the eternal world. Their so-called husbands only appear to be so due to the nature of the *lila*, just as for the same reason Krishna seems to be their secret lover since, in truth, Krishna is the natural lover of all souls. It is only to increase the intensity of the romantic love that *yoga-maya* creates the emotion of making the cowherd girls feel that they belong to someone else. In this way, Krishna enjoys all the flavors and psychologies of conjugal feeling: formal, informal, lawful, and forbidden.

Rasa-tattva (the philosophical concepts that sustain the essence of *krishna-lila*), and especially of romantic love relationships in transcendence, is a lofty subject, and it constitutes the essence of Vaishnava philosophy, which is exceptionally vast, profound, and detailed. Nevertheless, let us remember that what we present here is only a basic explanation of the topic, a drop of water drawn from the infinite ocean of spiritual, romantic feelings.

Krishna leaves Vrindavana

At around ten years and eleven months of age, Krishna leaves

Vrindavana and goes to the city of Mathura under the pretext of saving His parents, Vasudeva and Devaki. There He remains for eighteen years and carries out many other lilas. In Mathura, Krishna frees His parents from Kamsa's prison and changes His cowherd garb for that of royalty. Now, in the company of His "brother" Balarama, Krishna is surrounded and served by the inhabitants of Mathura. They love Krishna and Balarama with profound reverential affection, which differs from the spontaneous feeling of the inhabitants of Vrindavana. But the question is, why does Krishna, who infinitely loves the inhabitants of Vrindavana, abandon them, leaving them submerged in an ocean of lamentation over His separation?

In the Bhagavad-Gita, Lord Krishna declares that he descends to annihilate the wicked and redeem the pious when there is an increase in irreligion. This redemption of the world from evil hosts culminated in the battle of Kurukshetra, at the beginning of which Krishna spoke His instructions to Prince Arjuna, words that today are known as the Bhagavad-Gita. Releasing His parents from the prison of Kamsa and destroying the evil hosts were reasons for His departure from Vrindavana. However, we will mention a hidden reason for this shortly. Krishna never leaves Vrindavana even though He appears to do so. We said earlier that when Krishna crosses the boundary of His divine village to go to the city of Mathura, His original form becomes unmanifest. Instead, a replica of Him known as Vaasudeva gives continuity to the *lila* outside Vrindavana. This form of Vaasudeva lacks specific characteristics exclusive to His original form in Vrindavana since, in Mathura, the character of the *lila* is different.

In due course of time, Krishna also leaves the city of Mathura and manifests the magnificent city of Dvaraka, floating on the waters of the Arabian Sea. There He remains for the next 96 years with the members of His divine dynasty, including millions of His associates. Even today, archaeologists search for the remains of this city. In Dvaraka, Krishna manifests His divine opulence by multiplying Himself into sixteen thousand different forms that live in sixteen thousand palaces, with His sixteen thousand queens, and has ten children with each of them. It is not surprising that Krishna has wives and children. We have already explained the subject of the conjugal rasa, of how Krishna accepts as His eternal wives the souls who love Him with a marital romantic feeling. Nor does Krishna beget children in the way that ordinary human beings do. The Vedas themselves tell us that Krishna impregnates the material nature with living entities just by glancing at the moment of creation. Everything that exists is but a manifestation of His potencies, so the fact that His eternal wives conceive children in the divine *lila* that becomes visible in this world does not make Krishna an ordinary husband. After all, Krishna is the father of creation, and we all, without exception, are His children.

We also know that, unlike the pastimes of Vrindavana, which are brimming with childhood mood and romantic love, the nature of pastimes in Mathura, Dvaraka, and elsewhere is an unparalleled display of endless opulence that testifies to His divinity. In whatever form Krishna manifests, His associates (*parikaras*) always surround Him, many of whom do not belong to the category of soul (*jiva-tattva*) but are manifestations of His spiritual potency (*svarupa-shakti*), such as Nanda, Yashoda, Balarama, and many others.

Krishna was present in this world for 125 years, during which He always remained as a young man of only 16 years, which is His eternal identity. The closure of Krishna's pastimes in this world (*mausala-lila*) revolves around the destruction of His dynasty (known as Yadu), the consequent destruction of the city of Dvaraka, and His apparent death. Like all His pastimes, the *mausala-lila* is wrapped in the mystical veil of yoga-maya, giving it the final dramatic touch by resembling human nature (*nara-lila*).

Srimad Bhagavatam describes that just as human beings cannot trace the path that a lightning bolt will travel when it comes out of a cloud, even celestial beings could not trace the path that Krishna traveled when He left this world and returned to His eternal abode. When Krishna considered that the time to close His *lilas* had come, He informed the sages of His dynasty that He observed signs in the sky that heralded calamity, and He warned them that they should no longer remain in the city of Dvaraka. Once they left the city, *yoga-maya* caused the members of Krishna's dynasty to get drunk on rice wine and fight until they annihilated each other. We must remember that we should not look at the actions performed by the *yoga-maya* potency of Krishna in the light of everyday experience. The members of the Yadu dynasty are the eternal associates of Krishna; as such, they are not under the laws of material nature as ordinary souls. According to the great Vaishnava sages Jiva Goswami and Visvanatha Chakravarti, the destruction of the Yadu dynasty was not a historical event but a display of Krishna's internal potency to remove His dynasty from the earth. This implies that Krishna also displays illusory pastimes.

One of the causes of Krishna's descent into this world was to remove the excess burden of powerful military dynasties that populated the earth. Many kings who led these dynasties executed great penances in previous lives and possessed mystical powers (*yoga-siddhis*) through which they gained im-

arrow, Jara felt fearful and fell at the feet of Krishna, recognizing Him as the personality of Godhead. In fact, according to the sages, Yara is not an ordinary hunter but the mighty sage Bhrigu, who, in a previous birth, placed his foot on Vishnu's chest and had to be born once more to counteract his offense. Even today, the place from which Jara shot the arrow is known as Bhrigu-tirtha, a place of pilgrimage.

Also, the Vaishnava sages reveal that the divine Dvaraka returned to the spiritual world at the closing of Krishna's *lilas*. At the same time, a replica made of physical elements sank into the sea, thus giving a touch of terrifying human drama to the *lila*. Similarly, the members of the Yadu dynasty that annihilated each other, and the rest of Krishna's eternal associates, like Vasudeva and Devaki, that apparently died with the Dvaraka dynasty, were material replicas or representations of the original ones. These associates continue to exist in the eternal *lila* in the original and divine Dvaraka in the spiritual world, beyond the influence of the calamities of material nature. The sages recognize that being a display of Krishna's inner potency, the disappearance of His city and the destruction of His dynasty is shrouded in a mystical veil; it was but a display of His illusory power. The Acharyas tell us that in another parallel and unmanifest dimension of the *lila*, Krishna returned to Bhauma-Vrindavana and from there to Goloka-Vrindavana in the spiritual world together with His eternal associates, thus closing His *prakata-lila* or pastimes manifested in this mortal world.

However, Krishna does not have to descend into this world to cause the annihilation of all beings. We are all destined to die by the force of time, the unconquerable potency of Krishna. As we previously said, when Krishna personally removes a soul from his physical body (what we ordinarily call death), He awards him liberation from material captivity. Therefore, we must understand that such souls had an extraordinary accumulation of pious activities in previous births. Krishna is absolute—although His actions externally are different, the result is always positive. For a conditioned soul who has developed the tendency to confront Krishna, "dying" by engaging Him offers the same result as a yogi who has attained perfection: liberation from material bondage. Although externally, Krishna's activities are similar to human activities, they are always on the supramundane plane; they are divine, blissful, and perfect.

The battle of Kurukshetra

The whole plot in the Mahabharata is summed up in the great battle of Kurukshetra, at which point Krishna spoke His wise words to His cousin and disciple, Prince Arjuna. The fact that Krishna spoke the Bhagavad-Gita on a battlefield and encouraged Prince Arjuna to take part in it is surprising and contradictory to many people. The Mahabharata, or the history of Greater India, tells us of the attempt by some of the members of the Kuru dynasty to usurp the throne of the five Pandava brothers (of which Arjuna was one), who were the rightful heirs. This crisis constitutes the central drama of the Mahabharata. Logically, when power is usurped in society by questionable means, constitutional values are destroyed, and an illegitimate form of government reigns. Under such circumstances, citizens expect the military and legitimate rulers to do their duty. As a member of the martial class, Prince Arjuna found himself in a predicament to choose either fulfilling his duty or renouncing it to avoid a confrontation with his family members. At this time, Krishna spoke to Arjuna about the value of *dharma* and instructed him that, as a member of the ruling and martial class, it was his duty to put aside family sympathies and act as is expected of a rightful ruler.

The Bhagavad-Gita reveals that the fulfillment of duty (*dharma*) must be above the individual interest. Even in modern society, when a person gives up his comforts to pursue justice is considered an exemplary hero. If a police officer lets his son get away after committing a crime, it is considered dishonorable. The same is true if a judge dictates a sentence in favor of a criminal just because he is his relative. But if the policeman and the judge do their duty despite their family affection, they become an example of morality in society. For this reason, Krishna urges Arjuna to do his duty (*dharma*), recognizing that if he gives up the fight just because the greedy people who usurped the kingdom are his family members, without a doubt, this will constitute a dishonorable action. Another critical point is that to understand Bhagavad-Gita, we must at least theoretically accept Krishna's position as the supreme personality of Godhead.

As we previously explained, the different types of affections we manifest in this world originate in Krishna. This also includes the tendency towards heroic and martial sentiments. Krishna is not only the most beautiful cowherd boy of Vrindavana but also the greatest of heroes *(mahavirya)*. The heroic qualities we see in conditioned souls are but a slight vestige of this quality that originates in Krishna. On the battlefield of Kurukshetra and during His pastimes in this world, Krishna often enjoyed this heroic rasa by facing great warriors to reciprocate their fighting desires. In this way, Krishna satisfies liberated souls' romantic, brotherly, and parental love tendencies and the martial pride of great warrior heroes who wish to face Him in battle. Krishna is the personification of all forms of relationships. This heroic *rasa* is one of the seven secondary *rasas* we previously mentioned.

The primary cause of Krishna's appearance

Krishna tells us in His Bhagavad-Gita that His advent into this world is to redeem the earth from evil hosts and emancipate pious souls. However, the Vaishnava sages warn us that this is nothing more than an external cause. They tell us that Krishna comes to this world to show us the unique, supreme, and exclusive love of the inhabitants of Vrindavana (*vrajavasis*). The love of His parents, Nanda and Yashoda, of the cowherd boys (*gopas*), the cowherd girls (*gopis*), and especially the love of Radha, which is the highest form of love for Godhead. In the absence of Krishna, the inhabitants of Vrindavana exhibit the pinnacle of *prema* as *vipralambha-bhava*, feelings of separation rarely seen in human society. Krishna comes to this world to reveal this love for our benefit. By emulating such feelings of longing for God in His absence, we can attain the highest achievement possible for every soul.

We should remember that although such symptoms resemble ordinary anguish, the fortunate soul experiences the highest pleasure within the heart. Due to the absolute nature of Krishna, both His presence and His separation generate intense pleasure in the soul. Although enveloped in apparent pain, love in separation is the highest form of divine bliss and makes the experience of the consequent union more intense. Through this eternal dynamic of union-separation, Krishna extols the feelings of love of His devotees, taking them at every moment to a higher plane of divine bliss. Without developing an intense desire to obtain Krishna (*vipralambha-bhava*), achieving the exclusive love of Vrindavana (*vrindavana-prema*) is impossible. Simply put, Krishna came to this world to reveal the supreme love of Vrindavana. By opening a window to the spiritual world and allowing us to see the pure love of the liberated souls, Krishna invites us to awaken the desire to attain Him to return home, back to Godhead.

Part Four

The Historical Framework

Chapter 20

Cultural decline and rebirth of bhakti

The moment Lord Krishna closed His *lilas* to the common vision and departed from this world marks the beginning of the age of Kali, whose main characteristic is the drastic decline of good human qualities. Modern historiography extends to approximately four thousand five hundred years ago, beyond which it is almost impossible for historians to offer a reliable account of historical events. The Puranas (Vedic history books) and the well-known Mahabharata tell us about the great culture of wisdom that flourished in ancient India, significantly influencing neighboring cultures. According to the Vedas, in very remote antiquity escapes secular historical records, the world was under the influence of a predominant culture whose epicenter was in today's India. Many modern archaeological discoveries point at a unified world culture in a time so remote that it is almost impossible to frame. We dealt with all of this at the beginning of this book. Even the period from Krishna's departure to shortly before the Buddha's birth is quite dark and imprecise for historians. However, over time, a slow process of cultural decay and disintegration reduced the great Bharata (ancient name for India) to what is contemporary India, which in more recent times has continued to fragment into states like Pakistan and Bangladesh.

With the progress of the age of Kali, different prophets and religious reformers appeared in other parts of the ancient world, who, realizing the deplorable moral condition of their contemporaries, enunciated spiritual and ethical precepts for the revindication of society. During this period of cultural decline, India also saw the emergence of a multitude of reformers, the most prominent among them being Siddharta Gautama (Buddha, 563-483 B.C.), Vardhamana Mahavira (540-468 B.C.), founder of Jainism, and Goshala (484 B.C.E), the founder of the Ajivikas. Although important in his time, Goshala was the least influential of the three. The Ajivikas continued to exist for about a thousand years, but today they are an almost extinct subject in the religions of India. But if there is something in common between these three new religious movements, it is their purely anti-Vedic character.

Theistic or devotional traditions declined during this period, and many philosophical and ascetic spread systems came into vogue. Scholars estimate that by the time of the Buddha, there were more than seventy different types of ascetic sects in India, whose objective was the extinction of psychophysical desires through the practice of extreme asceticism. The young Siddharta Gautama (Buddha) also practiced this type of rigorous asceticism which he later abandoned in favor of his well-known Middle Way. As the most prominent among the anti-Vedic reformers, Siddhartha favored a system of thought in which human analytical ability constitutes the means of emancipation. His admirable will and effort to achieve enlightenment still have a stunning effect on those who hear it. His wisdom earned him the epithet of Buddha (the enlightened one), and although he was an atheist for some, others still consider him a skeptic. The well-known indeterminate questions attest to his often uncompromising position. "Is there enlightenment after death, or does it not exist?" "Does existence continue after we transcend the repeated births?" etc. Some say that Buddha often responded to these questions with profound silence or gave unintelligible answers like "What happens to the fire that goes out? Does it cease to exist? Does it transform? Does it enter an unknown state of existence?" By rejecting the decadent Vedic sacrifices, Siddharta sought his horizons independent of the Vedic version. One of the best-known teachings credited to him is his affirmation of the impermanence of all things, or the doctrines of *anicha* (the non-existence of an eternal, immutable, and divine substance) and *anatta* (literally, no soul)—that is, the spiritual non-identity of the self.

Unlike Siddharta Gautama, Vardhamana Mahavira preferred to lead a life of extreme penance, hence his epithet of *mahavira* (the great hero). The Jains see Mahavira as the twenty-fourth teacher of what they consider a long succession within their tradition (something similar occurs with Siddharta and the cycle of Buddhas that reflects the Vedic influence of the doctrine of the avatars of Vishnu). Although Vardhamana developed various doctrinal concepts, he emphasized the principle of *ahimsa* (non-violence) to an extreme. For Jains, the soul's liberation is possible when we stop the actions leading to the accumulation of *karma,* and the accumulated *karma* is removed. For the Jains, asceticism and non-violence are the ideal paths. Therefore, for the Jain, killing any creature is strictly forbidden, even unintentionally. For this reason, most Jains avoid agriculture and engage in commerce. Even today, they are a prosperous community.

Although they accept the existence of a paradise for pure

souls, they reject the existence of a supreme God. Therefore, paradise is where liberated souls dwell, not necessarily the kingdom of God. Buddhism and Jainism enjoyed the patronage of Indian kings and emperors who embraced their ideas. Chandra Gupta Maurya, the great emperor of India from the 3rd century BCE, converted to Jainism and sponsored this new faith that grew and spread, gaining significant influence. For its part, Buddhism obtained the patronage of Emperor Ashoka and developed an evangelistic character that took it to the most distant extremes of the Far East. While Jainism gradually lost influence, Buddhism became one of the most influential religions in India for several centuries. Although it subsequently succumbed to the rebirth of *bhakti*, it is now widely appreciated worldwide.

After this period, sects of very degraded consciousness also spread, such as the Kapalikas, Kalamukhas, etc., known to cover their bodies with crematorium ashes and use skulls as vessels to eat. Another anti-Vedic sect that for some time gained strength was the *vama-marga* (left path), named for its antagonism to Vedic regulations (considered the correct path). The practices and rituals of the followers of this path included eating meat, drinking liquor, ingesting aphrodisiacs, and practicing so-called tantric sex, often without kinship discrimination, even to the extent of practicing incest. Supposedly, this behavior aims to achieve liberation from dualities and psychosocial taboos of what is right and wrong, advocating the opposite of Vedic principles.

Besides these anti-Vedic traditions, there are other strands of Vedic or semi-Vedic thought known as *shaddarshanas* or the six philosophical systems of India. Each one of these paths is associated. They are 1. Kanada (Vaisheshika philosophy or atomic theory), 2. Akshapada Gautama (Nyaya philosophy or logic), 3. Kapila (Sankhya, the analytical process), 4. the well-known Patanjali (Yoga system synthesized), 5. Jaimini (Karma-Mimansa or Vedic rituals), *mimansa* means conclusion). This is a very peculiar system since it considers that the Vedas' ultimate purpose is to perform rituals (*karma*) to attain a higher form of life in a celestial world after death. It discards the transcendental objective of existence. For Jaimini, human destiny depends on the proper performance of Vedic rituals. Therefore, if there is a super cause (God), His will is subordinated to the rituals. Although these philosophical systems have independent bases, they often support their postulates and doctrines by relying on the Vedic version. Finally, we come to the best known of all these philosophical systems, 6. Uttara Mimamsa (commonly called Vedanta philosophy). It is the Vedic philosophy, as we find it in the Vedanta-sutra of Vyasa, the compiler of the Vedas.

It is noteworthy that by the time of Buddha, Mahavira, and the other non-Vedic reformers, the ancient ritualistic tradition of the Vedas was in decline, and animal sacrifice rituals came into vogue. Although the spiritual classes within the Vedic culture generally follow a diet that rules out the consumption of meat, there are certain concessions for those prone to consume it through the performance of specific rituals whose objective is to contain the indiscriminate slaughter of animals. One of the primary purposes of not eating meat is the practice of compassion to avoid causing unnecessary suffering to other sentient beings. However, by the time of Buddha and Mahavira, the indiscriminate performance of these animal sacrifices by the priestly class was excessive. This excess of violent sacrifices, extreme ascetic practices, and endless doctrinal sectarianism led these great reformers to reject the Vedas in search of new horizons. Despite the religiosity and popular culture continued being Indo-Vedic, these new ways of thinking that challenged Vedic hegemony dominated the intellectual scene of India for several centuries.

However, during the 3rd to 4th century BCE, there was a gradual revival of Vedic devotional traditions, or what scholars today call classical Hinduism. During this period, the Puranas, Agamas, Samhitas, Pancharatras, the Mahabharata, the Bhagavad-Gita, etc., reemerged and returned to occupy a unique place in the religious consciousness of India. For this reason, some modern historians consider "classical Hinduism" emerged during this period. However, this version differs from the Vedas themselves and their tradition of sages since spiritual knowledge is lost and reappears according to the conditions of human society, something that the Bhagavad Gita also confirms. Within the framework of the Vaishnava tradition, this rebirth of devotional fervor to Vishnu/Krishna is credited to great saints known as the Alvars.

The Alvars were twelve great Vaishnava saints of southern India from different social strata—from kings to simple commons. Among the most prominent Alvars was a great female saint named Andal. The Alvars were not only fervent devotees of Krishna but also great poets. The word *alvar* means "immerse" or "submerged." So they were known since they lived continually immersed in the deepest love for Krishna. The Alvars left behind a significant amount of devotional poems and songs to Krishna (more than four thousand poems) known as Divya-prabandham (divine prayers) and which the Vaishnava tradition holds in such esteem that it is called "the Fifth Veda."

The Divya Prabandham is the result of the devotion and mystical experiences of the Alvars. It contains a rich body of philosophical and theological ideas whose main characteristic is its emphasis on *bhakti* (devotion to Krishna). The biographies of the Alvars describe many miraculous anecdotes, including the extraordinary birth of Andal. The teachings of the Alvars do not differ from the Vedas. Still, their precepts are not given in Sanskrit, as the Upanishads and other Vedic mystical texts are, but in Tamil, the colloquial language of much of the Indian subcontinent. Because of this, its teachings were available to all—rich and poor, scholars and almost illiterate, men and women, pious and ungodly, etc. Unfortunately, historians have no unanimity about when the Alvars lived. Some sources suggest they may have existed as far back as 4200 to 2700 B.C., but the generally accepted date is between the fifth and ninth centuries of the Christian era. Of course, all these dates are debatable. Such chronological disagreements exist not only concerning the Alvars but also other Indian saints. This is because tradition often assigns similar names and titles to people who lived in different times. Something similar occurs with modern Indology's attempt to date the antiquity of scriptures and other historical events because many reference points are uncertain. What is known is that the Alvars lived before the great Vaishnava saint Nathamuni (823 AD), who lived in southern India before the construction of the famous temple of Paramesvara (770 AD). It is believed that some of the Alvars may have been partial manifestations of Vishnu/Krishna, who—at times—infuses His potencies into certain souls by endowing them with extraordinary spiritual power to reestablish Vedic religious principles.

The Alvars did not endorse the ascetic practices so popular in India, nor did they yield to social or gender considerations as a requirement for the path of *bhakti*. For them, the only requirement to reach God is the total and complete surrender of the soul, which is available to everyone without exception. Instead of asceticism, they emphasized the principle of Divine Grace, which descends to every soul who sincerely surrenders itself to the Lord. Divya Prabadham (the poetic song of the Alvars) is a source of inspiration for Vaishnavas, mainly from southern India. With the advent of these great saints, a spiritual revolution began in India that spread everywhere. However, although the Alvars revived Vaishnavism (devotion to Krishna) and their compositions reveal their profound love for God, they did not systematically outline the philosophical precepts that support the Vaishnava faith. The task of showing the harmony of Vaishnava devotion with the Vedas and the Upanishads was undertaken by holy men of great intellect and learning who continued this spiritual rebirth and whom history knows as Acharyas.

Chapter 21

The age of the Acharyas (holy teachers)

What is known as the age of the Acharyas ranges from the 8th to the 14th centuries A.D. One who possesses wisdom and sanctity is known as Acharya, which is why he fully represents the Vedic teachings. Like the Alvars, the Acharyas were great mystics. However, they systematized the Vaishnava philosophy and their commentaries on the Vedas, which until today are considered classics of Indian philosophy and religion. With their extensive scholarship, the Acharyas affirmed the Vedas' authority and systematized the *bhakti*'s principles. The most prominent Acharyas of this classical era of Vedic revival in medieval India were: Shankara (788-820), Ramanuja (1017-1137), Madhva (1239-1317), Vishnu Swami (13th century), and Nimbarka (13th century). Except for Shankara, each of these four Acharyas is the head of an apostolic lineage (*sampradaya*) that expounds a specific devotional theology within a unified Vaishnava tradition, each with its characteristics. The life and work of these mystics are so exceptional that it compels us to present at least a brief synopsis.

The Acharya Shankara

The most accepted date for Shankara's birth and disappearance is 788 to 820 A.D. in Kerela, southern India. He is primarily credited with restoring the validity of the Vedas to the society of the time. Shankara faced and converted many Buddhists, Jains, and followers of the Jaimini ritualistic tradition.

Although he only lived 32 years, his life was dazzling from the beginning, and his reform work was immense.

It is said that after many years of trying unsuccessfully to conceive a child, his parents visited a Shiva temple. That day they received the blessing that a child would soon be born to them; however, there was a condition; they should choose between an ordinary son who would enjoy a long life or an extraordinary son with a very short life. Knowing the value of bringing an exceptional being into the world, his parents chose the second option. Because of this, Shankara was born destined to live only 16 years, although sometime later, it is said that Lord Shiva himself doubled the length of his life.

Shankara showed signs of possessing great intellect and surprising abilities from his childhood. When he was just a 5-year-old boy, he asked his mother to allow him to renounce the world and enter the monastic order of life, something his mother naturally refused. The extraordinary boy insisted, but again and again, his mother tried to make him understand that the ascetic life was hard for a child his age. Finally, while the boy Shankara was playing in the river, a crocodile took him by the leg and threatened to devour him. Seeing his mother in despair, Shankara told her that only if she allowed him to enter the renounced order of life would the crocodile let him go. Seeing no other way to save her little son from a horrible death, his mother agreed, and the crocodile disappeared into the waters. At that moment, the admirable Shankara became a wandering monk, although he was barely five years old.

Shankara was a monist who debated Buddhist doctrine with great success. His work is extensive and complex. However, scholars consider that it is not free from ambiguity since his philosophy compromises between Buddhist nihilism, impersonal monism, and an occasional devotion to a personal God. Although allied to a monistic thought, the characteristic of his work is the introduction of a new concept of *maya* (illusion), which Shankara considers real and not real. This illusion, which exists from a relative point of view but not from the absolute one, has the power to cover pure Universal Consciousness (*brahman*). However, Shankara insists that Universal Consciousness is the only existing reality; surprisingly, this ignorance (*avidya*), whose origin is questionable, covers the *brahman* and makes Him forget his original condition as the only existing reality. As a result, this single reality experiences the false idea of existing as an infinity of individual souls within an unreal and purely subjective material universe. When we remedy this condition by cultivating knowledge, and our consciousness regains its original condition, we realize that neither the individual soul nor the physical universe exists but only *brahman*, a single inert Universal Consciousness with neither attributes (*nirguna*) nor potencies (*ashakti*).

The questions that traditionally arise due to this postulate are as follows. "How is it that this illusion (*maya*) simultaneously exists and does not exist?" "If the only existing entity is a consciousness without creative potency, what is the origin of the illusion?" "How can ignorance cover the Supreme Consciousness?" Even today, Shankarists cannot answer these questions satisfactorily. Some monists say it is a *brahman-lila* (pastime of *brahman*), but the nature of divine *lilas* is *ananda-maya* (overflowing with bliss and knowledge); therefore, *lila* does not subject *brahman* to the forgetfulness and suffering we experience in this world. This leads many commentators to consider that Shankara makes *maya* (the illusion) an even more mysterious substance than the *brahman* (the spiritual substance) he tries to define.

However, for Vaishnavas, this ambiguity is not an ineptitude of Shankara since his work serves a purpose. The society in which Shankara was born was almost entirely dominated by the Buddhist thought of emptiness and Jain relativism, so the validity of his work has a dual purpose. By compromising between the Buddhist doctrines of impermanence and the eternal Vedic brahman, Shankara contributed to restoring the authority of the Vedas. Many consider that he even cautiously advocated for the gradual reestablishment of theism. Shankara's work was undoubtedly an achievement worthy of his outstanding intellect and noble holiness. His disciplic succession is known as Shankara-sampradaya. Although he was an exponent of extreme monism, before leaving this world, Shankara revealed his theistic heart in his well-known verse Bhaja Govindam. Thus, he encouraged his followers who were immersed in the academic study of Vedanta philosophy to take the path of devotion to Govinda (Krishna) as the only means of emancipation.

> "You, foolish intellectuals, worship Govinda,
> worship Govinda, worship Govinda.
> Your knowledge of grammar
> will not save you at the time of death.

The Acharya Ramanuja

Shortly after Shankara's demise, also in southern India, the Acharya Ramanuja (1017-1137) was born. Unlike Shankara, Ramanuja lived a long life of 120 years. His intellectual abilities were also prodigious from a very young age, and countless miraculous events are attributed to him. Even when he was very young, Ramanuja could give explanations of very complicated texts in such a clear and explicit way that it fascinated the most illustrious Vedic scholars of the time.

Once at the parents' request of a young princess possessed by an evil spirit, Ramanuja put his feet on her head. The evil spirit left the girl's body, breaking a branch of the tree they were sitting on. One of his disciples contracted debts with a wealthy man on another occasion, but he couldn't repay him due to his extreme poverty. Because of this, the affluent man demanded that, in return, the poor man's wife should spend a night with him. Somehow this reached the ears of Ramanuja, who gave a portion of the remnants of his food to the young wife so that she could offer it to the petitioner, who, after testing it, immediately experienced a change of consciousness and began to lament his impious action and became a disciple of Ramanuja. On another occasion, Ramanuja met his disciples in Jagannatha Puri in northeast India for missionary purposes. One night while sleeping, Lord Vishnu took him back to his town of origin, and upon awakening, he was surprised to find himself hundreds of miles away.

As a young boy, Ramanuja once met a renowned Vaishnava saint named Yamuna, and from then on, he longed to see him again, but their itineraries and life courses never crossed again. A long time later, knowing that Yamuna was about to leave this world, Ramanuja rushed to meet him; however, fate had other intentions. Upon his arrival, Yamuna had already departed. Once there, Ramanuja noticed that three of the fingers of Yamuna's right hand were closed, and none of his disciples knew the cause. Ramanuja lost himself in a mystical trance and said those were the three wishes Yamuna wanted him to fulfill. To everyone's amazement, as he revealed each of these wishes, the fingers of Yamuna's lifeless body opened, returning to their natural state.

Hare Krishna

Ramanuja always wished to bless everyone by chanting the names of Vishnu (Krishna), but these *mantras* were confidential in his day. They were only revealed to those most advanced in devotional practice. Due to the spiritual nature of the divine name, if it is chanted without due respect or proper conscience, the chant is considered an offense to the Lord, so only when the practitioner is in a mature stage of devotion will he be given the *mantra* of the divine names. In this way, the *mantras* and Vedic knowledge descended through generations of devout saints for millennia. However, Ramanuja was not an ordinary saint but a *shakti-avesha-avatara*, a soul anointed with divine powers who descended from the abode of Vishnu, just as tradition had predicted would happen. As a great devotee, he knew that due to the influence of the current age of Kali, the general population could not successfully practice the purifying means to be initiated on the devotional path. He was also conscious that chanting God's names was the ideal process for spiritual perfection in this age. What in previous eras was the goal, in the age of Kali, also becomes the means. Before receiving the Vishnu *mantra*, his spiritual preceptor told him, "Only Lord Vishnu Himself is aware of the glories of this *mantra*; whoever chants it will go to Vishnu's supreme abode after death. This *mantra* is so pure and sacred that it should not be chanted by those desiring worldly enjoyment. Therefore, you must not reveal it to anyone." Saying this, his *guru* whispered Vishnu's secret *mantra*, "Om Namah Narayanaya," into his ear. After Ramanuja received this *mantra*, he went to the temple roof and addressed the crowd in the square. He told them, "Come all, come closer because I will give you a jewel of great value. You are all dearer to me than my own life, so I greatly desire to free you from the torments of this temporary world. Please recite this *mantra* that I have obtained. Do it, and the compassion of the Lord will be with you. He shouted several times at the top of his lungs: "Om Namah Narayanaya, Om Namah Narayanaya, Om Namah Narayanaya." At the same time, the crowd responded in unison each time Ramanuja chanted the sacred *mantra* hitherto confidential.

When his *guru* learned what had happened, he immediately reproached his action: "Get out of here! Do not force me to sin seeing your face. Someone like you is destined to live in hell for countless lives." However, Ramanuja replied with humble manners: "It is because I am willing to go to hell that I have disobeyed your order. You told me that whoever chants this *mantra* is freed from material suffering and returns to the supreme abode of Vishnu. Therefore, if a person as insignificant as me must go to hell, that does not matter if others get God's grace!" When his *guru* heard him, he was so moved that he replied: "My son, I have never met someone as generous as you. You will be my *guru* from today, and I will be your disciple because you are better than me." Ramanuja clasped his *guru*'s legs tightly against his chest and replied, "No, you are my eternal *guru*."

Something similar happened on another occasion with an impious priest. He tried to kill Ramanuja by adding poison to the water used to bathe the holy image of Vishnu, and the faithful regularly drank. Although Ramanuja sensed the priest's intention, he accepted the offering, telling him that he did not feel worthy of the honor of drinking the sacred water that had washed Vishnu's feet. Moments later, seizure-like tremors began to shake his body hard, and the priest guessed it was the effect of the poison. In reality, he was experiencing profound symptoms of love for God rarely seen in human society. The next day when he returned to the temple in perfect health, the priest threw himself to the ground and began to beat his head against the rocks until it bled, repentant of his impious act. Ramanuja pacified him as if nothing had happened and accepted him as his disciple.

On one occasion, during one of his missionary trips, he faced a great monistic scholar from the school of Shankara. For seventeen days, both sages debated establishing the superiority of their doctrines. But although Ramanuja tried his best, he could not convince him. His opponent refuted each of his arguments with his fantastic erudition. At the end of the seventeenth day, feeling somewhat puzzled, Ramanuja entered the temple of Vishnu and stopped to pray in front of the sacred image. "Lord, the truth revealed in the scriptures has been covered by the interpretations of Shankara, which can confuse even the great sages. How long will you allow this child of yours to stay away from the shelter of the shadow of your feet?" The following day, as Ramanuja was readying himself to debate, the public noticed a luminous aura surrounding his body and that his face revealed a profound peace. Everyone was astonished. Realizing that Ramanuja was not an ordinary soul, his opponent approached him and said, "Today, I will atone for my sins by becoming your disciple; only then can I destroy the root of my false pride." Many other accounts of his life are equally extraordinary. Such as the astonishing story of his disciple Kuresha. A cruel king plucked out Kuresha's eyes. Ramanuja prayed for the eyes of Kuresha in front of the sacred image of Vishnu, and they were reborn in their empty sockets.

Ramanuja wrote many comments and reflections on Vaishnava theology, clarifying the limitations of the work of Shankara. In a highly scholastic and pedagogical way, he advocated Vedic theism, holding that Vishnu/Krishna is the supreme person endowed with unlimited divine attributes and supporting each of his statements with quotes from the Vedas and the Upanishads. Days before leaving this world, he gathered his disciples to instruct them for the last time. In this assembly, he encouraged them to lead a pure life and carry the message of love for God to all. At the Shri Rangam temple in southern India, seated in a semi-lotus posture, even today, pilgrims revere an image of Ramanuja covered in sandalwood pulp. The local priests maintain that underneath this covering is the physical body of the Acharya Ramanuja. His disciplic succession is known as Shri or Laxmi-sampradaya, for his line of revelation begins with Laxmi, the majestic aspect of Radha, the pleasure potency of Krishna in Vaikuntha.

The Acharya Madhva

Around a century after the departure of the Acharya Ramanuja, near the village of Udupi, also in southern India, Madhva was born (1239-1317). Madhva was not only gifted with superhuman strength and intellect, but he was also capable of performing miraculous acts. For example, when Madhva was a boy, he collected dried tamarind leaves and turned them into gold coins in front of astonished creditors to pay for his father's debt, a miracle he did on more than one occasion to help godly people. He could also have a seed in his hand and make it sprout by chanting Vedic *mantras*. He could also defeat many fighters who challenged him and lift objects so heavy with one hand that otherwise took the cooperation of several dozen men to move. Once while crossing a jungle, his disciples were attacked by a tiger, which Madhva killed with bare hands.

Once someone stole his writings, and to win the king's favor to recover them, Madhva showed his strength by pressing his big toe against the ground and challenging the strongest fighters to lift it off. Even though several men were pulling his leg simultaneously, they could not lift it. Then, in a contest where people with surprising abilities participated, Madhva devoured more than a thousand twelve-inch long bananas and drank thousands of glasses of milk while smiling as if it were an ordinary event. Although they seem surprising, these abilities are possible through acquiring mystic perfections (*yoga-siddhis*).

Madhva was quite prolific, leaving many commentaries on the scriptures and other philosophical and theological treatises. Perhaps the most significant event in Madhva's life was his meeting with Vyasa, the compiler of the Vedas. On one of his trips to the Himalayas, he revealed to his disciples that he would meet the great sage Vyasa, who lives in the region of the Himalayas known as Badarika. Although situated in the Himalayas, Vyasa's abode exists on the transcendental plane and is not perceptible to ordinary vision; therefore, unseen to the human eye. Before meeting Vyasa at Badarika, Madhva fasted for forty-eight days in silence, absorbed in a trance. After wandering in that region for some time, he received the revelation of the transcendental Eden, where Vyasa dwells in the Himalayas, beyond physical laws. There he saw Vyasa, the Vedas compiler and Krishna's literary incarnation in all his glory, surrounded by great sages. Overwhelmed by a deep spiritual ecstasy, Madhva felt at the feet of Vyasa, who instructed him in spiritual science. Sometime later, between 1260 and 1271, he met again with Vyasa on his second trip to Badarika.

Like Ramanuja, Madhva successfully refuted both non-Vedic doctrines and the impersonal monism of Shankara by upholding the supremacy of Krishna as the Supreme Person.

His disciplic succession is known as Brahma-sampradaya since his line of revelation begins with Brahma, the first created being in the universe.

The Acharya Nimbarka

The Acharya Nimbarka was also born in South India, although the exact date of his birth is unknown. Some consider that he lived in the late 11th and mid-12th centuries. It is known that he flourished about 25 years after the departure of Ramanuja, which is why historians place his birthdate around 1162. Although his original name was Niyamananda, he received the name Nimbarka because of a miraculous feat accredited to him. It is said that Niyamananda once invited an ascetic to his house to offer him food as a charity, but by the time he finished cooking, it was very late, and the ascetic did not eat after sunset. Niyamananda begged Vishnu to remedy the situation so that this holy person would not feel inconvenienced. Even though the sun had already set, a yellow disk became visible in the sky, and Niyamananda showed the ascetic from the top of a Nimba tree as a sign that the sun was still visible. The ascetic took this yellow disk for the sun and ate the offering to his complete satisfaction. It was not long before he realized that what had happened was the result of the miraculous power of Niyamananda. Surprised at his power, he called him Nimbarka for having made him see the sun (*arka*) between the branches of a Nimba tree.

Nimbarka was a great devotee of Krishna known for his wisdom and holiness. He lived most of his life in the Mathura area where Vrindavana is located, where Lord Krishna manifested in this world more than five thousand years ago. Apart from some details, there is not much information about his life. Like the other Acharyas, Nimbarka presented his commentaries on the Bhagavad-Gita and the Vedanta philosophy, stating that Lord Krishna is the supreme personality of Godhead as the Vedas reveal. Nimbarka had many disciples who wrote commentaries about his teachings. His disciplic succession is known as Kumara-sampradaya since his line of revelation begins with four great sages called Kumaras. Some call it Hamsa-sampradaya because it was Vishnu, in the form of a divine swan, who originated the disciplic line of revelation.

The Acharya Vishnu Swami

Authoritative sources tell us that there were several Acharyas named Vishnu Swami. The oldest of them, Adi-Vishnu Swami (*adi*=first, original), is placed in the 3rd century BC. But over time, his apostolic line almost disappeared and was revived by a second Vishnu Swami (9th century AD), credited with converting many followers of Shankara to Vaishnavism. The third and last Vishnu Swami lived in the middle of the 13th century AD and had a great successor named Vallabha, whose *bhakti* school is known as *pushti-marga* (spontaneous devotion). The biographical data of Vishnu Swami is so scarce that his disciplic line today is represented by Vallabha Acharya. His disciplic succession is known as Rudra-sampradaya since his line of revelation originates with Rudra (also known as Shiva or Shankara), an aspect of Krishna involved in the destruction of material creation. Each of these four apostolic successions of revelation has its characteristics.

Chapter 22

Shri Krishna-Chaitanya Father of the Hare Krishna Movement

Shri Krishna-Chaitanya (1486-1534) is not considered one of the four classical Acharyas; however, He transcends them all. Shri Krishna-Chaitanya is the Father of the religion or spiritual path known as Hare Krishna. Vaishnava texts describe Him as *bhakta-avatara*—Lord Krishna Himself who descended (*avatara*) as His devotee (*bhakta*) to propagate the ideal way of practicing bhakti by loving Krishna with the sentiments of the inhabitants of Vrindavana. Because of this, his personality is not easy to comprehend even today. Nevertheless, Vaishnavas attest to His divinity with Vedic quotations to corroborate His identity, which—added to the symptoms of His person and His superhuman activities—leaves no doubt about His divine status. Shri Krishna-Chaitanya is also known as Mahaprabhu (the greatest teacher) or just as Shri Chaitanya. His disciplic succession is the same as the Madhva Acharya (Brahma-sampradaya). Still, because it has philosophical variants or characteristics that distinguish it from Madhva's, it is like a tree branch or a river tributary of his *sampradaya*.

Shri Chaitanya appeared in northeast India in what is now West Bengal, a region that was known by the name of Gauda. For this reason, His disciplic succession is known as Brahma-Madhua-Gaudiya-sampradaya or simply Gaudiya-sampradaya (*gaudiya*=of Gauda); thus, His followers (the devotees of the Hare Krishna movement) are known as Gaudiya-

Vaishnavas. As we previously explained, although the different Vaishnava *sampradayas* (apostolic lineages) focus on devotion to Vishnu/Krishna, each has its characteristics on account of its rasa or devotional sentiment and a particular form of worship. This implies that the Vaishnava philosophy we have explained in this work represents the disciplic succession of Shri Chaitanya—the Gaudiya-sampradaya, represented by the Hare Krishna Movement inside and outside of India.

Shri Chaitanya's activities were compiled in various biographies by great devout saints—eternal associates who descended into this world as part of His spiritual entourage. The foremost of these biographical works are Chaitanya-Bhagavata, Chaitanya-Charitamrita, Chaitanya-Mangala, and Chaitanya-Charita. The latter was written while Shri Chaitanya was still present in this world. Here we will not make a biographical description of Shri Chaitanya. We will only mention that He was in this world for forty-eight years and that as an *avatara* of Krishna, His descent, activities, and disappearance are as divine as those of Krishna Himself. To fully understand the personality of Sri Chaitanya Mahaprabhu, it is necessary to know the diversity of philosophical issues that we have previously explained, precisely the subject of spiritual *rasa*, which finds its peak in the love exchanges between Radha and Krishna.

Shri Krishna-Chaitanya, the combined form of Radha and Krishna

As a contemporary Vaishnava scholar informs us, the advent of Shri Chaitanya is not a simple historical event but the culmination of an eternal dynamism inherent in Krishna, a sort of transcendental dialectic that culminates in a divine *rasa*. We already know that Krishna is both *rasa-murti* (the personification of *rasa*) and *rasika-shekara* (the enjoyer of *rasa*). We also know that Radha and Krishna are the same entity, the Supreme Divinity, the same being who has eternally manifested in two bodies to enjoy the conjugal *rasa*. As His pleasure potency, Radha gives pleasure to Krishna, and Krishna enjoys Radha. In this exchange of love, Radha enjoys the infinite beauty and sweetness in Krishna—an experience unique to Her and no one else. For example, in ordinary life, the pleasure a woman experiences enjoying her lover and being enjoyed by him is outside her lover's experience. She only knows the joy that she derives from contact with him. In other words, the lover enjoys the person he loves, but what the beloved experiences when being enjoyed is not known to the lover. It is just like sugar, which does not know the experience of enjoying its sweetness since this pleasure belongs to the one who tastes it. If sugar wants to taste its sweetness, it must become the person who tastes it. This is precisely what Krishna does; He assumes Radha's feelings to savor Himself as Radha does and to experience what She experiences. Shri Chaitanya is the Enjoyer enjoying Himself.

The question may arise as to how it is possible that, being omnisciente, Krishna does not know something about Himself, being omniscient. But, of course, Krishna is omniscient, and such omniscience comes through His potencies. By assuming the position of His pleasure potency (Radha), Krishna enjoys Himself and thus experiences what His potency experiences by enjoying Him. In this way, Krishna practically gives a new dimension to *lila* unknown to the world—God savoring the pleasure of loving God! God savoring His beauty!

In divine *lila*, thoroughly enjoying the beauty of Krishna is the exclusive and unique experience of Radha, His pleasure potency, and not of Krishna, who is the object enjoyed. Therefore, Krishna assumes the position of His pleasure potency to enjoy His sweetness and beauty. This transcendent dynamic opens a new dimension in the divine *lila* and which Krishna savors three eternal desires that are inherent in Him:

1. To experience the glory of Radha's unique and unequaled love for Him at every moment.
2. To enjoy His excellent and infinite qualities that only Radha thoroughly enjoys through Her endless love.
3. To experience the bliss Radha experiences when She enjoys His unique qualities.

In simple words, Krishna's feeling is, "What does Radha experience when She enjoys Me and when I enjoy her?" How much beauty is there in Me that She only yearns for My company and love?" Since these experiences belong exclusively to Radha, His pleasure potency, Krishna assumes Her position to enjoy Himself. That is, Krishna endows Himself with the feelings of Radha. It is the *lila* or pastime of the lover becoming the one who loves him.

This eternal dynamism makes the Supreme Divinity, eternally manifested in these two divine forms (Radha and Krishna), again unite in a single form: Shri Krishna-Chaitanya. In other words, Shri Krishna-Chaitanya is the combination of Radha and Krishna in one body—or in a more specific sense, Krishna assuming the sentiments of His pleasure potency Radha. Being the complete whole (*purnam*), Krishna is both the supreme beloved object and the supreme loving subject—that is, the supreme beloved and the supreme lover. Shri Chaitanya is God in love with God; He is Krishna Himself as His devotee endowed with the sentiments of Radha to enjoy love and service to Himself. He is the combination of the eternal forms of Radha and Krishna.

Due to the eternal nature of the *lila*, these three questions or wishes did not arise in Krishna recently. Krishna did not have to wait from His departure more than five thousand years ago until His advent as Shri Chaitanya to experience this reality. These three "desires" exist in Krishna eternally, and Krishna fully satisfies them since eternity in His eternal form of Shri Chaitanya. This implies that the primary cause of His descent into this world of Shri Chaitanya is to teach us the love of Radha for Krishna as She experiences it—and, by extension, the shepherd girls of Vrindavana, that love Him in a similar way. Thus, Shri Chaitanya propagates the ideal process for attaining this kind of love for Krishna by chanting the divine names Hare Krishna Hare Krishna, Krishna Krishna Hare Hare/Hare Rama Hare Rama, Rama Rama Hare Hare.

This *mantra* is not ordinary but a *prema mantra*. It has the potential to awaken in each soul a pure love for God of the highest level, called *vrindavana-prema* (the love that the inhabitants of Vrindavana exhibit for Krishna), and specifically, the love of the cowherd girls (*gopi-prema*). For this reason, Shri Chaitanya is known as the most magnanimous *avatara* of Krishna, or *prema-avatara*. Without distinction of prior qualification, He freely gives away what no other manifestation of Krishna ever gave: the spontaneous love of the cowherd girls of Vrindavana for Krishna, the supreme and most confidential jewel of all forms of love for Godhead. This type of love is longed for by the great sages and is very rare in human society at any age. Still, by the grace of Shri Chaitanya Mahaprabhu, it is available to anyone who wants to take it and immerse himself in this infinite ocean of divine *rasa* that even Krishna Himself longs to taste. Lord Krishna, in His form as Shri Chaitanya, is so generous and compassionate because, in

His person, the sentiments of Radha predominate, among which Her compassion shines through with super excellence due to Her original feminine nature.

As Her pleasure potency, Radha's compassion for fallen souls knows no bounds, and at every moment, She yearns to touch them with a drop of Her infinite grace. It is by the blessing of Radha that a soul can engage in the service of Krishna. By engaging more and more souls in His service, She brings more and more pleasure to Krishna every moment. Although Shri Chaitanya is the *avatara* of love for Godhead, His personality is covered by a veil of mystery and can hardly be understood simply by studying the Vedas. Vaishnava sages and saints tell us that only through the company and the blessing of a devotee of Shri Chaitanya is it possible to understand this very esoteric personality. By assuming the sentiments of Radha, Krishna abandons the dark color of His divine complexion and takes on a hue like that of Radha, which has the radiance of molten gold.

For this reason, the devotees of Shri Chaitanya also call Him Goura (golden) or Gouranga (*anga*=body, limbs). Hence, His epithet of Golden Avatara. His advent in this world as the son of Sachi Devi and Jagannath Misra is a momentous event that occurs in the same way as Krishna's advent as the son of Nanda and Yashoda. Because He is Krishna Himself, Shri Chaitanya's body is not the product of physical nature but *sat-chit-ananda* (eternal, full of knowledge and bliss), personified tangible spirit. Like Krishna five thousand years ago, Shri Chaitanya appeared with His different potencies and confidential associates of His eternal abode, known as Pancha-Tattva *(pancha*=five, *tattva*=aspects, categories, eternal truths)—that is to say, the five aspects of Divinity.

Krishna's five aspects

These personalities accompanying Shri Chaitanya in His eternal *lilas* are not ordinary entities but five different aspects of His internal potency (*chit-shakti*). (1) First, we have Shri Chaitanya Himself, who is Krishna Himself, assuming the form of a perfect devotee (*bhakta-rupa*) with the feeling of Radha (*radha-bhava*), (2) Nityananda Prabhu, who is Balarama's expansion as a devotee (*sva-rupakan*), (3) Advaita Acharya, who is the incarnation of the devotee (*bhakta-avatara*), (4) Gadadhara Pandit, who is Radha Herself or the devotional energy (*bhakta-shaktikam*), and (5) Shrivas Thakur, the pure devotee (*bhakta-akhyam*) and the only one who belongs to the category of the individual soul. Among the Gaudiya-Vaishnavas (the devotees of Krishna in the disciplic line of Shri Chaitanya), it is customary to invoke the names of these five personalities (to recite the Pancha-Tattva-mantra) before beginning the chanting or recitation of the names of Krishna, in the following order:

> "*Shri Krishna-Chaitanya, Prabhu Nityananda, Shri Advaita, Gadadhara, Shrivas, adi goura bhakta vrinda.*"

Its translation is, "Glory to Shri Krishna-Chaitanya, Nityananda Prabhu, Shri Advaita, Gadadhara Pandit, Shrivas Thakur, and all the assembled devotees of Shri Chaitanya."

A short description will help us understand the importance of each of these personalities in Krishna's *lila* as Shri Chaitanya.

We already know that Shri Chaitanya is the eternal personality of Godhead, appearing as His devotee immersed in the feeling of Radha (*radha-bhava*). For his part, as the personification of Krishna's internal potency, Nityananda Prabhu (the second member of this Pancha-Tattva) is the same

Balarama we referred to in previous chapters and who acts as Krishna's older brother in the pastimes of Vrindavana. Balarama personifies Krishna's spiritual potency, and in His form as Nityananda Prabhu, He is the original spiritual master (*adi-guru*) of all souls. Like Shri Chaitanya, His body is *sat-chit-ananda*—eternal, full of bliss and knowledge. His name is Nityananda because He is immersed in the deepest love for Krishna (*nitya*=eternal, *ananda*=bliss). Shri Nityananda Prabhu (*prabhu*=master, teacher) is also known by the nickname "Nitai;" therefore, it is common to hear Gaudiya-Vaishnavas refer to Shri Chaitanya and Nityananda as "Goura-Nitai."

Shri Nityananda Prabhu's compassion has no limits, as He personifies Shri Chaitanya's love for fallen souls. Even today, Vaishnava saints and poets glorify the compassion of Nityananda Prabhu, whose pastimes have no end. Just as to attain Krishna, the blessing of Radha is needed; similarly, to reach Shri Chaitanya, it is necessary to receive the blessing of Nityananda Prabhu. During His *lila* in this world at the beginning of the 16th century, Nityananda Prabhu flooded Bengal with *krishna-prema* under the command of Shri Chaitanya. He went from house to house and implored even the most degraded souls to give up their sinful life and take the name of Krishna as their life and soul. If Nityananda Prabhu heard a person chant the names of Krishna just once, He would pour out an ocean of divine opulence in the form of *krishna-prema*. The episode of His meeting and the consequent salvation of Jagai and Madhai (two terrifying criminals) testifies to His compassion. Through Nityananda's grace, a spirit soul receives the fortune of *krishna-prema* as distributed by Shri Chaitanya Mahaprabhu. While Shri Chaitanya's divine body has the radiance of molten gold, just like Radha's, the complexion of Shri Nityananda Prabhu's divine body is snow white, just like Balarama in Vrindavana.

The third member of the Pancha-Tattva is Shri Advaita Acharya, who, according to the Vaishnavas, is a combination of Maha-Vishnu, the gigantic form of the four-armed Vishnu that manifests the material creation, and another aspect of Vishnu called Sada-Shiva residing in Vaikuntha. His body is also *sat-chit-ananda*, free from material duality, which is why he is known as Advaita (non-dual). Because he descended to this world to propagate *krishna-bhakti*, he is also called Acharya. Advaita Acharya came into this world long before Shri Chaitanya's advent. Aiming to redeem human society from its wretched condition in the age of Kali, this powerful personality incited Shri Chaitanya to descend and spread the *yuga-dharma*, the means for spiritual emancipation for the era, the chanting or recitation of Krishna's names. Shri Advaita Acharya and Shri Nityananda Prabhu are the two main branches of the tree of Shri Chaitanya. Through them, Shri Chaitanya carried out His mission of bestowing *krishna-prema* (love for Krishna) on the fallen souls of this age by the congregational chanting of Krishna's names (Hare Krishna, Hare Rama). In the works of art showing the Pancha-Tattva, we always see Nityananda Prabhu and Advaita Acharya to the right of Shri Chaitanya, respectively. As with Nityananda Prabhu, Shri Chaitanya commanded Advaita Acharya to spread *krishna-bhakti* to fallen souls.

The fourth member of the Pancha-Tattva is Gadadhara Pandit. He is the devotional manifestation since He is none other than Radha Herself, the pleasure potency of Krishna. Since in His form as Shri Chaitanya, Krishna tastes His beauty by experiencing what Radha experiences, Radha assumes the eternal form of Gadadhara Pandit and always accompanies Him, providing the necessary emotions to fulfill this purpose. Whenever Shri Chaitanya immersed Himself in the sentiments of Radha, Gadadhara Pandit (Radha) would recite specific verses from Srimad Bhagavatam describing the qualities of Krishna to elicit in Shri Chaitanya sentiments like those of Radha's for Krishna. Gadadhara Pandit (Radha) was assisted by two great associate saints of Shri Chaitanya, Ramananda Raya, and Suarupa Damodara. Both are cowherd girls (*gopis*), intimate friends of Radha in their eternal forms in Vrindavana. In their company, Shri Chaitanya manifested the highest symptoms of love for Krishna (*maha bhava*) that are unique to Radha and impossible for individual souls to attain.

Finally, we have Srivas Thakur, the fifth member of the Pancha-Tattva, who, unlike the others, is an individual soul (*jiva*) and is the emblem of the pure devotee. It was in the house of Srivas Thakur that, with His devotees, Shri Chaitanya began the congregational chanting of the names of Krishna, dancing day and night in such a way that no ordinary soul can imitate. In the historical context, this is the beginning of the Hare Krishna religion or Movement, which is a manifestation in this world of the eternal pastimes of Shri Chaitanya in His divine abode. Vaishnava sages identified Shrivas Thakur with Narada Muni, a celestial sage of great prominence in the Vedas and referred to by Krishna in the Bhagavad-Gita. Even in His *lila* as Shri Chaitanya, Krishna is surrounded by His associates and His different potencies who serve Him in different ways.

When Europe was just awakening from the Dark Ages, these five divine personalities—accompanied by many liberated souls who descended to this world in the company of Shri Chaitanya—carried out an unprecedented spiritual revolution in medieval India. Not only prominent biographers and historians of the time but also ordinary people whose accumulation of piety allowed them to be eyewitnesses of the events left behind diaries that speak of marvelous occurrences. Shri Krishna-Chaitanya manifested His *lilas* for forty-eight years, spending twenty-four of them in the Navadvipa area on the banks of the Ganges in what is now West Bengal. His eternal parents, Jagannath Misra and Sachi Devi, named Him Visvambhara, although, during this period of His childhood pastimes in Navadvipa, He was known by the nickname Nimai. After twenty-four years in this world, Nimai accepted the renounced order of life (*sannyasa*) and left Navadvipa. It was from that moment that He became known as Shri Chaitanya. During the first six years of His *sannyasa* life, He toured much of India, including Vrindavana, Benares, etc. He then remained at Jagannath Puri in Orisa, on the shores of the Indian Ocean, for the last eighteen years of His *lila* in the company of His associates absorbed in Radha's most intense feelings of love for Krishna.

In 1532 Shri Krishna-Chaitanya closed His *prakata-lila* (pastimes manifested in the world) mysteriously. Absorbed in the feelings of separation from Radha for Krishna (*vipralambha-bhava*), He entered the temple of Krishna known as Tota-Gopinath, ran towards the *archa-vigraha* (the worshipable form of Krishna) and disappeared from ordinary vision. Other versions tell us that He entered the ocean or the temple of Puri and never again came out. However, Vaishnava saints acknowledge that all of them are possible due to Chaitanya's divinity and for the pleasure of the many faithful devotees. Shri Nityananda Prabhu also similarly closed His *lila* by entering the image of Krishna called Banke-raya. Advaita Acharya and Gadadhara Pandit left the world in an equally mystical way, with neither of them leaving a mortal body behind

Goura Mandala: Shri Krishna-Chaitanya's abode

Shri Chaitanya's eternal abode is Navadvipa. It is situated in Goloka-Vrindavana, the supreme spiritual world. In the same way that Vrindavana manifests itself in this world, Navadvipa is also present in material creation. In its spiritual essence, Navadvipa is not different from Vrindavana. It is another dimension or aspect of it, just as Shri Chaitanya and Nityananda Prabhu are not different from Krishna and Balarama. Navadvipa is the same Vrindavana with the same eternal associates of Krishna, enjoying the *lila* in a different dimension and flavor. The area where Navadvipa manifests in this world is known as Goura-mandala, situated on the banks of the Ganges in Bengal. There, Shri Chaitanya, Nityananda, and their infinity of associates carried out their eternal pastimes in an unmanifested way (*aprakata-lila*), just as Radha and Krishna do in Vrindavana.

When Shri Chaitanya and Nityananda (Goura-Nitai) manifested their pastimes in this world, Navadvipa was renowned as a settlement of wisdom due to its many schools and academies meant for the study of all kinds of philosophies. Sages of great erudition roamed its streets, debating the different doctrines. As its name indicates (*nava*=nine, *dvipa*=island), Navadvipa consists of nine islands naturally configured in the shape of a great lotus bathed by the waters of Ganges and in whose center lies Antardvipa (the inner or central island) as an expression of the eternal Navadvipa in the spiritual world. What distinguishes Navadvipa from Vrindavana is that, while in Vrindavana (the abode of Radha and Krishna), the *madhurya* of Krishna (His sweetness) predominates. However, in Navadvipa (Shri Chaitanya and Nityananda's abode), what prevails is the *audarya* (the generosity) of the love for Krishna.

From this earthly Navadvipa, Shri Chaitanya and Nityananda freely give the most fallen souls of the Kali age the rare opportunity to learn to love Krishna with the sentiment of the inhabitants of Vrindavana, and especially the feeling of the cowherd girls for Krishna (*gopi-bhava*). The only condition is a sincere dedication to the chanting, recitation, or meditation of the names Hare Krishna Hare Rama (Hare denotes Radha)—without demanding any prior qualification and without considering anyone's condition of life. While in Vrindavana, Krishna is loved in union (*sambhoga*), in Navadvipa, Krishna is loved in separation (*vipralamba-bhava*) or the intense eternal longing to attain Him. Just as Radha and Krishna complement each other as divine counterparts, Navadvipa and Vrindavana complement each other in this inexhaustible dynamism since union (*sambhoga*) is experienced with more intensity when the sentiments of longing for Krishna (*vipralambha*) increase.

Shortly after Shri Chaitanya left this world with His associates, the waters of the Ganges flooded the area, and the earthly Navadvipa disappeared from the worldview for about a hundred years. By the time the water of the Ganges recessed, the geography had changed. Over time people settled again in the place. In the earthly Navadvipa, where Shri Chaitanya carried out His pastimes, there is an area known as Mayapur. The main center of the Hare Krishna Movement or the International Society for Krishna Consciousness (ISKCON) is situated there. As we know, A.C. Bhaktivedanta Swami Prabhupada is its founder-*acharya*. Annually, between February and March, Gaudiya-Vaishnavas of all nationalities gather at this place to celebrate the advent day of Shri Krishna-Chaitanya, which occurred in 1486. As we write this work, we celebrate the 532 anniversary of His advent.

Shri Chaitanya (right) and Shri Nityananda (left) advent into this world to propagate the chanting of Hare Krishna, the easiest and most elevated process of attaining love for Krishna with the sentiment of the inhabitants of Vrindavana.

Chapter 23

The Apostolic Heritage

Except for eight verses about the wonderful potency of Krishna's name, Shri Chaitanya wrote nothing more about the philosophy of *bhakti*. His closest associates and disciples were the ones who compiled his teachings. As we already know, these disciples and associates were not ordinary people but the eternal associates of His abode who descended to accompany Him in His *lilas*. Therefore, the liberated souls can simultaneously dwell in the company of Radha and Krishna in Vrindavana as well as with Shri Chaitanya and Nityananda in Navadvipa. According to the teachings of the Vaishnava sages, those who are exclusively attracted to the forms of Radha-Krishna or Krishna-Balarama attain their eternal companionship in Vrindavana. At the same time, those whose attraction draws them towards Chaitanya and Nityananda enter their eternal realm of Navadvipa, both in the spiritual world. However, when leaving the physical body, those who develop a dual and balanced attraction for both *rasas* (love in union and separation) assume a dual spiritual existence. In this way, while in an eternal spiritual body, they render loving service to Radha and Krishna in Vrindavana, and in another body, they do so as a devotee in the perpetual company of Shri Chaitanya and Nityananda in the eternal Navadvipa. Simultaneously, in a third spiritual body resembling the one they had in this world as Acharyas, these souls dwell for eternity in these sacred places in the physical world that are replicas of the divine abode.

These extraordinary personalities who accompanied Shri Chaitanya and Nityananda as their companions, servants, and disciples are none other than the cowherd girls (*gopis*) and cowherd boys (*gopas*) of Vrindavana who participated in Krishna's *prakata-lila* (pastimes in this world) five thousand years ago. Therefore, they knew the esoteric aspects of love relationships in transcendence (*rasa*). Their lives are so admirable that such a small biographical presentation as the one we present here is nothing more than a tiny glimpse.

The six Goswamis: The first generation of apostles

The members of the Pancha-Tattva are like the major branches, the minor branches, leaves, flowers, and fruits of the great tree of Shri Chaitanya. However, it is accepted that the main and most prolific were the well-known Six Goswamis of Vrindavana. Therefore, whenever we study the teachings and life of Shri Chaitanya, their names become evident: 1. Rupa Goswami, 2. Sanatana Goswami, 3. Raghunath Dasa Goswami, 4. Raghunath Bhatta Goswami, 5. Gopala Bhatta Goswami, and 6. Jiva Goswami.

Shri Chaitanya sent them to Vrindavana to rediscover the exact places where—four thousand five hundred years before—Krishna manifested His pastimes. By then, Vrindavana, in addition to its abundant dangerous predators, was covered by very dense forests that made it almost impossible to recognize the exact places where Krishna performed His *lilas*. However, being eternal associates of Radha and Krishna and participants of Their eternal *lilas*, the Goswamis rediscovered these places that today receive countless pilgrims from all over the world, which is why it is often said that today's Vrindavana is a gift from the Goswamis. Attracted by their holiness, many people from all walks of life became their disciples. Gradually, a large community of Gaudiya-Vaishnavas grew in Vrindavana, making it a great center of scholarship. With the support of wealthy people, the Goswamis built temples of great magnificence. They also established the sacred forms (*archa-vigraha*) of Radha and Krishna, attracting millions of pilgrims annually even today. The flourishing of Vrindavana was such that it even drew the attention of the Mughal Emperor Akbar, who was a great admirer of the work of the Goswamis to the point that, according to several of his biographers, he asked Jiva Goswami for a personal audience. Unfortunately, several decades after his death, his extremely cruel-hearted great-grandson Aurangzeb was crowned emperor. Unlike Akbar, a great universalist, Aurangzeb was a fanatic of his Muslim religion. He destroyed many of the Goswami temples in Vrindavana. Their ruins, even today, testify to its splendorous past.

The life, holiness, and scholarship of these Six Goswamis are astonishing. Their level of renunciation, penance and mystical potential speaks for themselves. For years they traveled the forests of Vrindavana, where frightening beasts abounded, slept each night under a different tree, dressed in rags, and begged their sustenance from the forest dwellers. Stories abound about how Radha and Krishna protected and provided for their every need. Minimizing eating, sleeping, and other physical activities to levels impossible for ordinary humans, the Goswamis wrote many books on the pastimes of Radha and Krishna and the teachings of Shri Chaitanya.

The most cited among the Six Goswamis are the two brothers Rupa Goswami (1489-1564) and Sanatana Goswami (1488-1558), Jiva Goswami (1513-1598), and Raghunath Dasa (1495-1571) due to their immense literary contribution.

Among them, Raghunath Dasa was a vitally important factor in the compilation of the most important biography of Shri Chaitanya called "Shri Chaitanya Caritamrita." He was an eyewitness of Chaitanya's *lilas* during the eighteen years He remained in Jaganath Puri, absorbed in Radha's feelings for Krishna (*maha bhava*).

The Hare Krishna Movement worldwide descends directly from these Six Goswamis, especially Rupa Goswami, which is why its members are known as *rupanugas*, or followers of Rupa Goswami. Rupa and Sanatana were cultured and learned; they knew many arts, such as architecture, counseling, administration, foreign languages, etc. Their education was so refined and their intelligence so brilliant that in their youth, they were the advisers and prime ministers of the powerful Muslim emperor Hussain Shah. The luxury, splendor, and riches they enjoyed are difficult to describe; however, against the emperor's will and by overcoming insurmountable obstacles, they abandoned their life of luxury—like one who abandons pebbles—to join Shri Chaitanya Mahaprabhu, their only eternal treasure. Shri Chaitanya personally instructed Rupa and Sanatana in the Vaishnava philosophy, which is why they are considered the highest authority among the followers of Shri Chaitanya. Rupa Goswami especially wrote extensively on the subject of *rasa*, loving exchanges in transcendence, and for this reason, he is known as *rasa-acharya*. For his part, Sanatana delved into different topics of *bhakti*, such as the activities and exemplary behavior of a Vaishnava. Their work is pervasive, not only in their writings but also in their efforts to discover the places of Krishna's *lilas*. At the same time, they spent much of the day meditating (or reciting) more than one hundred thousand names of Krishna each day and sleeping only one to three hours each night.

As for Jiva Goswami, among an infinity of other works, he also wrote six philosophical treatises (*sat-sandarbhas*). In the *sandarbhas*, Jiva systematized and outlined vital aspects of the teachings that Shri Chaitanya imparted to his uncles Rupa and Sanatana. For this reason, Jiva is considered the supreme authority of the Gaudiya-Vaishnavas on philosophical matters. His work is so voluminous that it is second only to Vyasa, the compiler of the Vedas. Jiva Goswami's intellect and genius surpass even the extraordinary. His accomplishments include creating a system for studying Sanskrit grammar while remembering Krishna's names. His love for Krishna was so profound that his eyes were always reddish with tears, as if he were about to cry. Some biographers consider that Jiva possibly never had personal contact with Shri Chaitanya; because of this, some compare him to Saint Paul, the apostle of Christendom, who is known to have never met Jesus.

However, other biographers tell us that when Rupa and Sanatana went to meet Shri Chaitanya in the village of Ramakeli, they took young Jiva with them. What is known is that Jiva enjoyed the direct company of Nityananda Prabhu. Whatever the case, it is a fact that Jiva grew up and studied under the guidance, wisdom, and sanctity of his uncles, who were direct disciples of Shri Chaitanya. When Jiva Goswami was still very young, Nityananda Prabhu took Him to Navadvipa, where Shri Chaitanya manifested His *lilas* during His first twenty-four years in this world. In Navadvipa, Jiva Goswami met many of Shri Chaitanya's associates, including His transcendental mother, Sachi Devi, who is the manifestation of Yashoda, the eternal mother of Krishna. When Rupa and Sanatana left this world, Jiva Goswami became the leader of the Vaishnava community of Vrindavana, while in Navadvipa, Virabhadra, the mighty son of Nityananda Prabhu, became its leader. According to the devotees and closest associates of Shri Chaitanya, the Six Goswamis are *manjaris*, very young *gopis* who are the most intimate friends of Radha in Goloka-Vrindavana; therefore, they are witnesses of the eternal loving pastimes of Radha and Krishna.

The spiritual identities of these Six Goswamis in the eternal abode of Vrindavana are followed by their names in this world: 1. Rupa Goswami (Rupa Manjari) 2. Sanatana Goswami (Labanga Manjari) 3. Ragunath Dasa Goswami (Rati Manjari) 4. Ragunath Battha (Raga Manjari) 5. Gopal Battha Goswami (Guna Manjari) and 6. Jiva Goswami (Vilasa Manjari).

The second generation

As we have mentioned, after the departure of the older Goswamis, Jiva Goswami remained at the head of the community of Vaishnavas in Vrindavana and was in charge of training the new generation. The other prominent community was found in Navadvipa, in the Bengal area, generally under the guidance of the descendants of Nityananda Prabhu. Under Jiva Goswami's care and that of other prominent Goswamis emerged the second generation of great Vaishnavas, who preserved and disseminated the teachings of Shri Chaitanya. The most notable were Narottama Dasa, Shyamananda Pandit, and Srinivas Acharya due to their sanctity and missionary activities to propagate the teachings of Shri Chaitanya for the benefit of fallen souls. The exact dates of their births and departures from this world are unknown with certainty, but they are between the beginning and end of the 16th century.

Once, Shri Chaitanya—overcome with spiritual emotions—began to shed tears and repeat the word "*narottama, narottama,*" which means first-class person. Although no one understood the reason for this, shortly afterward, Shri Chaitanya revealed that a great devotee named Narottama Dasa would be born to spread the congregational chanting of the names of Krishna (*kirtana*). The following day, Nityananda Prabhu announced to the Vaishnavas present that Shri Chaitanya would deposit His love for Krishna (*krishna-prema*) in the waters of the Padma River. When Shri Chaitanya entered the water, He caused the river to overflow and said, "When someone enters your waters and causes you so much joy that it makes you overflow, that person is Narottama Dasa." Years after Shri Chaitanya left this world, Narottama Dasa, as an adolescent, had a dream in which Nityananda Prabhu ordered him to bathe in the waters of the Padma River. At that time, Shri Chaitanya appeared before Narottama and embraced him. At that moment, Narottama Dasa's body took on a golden hue similar to Shri Chaitanya's. Despite coming from a highly prestigious social class, Narottama Dasa left his comfortable life and went to Vrindavana to lead an ascetic life in the company of the Goswamis. There he became a disciple of Lokanath Dasa, one of the associates of Shri Chaitanya. Seeing Narottama's great love for Krishna and his humility, Lokanath placed him under the care of Jiva Goswami.

It should be mentioned that even though Krishna's associates are present in this world, simultaneously in their divine spiritual bodies, they continue serving the Divine Couple Radha-Krishna in Goloka-Vrindavana. Once, while contemplating his eternal form in Goloka-Vrindavana in mystical meditation, Narottama Dasa saw himself boiling a pot of milk for Radha. Still, seeing that the hot milk began to spill, he stopped it with his bare hands. After coming out of his trance, the young mystic noticed that his hands were burned since what happened in the spiritual plane also took place in the physical plane. Although he covered his hands with a cloth, Jiva Goswami, of a similar spiritual category as Narottama Dasa, could intuit what happened. So, taking him by the hands, he said, "You are the manifestation of Shri Chaitanya Mahaprabhu's love, and with this love, you will flood the whole world."

Besides being a devout scholar of great holiness, Narottama Dasa was also a great singing poet. His songs, composed in simple Bengali language, are full of sentiments that touch the depths of the heart and contain the essence of the teachings of Shri Chaitanya's religion of love. Narottama Dasa was the one who organized the first festival to celebrate the advent of Shri Chaitanya in this world years after His departure. Tens of thousands of people attended, many of whom were associates of Shri Chaitanya, by then very old. Narottama is accredited with the miracle (among many others) of causing the reappearance of Shri Chaitanya and His associates (Pancha-Tattva) while singing. Since he was an unparalleled singer, his voice and melody were extremely attractive. When overflowing with emotions, Narottama Dasa began to sing, Shri Chaitanya and other members of the Pancha-Tattva appeared before everyone present. Once more, They danced to the rhythm of the congregational chanting of Krishna's names. The Vaishnavas considered Narottama Dasa the personification of Nityananda Prabhu's ecstasy.

....

The second of these three great Vaishnava saints was Shyamananda Pandit, whose life is no less admirable. His original name was Dukhi-Krishna Dasa. Dukhi means afflicted. His parents named him Dukhi, hoping that death would not take him away since, before conceiving him, several of his siblings had died at birth. His guru was a great Vaishnava saint named Hridaya Chaitanya, a prominent associate of Shri Chaitanya and Nityananda in Navadvipa. Contemporary sages tell us that Hridaya Chaitanya is an eternal associate cowherd boy of Krishna and Balarama in Goloka-Vrindavana; therefore, his rasa (affective mellow) towards both Krishna and Shri Chaitanya is by nature brotherly. His relationship with Shri Chaitanya was so intimate that on one occasion, Shri Chaitanya once entered his heart (*hridaya*). Since his disciple Dukhi-Krishna Dasa in his original form is a cowherd girl (*gopi*) of Vrindavana, his spiritual relationship (rasa) with Krishna is one of conjugal love. Because of this, his *guru* allowed him to live under the guidance of Jiva Goswami (whose love for Krishna is also conjugal) to receive instructions on the spiritual practices he should follow appropriate to his *rasa*.

On one occasion, a very special *lila* occurred between Dukhi-Krishna Dasa and Radha, which moved the community of Vaishnavas. While walking through one of the forests of Vrindavana, Dukhi-Krishna Dasa found such a splendid anklet that it made the whole place glow. He was convinced that it was not an ornament of this world, brought it to his forehead, and immediately felt such intense feelings of *prema* that he lost consciousness. When he regained composure, still delirious with *prema*, he hung the anklet around his neck and buried it in a secluded place. Shortly after, a beautiful *lila* took place, culminating in the appearance of Lalita Devi, one of the eight intimate associate *gopis* of Radha and Krishna. Dukhi-Krishna Dasa gave her the divine anklet. Lalita Devi touched his forehead, making two vertical lines appear joined in a U-shape between the eyebrows and extending to the upper forehead, decorated with a point between both lines. Lalita Devi told Dukhi-Krishna Dasa that from that moment, he would be known as Shyamananda since his service had given pleasure to Radha. She ordered him not to reveal what happened to anyone except Jiva Goswami. On his return, Jiva Goswami noticed that the body of Dukhi-Krishna Dasa had a golden effulgence and that his eyes emanated bliss. So Dukhi-Krishna Dasa revealed what had happened. From this moment, everyone began to call Dukhi-Krishna Dasa, Shyamananda. However, a controversy arose because his new name and the mark on his forehead that distinguished his disciplic line differed from the rest of the Gaudiya-Vaishnavas.

Tradition considers it inappropriate for a disciple, after receiving his new name upon initiation, to receive a different name from another spiritual instructor, which led Hridaya-Chaitanya to believe that Jiva Goswami had acted in an unexemplary way. However, Jiva Goswami received the emissaries of Hridaya-Chaitanya with the great humility that characterized him, informing them that he had nothing to do with the name change nor with the new design of the mark on the forehead (*tilaka*) of Dukhi-Krishna Dasa. When the emissaries returned with the news, Hridaya-Chaitanya, who lived in distant Navadvipa (Bengal) —very surprised by his disciple's behavior—decided to go to Vrindavana. After his arrival, Dukhi-Krishna Dasa (now Shyamananda) related what happened to his *guru*, but Hridaya-Chaitanya, instead of believing the wonderful story, considered that Shyamananda was lying; therefore, the tension increased. In search of help, Shyamananda mystically accessed his divine identity in Goloka-Vrindavana as a cowherd girl. Such an event gave rise to a beautiful *lila* in the spiritual world between Shyamananda and Radha, where Radha and Krishna's associates assured him that the new mark on his forehead would never be erased.

Back in external consciousness, Shyamananda invited his

guru Hridaya-Chaitanya to write the name Shyamananda on his body and try to erase it as proof of its divine origin. Despite Hridaya-Chaitanya's attempts, each time he erased it, again and again, the mark on the forehead and the name Shyamananda became vividly visible. Finally, realizing that Shyamananda's words were true, Hridaya Chaitanya was pleased to have such an exalted disciple. This *lila* of an apparent dispute between Jiva Goswami and Hridaya Chaitanya, both backed by their disciples, is a replica in this world of the divine quarrels in Goloka-Vrindavana between Radha and Her cowherd girlfriends against Krishna and His cowherd boyfriends. Such dive disputes overflow with divine bliss, for they always culminate in wonderful pastimes of love between Radha and Krishna. Many other events in Shyamananda's life speak of his exalted personality. Some Vaishnavas consider Shyamananda Pandita to be the personification of the spiritual ecstasy of Advaita Acharya, the third member of the Pancha-Tattva.

....

The third of these three great Vaishnavas was Shrinivas, a disciple of Gopala Bhatta, one of the Six Goswami of Vrindavana. His admirable life speaks of his status as an eternal associate of Radha and Krishna. Like Narottama and Shyamananda, Shrinivasa carried out many missionary activities to spread the teachings of Shri Chaitanya everywhere. A well-known event in his life occurred when Birhambir, then king of the city of Vishnupura, heard from his astrologer about pilgrims transporting a great treasure through his kingdom. Without hesitation, he sent raiders to steal it. But when the king opened the chest, he marveled to see that the treasure was none other than the original manuscripts of the

Goswamis, many of them signed by the great sage and saint Rupa Goswami, recognizable by his exquisite calligraphy. As he examined them, his heart was touched by the philosophy that revealed the teachings of Shri Chaitanya. That same night, Shrinivas appeared before the king in a dream, announcing that he would soon go to his kingdom to meet him. Days later, in the hall of his palace, King Birhambir heard Shrinivas recite the most esoteric verses of Srimad Bhagavatam. He explained them so profoundly that the king not only returned the chest with the manuscripts of the Goswamis, but he also became his disciple. During his lifetime, Shrinivas attracted countless people to Shri Chaitanya's path of love.

Shrinivas was also known for his prolonged trances, often bringing tangible objects from the spiritual realm to the physical world. Once, he fell into such a deep trance for three days that his disciples feared that his physical life would end. On another occasion, in his meditation, he saw Shri Chaitanya putting a garland of flowers around his neck that previously Shrinivas had offered him. When he came out of his trance, everyone saw that a garland had appeared around his neck. His contribution to the *sampradaya* (disciplic succession) of Shri Chaitanya is immeasurable.

For this reason, the Vaishnavas consider Shrinivas to be the personification of Shri Chaitanya's ecstasy or an empowered portion of His Self as His devotee. While the Goswamis wrote down the teachings of Shri Chaitanya, Narottama Dasa, Shyamananda Pandita, and Srinivas Acharya spread these teachings throughout various parts of India despite facing great vicissitudes. Even today, the glory of their missionary work is the subject of admiration among the faithful of Chaitanya.

Later generations

These three personalities were followed by generations of prominent disciples of great sanctity and wisdom who continued the apostolic line of Shri Chaitanya. The most notable of this new generation was Visvanatha Chakravarti. His commentaries enormously contribute to Vaishnava philosophy since they elucidate the esoteric meaning of Radha and Krishna's loving pastimes. His contribution to the explanations of *krishna-lila* is as respected as that of the Six Goswamis. The most recognized of his disciples and who was part of the following generation was the great Baladeva Vidya-bhushana, who, from his youth, showed great sanctity and a privileged intellect. Baladeva Vidya-bhushana wrote the commentary on the Vedanta philosophy that represents the Gaudiya-sampradaya, as the disciplic succession of Shri Chaitanya is known. At the beginning of this work, we explained that the Vedanta-sutra synthesizes the Upanishads' philosophy, which is the philosophical essence of the four Vedas. Medieval Indian orthodoxy does not consider a disciplic succession authentic unless it presents a coherent commentary on the Vedanta-sutra that supports its postulates.

The Srimad Bhagavatam, the ripened fruit and essence of the Vedic tree of knowledge, tells us that it was compiled by Vyasa, the compiler of the Vedas; therefore, it is the natural commentary on Vedanta, something that Shri Chaitanya ratified. Because of this, neither the Goswamis nor their successor disciples wrote a commentary on the Vedanta-sutra. However, in the middle of the 18th century, in the city of Jaipur, the Ramanandi Vaishnavas (a branch of the *sampradaya* of Ramanuja) wanted to take charge of caring for the *archa-*

vigraha (adorable form) of Radha and Krishna known as Radha-Govinda. This *archa-vigraha* belonged to Rupa Goswami. However, the authenticity of Shri Chaitanya's *sampradaya* was questioned since it lacked a commentary on the Vedanta-sutra. Years before, when the fanatical Mughal-Islamic emperor Aurangzeb invaded Vrindavana, these famous forms of Radha-Govinda were removed to prevent their destruction. Because they descended in apostolic succession in the line of Rupa Goswami, the Gaudiya-Vaishnavas were undoubtedly the rightful heirs of these beautiful forms of Radha-Govinda.

The king of Jaipur, a faithful follower of Shri Chaitanya's apostolic succession (Gaudiya-sampradaya), found himself in a dilemma and sent an emissary to Vrindavana requesting the intervention of the great sage Visvanatha Chakravarti. However, Visvanatha Chakravarti's extreme old age prevented him from making such an eventful journey, which is why he entrusted the task to his young disciple Baladeva. In Jaipur, the Gaudiya-Vaishnava community was preparing to receive the great and famous sage Visvanatha Chakravarti who would represent them. However, to their surprise, they saw that this youngster who would represent him had arrived in his place! With their hopes dashed, anxiety took hold of their hearts. What was at stake was nothing more and nothing less than the authenticity of Shri Chaitanya's *sampradaya* and the sacred forms of Radha-Govinda that once belonged to Rupa Goswami. But, aside from being a disciple of the great Visvanatha Chakravarti, what else could be said about this unknown youngster?

Despite the arguments made by young Baladeva about the authenticity of Shri Chaitanya's *sampradaya*, the Ramanandi Vaishnavas demanded a commentary on the Vedanta-sutra, an undertaking entrusted only to the most experienced Vedantists. Faced with this inconvenience, the young Baladeva approached the sacred forms of Radha-Govinda and expressed his feelings: "Why do you want to separate us from Your service? What serious offense have we committed? Why do you want to leave us?" That same night, while he was sleeping, Govinda (Krishna), under the pretext of a dream, appeared before Baladeva and told him that He did not have to worry since He would dictate the required commentary. Baladeva only had to pay attention and write. In a matter of days, young Baladeva presented his commentary. It was so convincing and exquisite that it surprised even the best among Vaishnava Ramanandi scholars. With great pleasure, they accepted the authenticity of Shri Chaitanya's *sampradaya* and even wished to convert and become disciples of Baladeva. However, the young sage considered it unnecessary since the Ramanandis are an authentic disciplic succession. Out of respect and admiration for the prodigious intellect of the young Baladeva, the Vaishnavas Ramanandi bestowed upon him the title of *vidya-bhusana*, "ornament of wisdom." In Shri Chaitanya's disciplic succession, Baladeva Vidya-bhuhsana is known as Gaudiya-vedanta-acharya (the *acharya* of the Vedanta philosophy). However, recognizing Krishna as the work's actual author, Baladeva named his commentary Govinda-bhashya, "Govinda's commentary," or in other words, what Govinda spoke.

....

After Baladeva Vidya-bhushana the most recognized *acharya* in this apostolic line was an ascetic known as Jagannath Dasa Babaji (1776? -1894). Jagannath Dasa had an extremely long life of about 120 years. His life of holiness and renunciation was a great inspiration to the Gaudiya-vaishnavas, as all the symptoms of a *maha-bhagavata* (saint of the highest level) were visible in his person. Jagannath Dasa spent his entire life between Vrindavana and Navadvipa and had two disciples who were part of the next generation. Both are of unparalleled importance for the modern era: Goura Kishora Dasa Babaji and Bhaktivinoda Thakur. The latter often carried his old *guru* inside a basket tied to his back.

At the gates of the 20th century

Bhaktivinoda Thakur (1838-1914) was born under the name Kedarnath and is considered the great-grandfather and forerunner of the Hare Krishna Movement worldwide. In addition to his immense nobility and compassion for the wellbeing of his humanity, Bhaktivinoda was a great intellectual, philosopher, thinker, writer, poet, visionary, prophet, and social reformer. He was also a highly respected magistrate of his day in times when the British crown reigned over India. However, these qualities were the natural ornaments of his virtue and holiness. He was such a dazzling and virtuous personality that Shri Chaitanya's followers call him "the Seventh Goswami" since his life and work are similar in stature to both the Goswamis and Visvanath-Chakravarti.

As with the previous Acharyas, it is impossible to reduce his life to a just synopsis. Born into a highly respectable family, Bhaktivinoda attended British educational institutions, thus becoming familiar with Western philosophy and other prevailing ideas of his day. In his youth, he devoted himself to researching the different philosophical and religious systems of the West and India to find a comprehensive path that reconciled reason and traditional beliefs, differentiating the mundane from the spiritual aspect of religion. By so doing, he opened the way for modern critical analysis and appreciation of Vaishnava mysticism. Finally, at age 29, his spiritual quest led him to Shri Chaitanya's religion of universal love.

In the years to come, almost wholly abandoning sleep, Bhaktivinoda Thakur wrote many books in which he outlined the philosophy of Shri Chaitanya delightfully and pedagogically. The influence of Bhaktivinoda was to the land of Shri Chaitanya (Navadvipa), what the Goswamis were to Vrindavana centuries before. Bhaktivinoda rediscovered the places of the *lilas* of Shri Chaitanya by then lost to ordinary vision. Bhaktivinoda wanted to rediscover Shri Chaitanya's place of advent in this world for a long time. Absorbed in this thought, once, while observing the horizon of Navadvipa from his home, he had a mystical vision that gave him indications of the exact place of advent. The next day, carrying his *guru* Jagannath Dasa in a basket tied to his back (who was over a hundred years old and disabled), he approached the site of his vision. Sensing the divinity of the place, Jagannath Dasa jumped out of the basket and began to dance in divine ecstasy, something normally impossible for his physical condition, thus confirming the authenticity of the place. Later, Bhaktivinoda verified this finding using other sources and ancient maps. He also discovered where Shrivas Pandita's house was—the site where Shri Chaitanya began the movement of congregational chanting of the names of Krishna in this world.

Bhaktivinoda's work of reform was not easy. Shortly after the departure of Shri Chaitanya, the pseudo-spiritualists distorted His teachings. Under the pretext of imitating Radha and Krishna's divine loving affairs, which they considered an authentic method of spiritual practice, they engaged in immoral practices. Not surprisingly, various sects emerged propagating philosophical concepts foreign to Shri

Chaitanya's teachings. Amid this sea of heresies, the few genuine saints and practitioners were like needles in a vast haystack, which is why the educated society of the time developed a negative opinion of the religion and teachings of Shri Chaitanya. Seeing this painful condition, Bhaktivinoda Thakur undertook the arduous task of rescuing the prestige of these teachings. With his great talent, scholarship, writings, and the perfect example of his virtuous life, he gradually restored the purity of the teachings of the Goswamis by attracting large numbers of people of good education and social standing to the Shri Chaitanya's path. Like Narottama Dasa, Bhaktivinoda Thakur was a great poet who composed countless devotional songs in simple Bengali language, brimming with spiritual sentiments embodying the essence of Shri Chaitanya's teachings. Personally bringing the chanting of Krishna's names to each house, Bhaktivinoda revived the work of Shri Nityananda Prabhu and was the pioneer in blessing the world with the teachings of Shri Chaitanya.

In 1880 he sent some of his writings to well-known thinkers, such as Ralph Waldo Emerson in the United States, Reinhold Rost in Europe, and various academies and bookstores in Canada, England, and Australia. Convinced of Shri Chaitanya's prophecy that the chanting of His holy name would be heard in every town and village in the world, Bhaktivinoda once wrote: "When in England, France, Russia, Prussia, and America will all the fortunate people sing, with cymbals and drums, the name of Chaitanya again and again in their countries, raising the waves of the congregational chanting? When will that day come? When will that day come when white-skinned foreigners speak about the glories of Shri Chaitanya and, with this chanting, extend their arms to embrace the devotees of other countries in brotherhood? When will that day come?" In 1895, he announced that the person who would carry the teachings of Shri Chaitanya worldwide was about to appear. A few months later, in Kolkata, A.C., Bhaktivedanta Swami Prabhupada, the founder of the Hare Krishna Movement, was born. Bhaktivinoda Thakur had a large family, which he maintained with his profession as a magistrate, thanks to his extraordinary capacity for work. He only slept two to three hours a day, wrote for about six hours, studied, and prayed for four and a half hours while dedicating six hours a day to his work at court. Here is the tentative schedule of his regular life.

8:00 pm – 10:00 pm sleeps

10:00 pm – 4:00 am, writes

4:00 am - 4.30 am, short rest

4.30 am – 7:00 am, prays

7:00 am - 7.30 am, answers his correspondence

7.30 am - 9.30 am, studies the scriptures.

9.30 am – 10:00 am, takes a bath and breakfast

10:00 am – 1:00 pm, magistrate duties at the court

1:00 pm – 2:00 pm, comes home for lunch

2:00 pm – 5:00 pm, back to the court

5:00 pm – 7:00 pm, writes and translates ancient texts.

7:00 pm – 8:00 pm, takes a bath, supper, and rest.

In 1874, after praying for some time to conceive an empowered soul capable of continuing his mission, a son was born to him whom he named Bimala-prashad. He was later known as Bhaktisiddhanta Saraswati. Aware of the extraordinary personality that had descended as his son, from an early age, he called him "Ray of Vishnu" and *"acharya* sun." At the beginning of the 20th century, his son, Bhaktisiddhanta Saraswati, would become the spiritual master of A.C. Bhaktivedanta Swami Prabhupada.

....

Goura Kishor Dasa Babaji (1838-1915) was a continual companion of Bhaktivinoda Thakur and was recognized as a Vaishnava *mahatma* among the descendant apostles of Shri Chaitanya. Like his *guru* Jagannath Dasa, Goura Kishor was a great ascetic of unfathomable spiritual power. He left home at an early age to lead the life of a spiritual mendicant absorbed in reciting the divine names of Radha and Krishna. Although he never learned to read or write, the Vaishnava sages of his day recognized him as an enlightened soul, an eternal associate of Shri Chaitanya, whose discernment and spiritual wisdom transcended the barriers of worldly scholasticism. Aware of his profound spiritual achievement, Bhaktivinoda Thakur urged the most exalted among his sons, Bimala-prashad, to become Goura Kishor's disciple.

Contemporary Acharyas

Bhaktisiddhanta Saraswati (Bimala-prashad, 1874-1937) is the most outstanding contemporary Vedic scholar. At the moment of his birth, the experts discovered signs on his body that announced his condition as a liberated soul according to Vedic astrological principles. Once again, it is necessary to say that no biographical synopsis, however fair it may be, can express the exceptional nature of his life. Bhaktisiddhanta Saraswati was a celibate monk throughout his life; his contemporaries called him "lion *guru*" (*acharya-keshari*) for his memory, intelligence, and unfathomable wisdom. Others called him the "human encyclopedia" since there was no branch of knowledge on which he could not debate. Despite his being an adolescent, the scholars offered him the prestigious title of Saraswati due to his immense wisdom. While still very young, he vowed to recite a billion names of Krishna by leading a life of intense austerity, a vow he completed after nearly ten years wherein he engaged in prayer for twenty-two hours a day.

In 1918, after the departure of his father Bhaktivinoda Thakur, and his *guru* Goura Kishor, Bhaktisiddhanta accepted the renounced order of life, and later, he founded the prestigious Gaudiya-math religious society to spread the teachings of Shri Chaitanya throughout India and beyond. Bhaktisiddhanta Saraswati was a dynamic preacher who continued his father's work since he was also a prolific reformer and writer. Throughout his life, he strongly opposed the erroneous idea that only those born into priestly families can be ordained as such and act as spiritual mentors. Due to this, he faced great opposition from the priestly class that monopolized this right. They even attempted against his life on several occasions. Realizing that the new world social order revolved around modern technology, Bhaktisiddhanta Saraswati coupled the Vaishnava standards of life with modernism, breaking many of the classical taboos of the time. In this way, he opened the way to lead a Vedic way of life while conforming to the way of life of modern society. He introduced reforms that revolutionized the static concepts of the renunciate's life by dynamic and practical principles according to time, place, and circumstances, emphasizing the essence of Sri Chaitanya's teachings beyond forms and archaic formulas. Accepting the principle of practical renunciation described by Rupa Goswami centuries ago, Bhaktisiddhanta showed how to use all modern technology in the service of Shri Chaitanya's teachings for the benefit of humanity. In this way, he broke with ancient meaningless formalities by adopting norms that would appeal to the modern human being, such as the way of dressing and lifestyle in general, while preserving the essence of *bhakti*.

He sent his disciples to Europe on missionary activities to propagate the teachings of Shri Chaitanya. More than once, he mentioned that one of his disciples would fulfill Shri Chaitanya's prophecy that Krishna's names would be chanted worldwide. If we remember, it was in Calcutta in 1922 when for the first time, he met the young Abhay Charan De, who, ten years later, in 1932, would become his formally initiated disciple. Abhay would eventually be known worldwide as A.C. Bhaktivedanta Swami Prabhupada, the founding *acharya* of the International Society for Krishna Consciousness (ISKCON)—or the Hare Krishna Movement, as it is popularly known. Before leaving this world, Srila Bhaktisiddhanta noted with disgust that many of his senior disciples were arguing about who would be the next *acharya* of the mission he had founded. On a particular occasion, while on pilgrimage with his disciples in Vrindavana, he told Abhay Charan that after his departure, there would be a schism in the Gaudiya-math, the society that he had founded.

Knowing Abhay's innate virtue, he told him, "You are different if you ever have money print books." Sometime later, anticipating his departure from this world, Abhay wrote him a letter. He wanted to know the last instruction that his *guru* had for him. The answer was the same instruction he had received in 1922 when they first met in this world, "Preach the message of Shri Chaitanya in the English language." The departure of this luminary was a severe blow for the prestigious Gaudiya-math Mission and Abhay Charan. As expected from a genuine disciple who feels the pain of separation from a great soul, years later, Abhay confessed that upon hearing the news, he wept. Since then, Abhay Charan adjusted his life to fulfill the wish of his *guru* and the apostles who preceded him to carry all over the world the teachings of the universal love of Shri Chaitanya in the form of the divine names of Krishna. Before leaving this world, on November 14, 1977, Abhay Charan, who was then known as A.C. Bhaktivedanta Swami, left his legacy in the care of his disciples, who from the very beginning preferred to call him by the prestigious title of Srila Prabhupada. However, how this extraordinary personality came to America at the advanced age of 70 years during the tumultuous decade of the sixties, alone, penniless, and in poor health, and how he made Shri Chaitanya's prophecy come actual leads back to the introduction of this book.

> "He reasons ill who tells that Vaishnavas die
> When thou are living still in sound!
> The Vaishnavas die to live,
> and living try to spread the holy name around!"
>
> Bhaktivinoda Thakur

Appendix

Hare Krishna today: Integration or isolation?

A distinctive feature of every genuine spiritual movement is its inner dynamism and human disparity. This diversity of opinions and procedures injects life into such movements. The functionalism of ideas survives when we adjust to the generational changes preserving the essence of a message and discarding the externals when they lose their reason for being. Thus, we can project our teachings beyond our times and last through millennia.

However, since humans fear change by nature, such metamorphoses are always controversial. As a result, we easily cling to external forms at the risk of forgetting the essence. Hence, the outward forms become sacred.

In this regard, we find an example of the perennial tension between preservation and adaptation in the society of Krishna devotees in the West—the now well-known Hare Krishna Movement. The diversity of opinions among its members reveals their human texture and sincere attempts to rectify their ideas and points of view. Some may question the need to address a controversial issue in this work; however, it is precisely the positive dynamics of the controversies that motivate us. In his masterful work, the great sage Krishna Dasa Kaviraja, author of the leading biography of Shri Chaitanya, advised us that a sincere seeker should not put controversial issues aside since they strengthen the mind and make one more attached to Krishna.

The reason that compels us to present such internal controversy in this society is not difficult to intuit. From the early 1960s to the mid-1970s of the 20th century, the American youth revolted against the lifestyle of their parents. Out of this rejection sprang the *hippie* movement, marked by its psychedelic music, bizarre fashion, drug abuse, sexual debauchery, and moral liberalism. However, the interest in poetry, literature, and the exotic superficiality of Eastern mysticism was another hallmark. While one part of American society fought for its civil rights and another bled in Vietnam, the world lived under the continuous threat of a nuclear holocaust. The Cold War between the extinct Soviet Union as leader of the Socialist Block and the United States in alliance with the democracies of the Free World was at its zenith.

During this unconventional and tumultuous period for the traditional way of life of the Americans, Bhaktivedanta Swami Prabhupada arrived in the United States. With his elegance, refined manners, and deep piety, he soon attracted a misled youth who would make Hare Krishna a prevalent phrase. Under his influence, his followers gradually abandoned the threadbare clothes of a rebellious generation that liked everything strange and exotic, adopting garments like those of this old saint who was to become their spiritual mentor. By dressing in the classical Indian style, they catalyzed their rejection of social norms. This is perhaps the cause why the nascent International Society of devotees of Krishna was made up almost exclusively of young people from the *hippie* culture. In this way, the Hare Krishna movement became known for its multi-colored Hindustani dress.

A wise saying says that time and tide wait for no man. In 1977 at the age of 81, Bhaktivedanta Swami Prabhupada left this world, leaving behind a vast legacy that his disciples were to carry on, even though most were in their twenties. Orphaned at such an early age and with such a burden of responsibility, these young men and women were responsible for the great successes and significant failures that resulted from a long and tortuous but natural maturation process, both individually and collectively. Gradually, the historical window of this era of rebellion and exoticism that characterized the sixties closed, and the collective intoxication with the orientalist mystique ended. The garments that served as an attraction for the great Hare Krishna explosion lost their charm and appeal to a new and somewhat apathetic and disinterested audience. Gradually, the new generations left behind the *hippie* utopia of their parents and took up the norms of life centered on material success. As a result, their interests, concerns, tastes, styles, and preferences changed dramatically. Today's India, archaic and decadent, devoured by its social ills and eager to imitate European culture, hardly inspires. Even today, words like yoga and meditation are synonymous with psychophysical benefits far removed from their spiritual dimension. Those who try to promote these disciplines do so in a way that appeals to current dynamics, no matter how trivial. The 21st century opened its doors more than two decades ago, and the romantic legacy of the sixties is now the nostalgia of the elderly. And what happened to that dynamic movement of young people wrapped in their white and saffron robes dancing with joy in the squares of North American cities and the great European capitals to the beat of the chanting of Hare Krishna? Despite being the heirs of authentic and profound spiritual science, most people know the "Hare Krishnas" for their distinctive and somewhat anachronistic dress rather than for the generosity of their message.

However, most members of the International Society for

Krishna Consciousness and other societies that sprout from it still keep the same social projection they had at the dawn of this movement, although, according to many, today has a discordant effect. Those who still carry the chant of Hare Krishna to public squares wearing the garb of that longed-for India of the sixties recognize that they do not receive the same reception as more than half a century ago. Young college dropouts do not join by the dozens in search of a spiritual adventure, but quite the opposite. The times have undoubtedly changed. Today's society does not take the Hare Krishna devotees in the same mood as it did in the roaring 1960s. What has happened?

This reality has not escaped the vision of some leaders and members of this Krishna Consciousness Movement. In 2013, after many years of reflection and maturation, Hridayananda Dasa Goswami (Dr. Howard Resnick), a prominent disciple of Bhaktivedanta Swami and one of the most senior spiritual leaders of ISKCON, launched an internal reform mission under the name of Krishna West. To his credit, Hridayananda Dasa Goswami holds a Ph.D. from Harvard University in Sanskrit and Indian studies and is an ex-member of the Governing Body. His mission aims to promote the Hare Krishna movement in modern society while preserving the essence of its practices and teachings for the spiritual welfare of the individual and the community.

Like everything in this world, this postulate of preserving and adapting has supporters and detractors. The debate revolves around the essential and peripherical aspects of devotion to Krishna. In other words, it attempts to separate what is integral to the spiritual process of *bhakti* from that which is simply a cultural aspect of India.

One of the most emphatic teachings of the Hare Krishna

movement is the distinction between what is Hindu religion and what is *sanatana-dharma* (the eternal function of the soul in its relationship with God), something that transcends all cultural and ethnic barriers. Therefore, any person who knows the Vaishnava philosophy would never present the teachings of the Bhagavad-Gita as Hindu philosophy. Calling *krishna-bhakti* Hinduism is not to understand its metaphysical dimension. However, from the very beginning, the young members of the Hare Krishna Society mistook India's cultural elements as an intrinsic part of *bhakti*.

Despite being faithful to the principles of *bhakti*, most practitioners are not historians; hence, they are unaware of India's socio-political history. Therefore, many elements they consider essential to the Vaishnava culture are not from India but imported by the colonizers who came to India in the last thousand-odd years.

In his lectures and writings, Hridayananda Dasa Goswami, the promoter of internal reform within the Hare Krishna world, presents several points of interest. He postulates that its members must integrate effectively into modern society for this movement to be correctly appreciated. They also must understand the meaning of Vedic culture to avoid clinging to the customs and norms of ethnic India. Hridayananda Dasa Goswami postulates that although the Krishna Consciousness movement tries to spread Vedic culture to modern society, it is a fact that the term "Vedic culture" does not appear in the Vedic scriptures. Therefore, (and above all) its members must define the term Vedic based on the principles given in the Vedas; otherwise, our concept may be whimsical and lacks spiritual authority.

However, since Bhaktivedanta Swami Prabhupada often used the term "Vedic culture," it must be accepted as long as we use it in a way that the Vedic scriptures intend it.

As we already know, the word *veda* means knowledge. Therefore, Vedic culture is a standard of life that elevates us to the platform of knowledge—specifically spiritual knowledge, and not simply an imitation of the clothing, cuisine, dance, music, architecture, and other traditional customs of an ethnic group. For this reason, considering something Vedic simply because it comes from India is wrong. According to Hridayananda Dasa Goswami, it is a mistake to think that if someone practices devotion to Krishna but does not adhere to Indian ethnic customs is not a serious practitioner of the Vaishnava religion. This idea is a mistake that the Hare Krishna society still clings to after more than four decades after its founder's departure.

Hridayananda Dasa Goswami (Dr. Howard Resnick) postulates the prominent Vaishnava scripture, such as Srimad Bhagavatam, Bhagavad-Gita, Mahabharata, etc., do not describes a sort of clothing, architecture, food, music style, etc., as an eternal Vedic prototype. Instead, the scriptures show different cultural forms within "Vedic culture." An example is the difference between the cultures of the big cities and the small rural towns, even in Krishna's time. When Krishna left the simple village of Vrindavana, the *gopis* lamented, thinking that because Krishna now lived in a sophisticated city with different cultural preferences and values, He would never think about them again. Such difference in cultural values is natural because of region and climate. It is a fact that people who live in mountainous areas do not dress in the same way as the inhabitants of tropical forests, towns, deserts, or coastal areas. According to the Vedas, the Vedic culture (or Aryan culture) existed in very remote times in various parts of the world. However, those who inhabited the cold or forest areas of Europe did not dress precisely the same as those in tropical India. There is also no evidence that Shri Chaitanya commanded his followers to dress differently from society in general, nor did He ever state that the external cultural norms of Bengal in India at the time corresponded to an eternal Vedic ethnicity or prototype.

Shri Chaitanya Himself adhered to the moral principles of the time when He appeared. We find an example of this in that Shri Chaitanya accepted the monastic order of life from an institution opposed to *krishna-bhakti* because it was a prestigious monastic order of the time. Also, when the great devotee Sanatana Goswami joined His movement, he abandoned his luxurious way of life and, under the inspiration of Shri Chaitanya, dressed in a way that complied with the cultural norms of the society of the time expected from an ascetic of his spiritual status. Also, Shri Chaitanya only ate in the houses of brahmans (priests), which is compatible with the custom of the time for those in the renounced order of life.

In essence, Hridayananda Dasa Goswami (Dr. Resnick) postulates that Vedic culture is a way of life that teaches general and cultural principles to help us lead a higher life. Vedic culture is not ethnic Indian cultural details, like the dress, culinary recipes, etc. Vedic means something spiritually uplifting and appropriate for time and place, not necessarily a replica of India's culinary recipes and dress. This initiative by Hridayananda Dasa Goswami received much criticism. However, both A.C. Bhaktivedanta Swami and his spiritual predecessor also received criticism from their contemporaries for their initiatives to adjust the way of implementing the Krishna Consciousness movement inside and outside India.

In many of his comments, Bhaktivedanta Swami confirms the authenticity of such adjustments, which we can appreciate in his explanation of verse 4.8.54 of Srimad Bhagavatam. Let's read:

> "It is specifically mentioned in this verse that one should take into consideration of the time, place, and available conveniences. Our Krishna consciousness movement is going on throughout the entire world, and we also install Deities in different centers. Sometimes our Indian friends, puffed up with concocted notions, criticize, 'This has not been done. That has not been done.' But they forget this instruction of Nārada Muni to one of the greatest Vaishnavas, Dhruva Mahārāja. One has to consider the particular time, country and conveniences. What is convenient in India may not be convenient in the Western countries. Those who are not actually in the line of *ācāryas,* or who personally have no knowledge of how to act in the role of *ācārya,* unnecessarily criticize the activities of the ISKCON movement in countries outside of India. The fact is that such critics cannot do anything personally to spread Krishna consciousness. If someone does go and preach, taking all risks and allowing all considerations for time and place, it might be that there are changes in the manner of worship, but that is not at all faulty according to *śāstra* [scripture]."

As we mentioned earlier, during the 1960s and 1970s, the social psychology of the younger generation, shaped by the *hippie* counterculture, was drawn to India's flamboyant dress and mystique. Perceiving this hippie mentality in his disciples, Bhaktivedanta Swami Prabhupada often expressed that they should dress like gentlemen. However, as expected, from the beginning, his disciples channeled their youthful energy by wearing typical Indian clothes, opting to imitate the Hindustani appearance of their mentor. The difficulty for Prabhupada did not consist in getting his disciples to dress in a way that would be extravagant to Western society but in preventing them from doing so. For a rebellious and radical youth that broke with their parents' norms, the option to dress like a gentleman (as Prabhupada often said) implied maintaining the dress code of the 1950s amid an era dominated by the psychedelic counterculture. This was an unattractive option. However, this way of channeling their youthful extravagance into the Indian dress led them to abandon their threadbare hippie clothes; therefore, Bhaktivedanta Swami did not object. "It is good to imitate what is good," he responded once when a reporter mentioned how his disciples tried to imitate him. Before long, in the society of Western devotees, Hindustani clothing such as the *dhoti* (male lower garment), the *kurta* (shirt), the *sari* (female clothing), and the *choli* (tight-fitting short blouse) were the undeclared uniform of the sincere devotee of Krishna. They even took on the connotation of "devotional clothing," though such words do not exist in the Vedic texts. Nevertheless, neither the scriptures nor the history of India indicates that this type of clothing was exclusive and distinctive of Krishna's devotees nor the spiritual class or that it was considered a type of spiritual or devotional clothing as claimed by many of the leaders within the Hare Krishna world.

To further complicate matters, the opponents of the Krishna-West reform argue that this type of Hindustani clothing (*dhoti*, *sari*, etc.) is how Lord Krishna dresses in His abode, Goloka-Vrindavana. However, as we said, in the Vedic-Vaishnava texts themselves, we do not find these words. The counterargument is that we find words like *dhoti*, *sari*, etc., in the Acharyas' descriptions of Krishna and His divine world. However, Dr. Hridayananda Dasa Goswami considers that if this way of dressing is an intrinsic part of devotion to Krishna, we should find such a statement in the scriptures and the instructions of the great Vaishnava sages when they delineate the fundamental principles of *bhakti*. And yet they do not appear. Instead, we find the opposite. To carry out their mission, many great contemporary Vaishnavas dressed in a way that was considered respectable in their respective times. It is a fact that the scriptures do not mention that Radha and Krishna dress in a Hindustani way (with *dhoti*, *sari*, etc., which are not Sanskrit words). Instead, the scriptures use the term *avesha* (garment). Therefore, we should understand that when Acharyas use words like *dhoti*, *sari*, etc., they are simply using contemporary language to describe eternal truths. For example, some Upanishads, despite being ancient wisdom, are presented in a much more modern Sanskrit. We also hear from Srila Prabhupada that the great saintly king Dhruva, who lived in an age before the current age of Kali, was not interested in listening to cinema music. The cinema is a modern phenomenon, implying that Prabhupada undoubtedly uses contemporary language to express universal teaching: the disinterest of liberated souls in the world's pleasures. There are many other similar examples.

However, even if Radha and Krishna in the divine world wear outfits similar to the Hindustani dhotis and saris of this world, it does not necessarily indicate that they are precise of the exact spiritual nature. On the other hand, if these garments are worn by the Hare Krishna devotees of today in the West just because it is how Krishna dresses, and subsequently, they are spiritual, then why limit them to the dress? Doesn't Krishna carry a flute and wear peacock feathers, earrings, etc.? We will also have to accept these objects if we follow the same logic. Furthermore, just because Krishna wears a particular garb and carries a flute in the divine world, does this mean that the garments and flutes of this world are spiritual objects? It is not so because there is no such thing as clothing that is spiritual in itself. Spiritual is our consciousness.

Many of the verses of Srimad Bhagavatam inform us that Krishna and His associates wore clothing that required belts, something to note since Hindu *dhotis* and *saris* do not require a belt. For example, in verses 2.2.11, 8.3.28, 14.8.25, 20.8.32, and 10.88.28, the Srimad Bhagavatam speaks of Krishna's belt. Moreover, verse 10.33.13 mentions the belt of Vrindavana cowherd girls, 11.17.23 mentions the belt of celibate students, and 10.75.24 mentions the belt of other associates of Krishna. Therefore, Hridayananda Dasa Goswami argues that it is not clear that 5000 years ago, when Lord Krishna descended into this world, men wore *dhotis* just like the Hare Krishna devotees of today wear.

Undoubtedly, the dress codes mentioned in the scriptures are not universal. They are not for all times but destined for a specific time and place since the scriptures do not impose wearing ethnic Hindostanic clothing as an essential part of *bhakti*. For example, historical evidence shows that the *choli* (Hindustani tight blouse) originates from the Chola kingdom in medieval southern India; therefore, they would not have existed in northern India during Krishna's time. Despite this, all Indian art of the Hare Krishna movement shows the ladies of India north 5000 years ago wearing cholis, and often Lord Krishna himself wearing Islamic clothing in the style of the Mughal empire.

Due to the emphasis on the Hindustani dress, the western Hare Krishna devotees created two clothing categories, hitherto non-existent in the Vaishnava religion, erroneously called "devotional clothing" and "*karmi* clothing." The first is for Hindustani attire, and the second is for Western clothing. A *karmi* is a person who does not care about the spiritual life. The categorization is surprising if we consider that Prabhupada never used the terms for that purpose. Instead, his disciples used them as the dressing codes of western Hare Krishna society. There is no doubt that Prabhupada liked his disciples' preference for such Hindustani garb rather than the shabby *hippie* dress since it channeled the impetuous for dressing in an exotic way typical of the 60s. It also served to attract the public's attention at a certain point in history, which proved to be a great success. However, it is a fact that half a century later, both the world and social psychology are very different and this no longer works. Even Prabhupada varied his way of doing things when something did not work as expected or became obsolete.

However, those who still advocate the classical clothing of medieval India consider that just as people recognize a police officer by his uniform, they also recognize a spiritual practitioner for his dress. The deficiency in this argument lies in the fact that people know in advance that a policeman is a civil authority, and he only needs the uniform to be recognized. Such a uniform was designed to inspire trust and respect for a particular society's cultural norms. On the contrary, very few people in the West accept someone dressed in Hindustani clothing as a spiritual authority. Instead, often this has the opposite effect. It is a fact that many people consider the members of this movement strange and unbalanced, remnants of the *hippies* who live on the fringes of the predominant culture. For the exponent of the Krishna-West reform, the entrenchment in the ethnic customs of India, instead of representing the universal nature of Shri Chaitanya's religion, serves as a barrier to distance the Hare Krishna devotees from the rest of society that they attempt to transform in search of a better world.

Another relevant aspect that Hridayananda Dasa Goswami cites is that many of the Hare Krishna devotees are unaware of Islamic culture's influence in India after several centuries of domination. Therefore, they consider Vedic things that come from non-Vedic cultures. A classic example of this is a typical dessert in Krishna temples in the West called halvah, which originates from the Middle East and ironically has become almost a culinary symbol of the Hare Krishna society in the West. Likewise, few know that the men's shirt (*kurta*), mistakenly called "devotional clothing," was brought to India by the Islamic invaders. In fact, *kurta* is a Persian word, a language that permeates Hindi, the official language of India. The most prominent classical musicians of India are Muslim. The Sangeet Research Academy tells us: "The music of India has developed through very complex interactions between different peoples of different races and cultures over thousands of years."

Much of the classical architecture that represents the India of today to the world is nothing more than an amalgam of foreign influences, especially the Muslim culture of the Islamic-Mughal period. For example, the famous Rupa Goswami's temple in Vrindavana is a perfect example of Mughal architecture, very much in vogue in his time. In short, there is abundant evidence of how many foreign customs and ethnic groups have influenced the culture of India in the last thousand years.

The Krishna-West reform attempts to "de-Hinduize" the

Hare Krishna movement to flow with the universal nature of *bhakti* (devotion) and in harmony with the best aspects of the Western culture. The seed of this idea comes from the words of Bhaktivedanta Swami Prabhupada himself, the founder of this movement. After all, the mission of Bhaktivedanta Swami Prabhupada was not to "Hinduize" the westerners but to make them Krishna conscious.

For example, the first significant temple that the Hare Krishna Movement acquired was an old Christian church in Los Angeles, California. Instead of placing the forms of Krishna in the grand and majestic shrine, Prabhupada preferred to put them in a small space somewhat more separate, in a way that the guests could sit on the benches as it is done in churches to hear about Krishna. Prabhupada gave the Sunday talks at the shrine and not in front of the Radha-Krishna forms to make it more comfortable for Western guests. A disciple named Gargamuni Dasa, who was serving as the temple president at the time, tells us a story about it:

> "The current temple room in L.A was not what Prabhupada intended to be the temple room... Prabhupada had another idea that wasn't our vision. His vision was to have mainstream America come in with their shoes on and sit in the pews and hear Bhagavad Gita and kirtan on the stage. We put Prabhupada's Vyasasana on stage and he had Visnujana play the organ... Prabhupada didn't want the stained glass windows removed. "Don't touch anything," he said. Even where the minister spoke, the pulpit, he kept that. It was so surreal to sit in the pews and hear *Bhagavad Gita* and Visnujana [a devotee] singing *Jaya Radha-Madhava* on the organ. Even Prabhupada would play

the organ. Prabhupada said, "They are inclined to come to church. So let them come back to this church, but hear *Bhagavad Gita* and *kirtan*." Prabhupada was thinking of mainstream America, not hippies. Prabhupada's vision wasn't that we all become monks. He wanted judges, politicians, doctors to come to the temple. They weren't going to become monks and shave up. But we had another vision—come to the temple and shave up." [Gargamuni Prabhu, Disc 3 in "Following Srila Prabhupada" DVD series].

Dr. Hridayananda Dasa Goswami unearthed many other quotes little known to the generality of the members of the Hare Krishna movement. They reveal that despite the youthful impetus of his disciples to dress similarly to their spiritual guide, Prabhupada had a different, universal, and much less Hinduized vision to carry out his mission of spiritual reform of society. Some of his conversations and writings reveal this reality:

"The real principle is to spread the Krishna consciousness movement, and if one has to change into regular Western dress for this purpose, *there should be no objection*." [CC 2.14.5 Purport]

....

Allen Ginsberg: "Yes, but what [ISKCON] requires is an adaptation of Indian dress…"

Prabhupāda: "That is not very important."

....

"Our only concern is to attract people to Krishna consciousness. We may do this in the dress of sannyasis or in the regular dress of gentlemen. *Our only concern* is to spread interest in Krishna consciousness." [SB 7.13.10 Purport]

....

"So if you don't accept this dress, that does not mean you cannot be in Krishna consciousness. Krishna consciousness can be achieved in any condition of life. It doesn't matter whether you are dressed in this way or in your American way or any way. That doesn't matter. It has nothing to do... Krishna consciousness is different from this dress or that dress." [Lecture — Boston, May 3, 1969]

....

"Dress has to be accepted according to the taste of others and foodstuffs accepted according to the eater's taste. So, if you think this kind of dress will attract more people, you can dress yourself in that manner." [Prabhupada Letters: 1969]

....

"*Sadhu* [holy man] does not mean a kind of dress, or kind of beard. No. *Sadhu* means a devotee, perfect devotee of Krishna. That is a sadhu." [Sydney, February 16, 1973]

....

Disciple: "Speaking about clothes, Monsieur le President says that he has been to India, and he understands that one dresses like this in India. But why would the disciples dress in America or in Europe in this way? Is it necessary?"

Prabhupada: "No. It is not necessary. Dress you can have as you like. It doesn't matter, because *dress is a dead thing*. Real thing is that we want a living being who can understand. That is the real position." [Srila Prabhupada Welcomed by Governor at Hotel De Ville — Geneva, May 30, 1974]

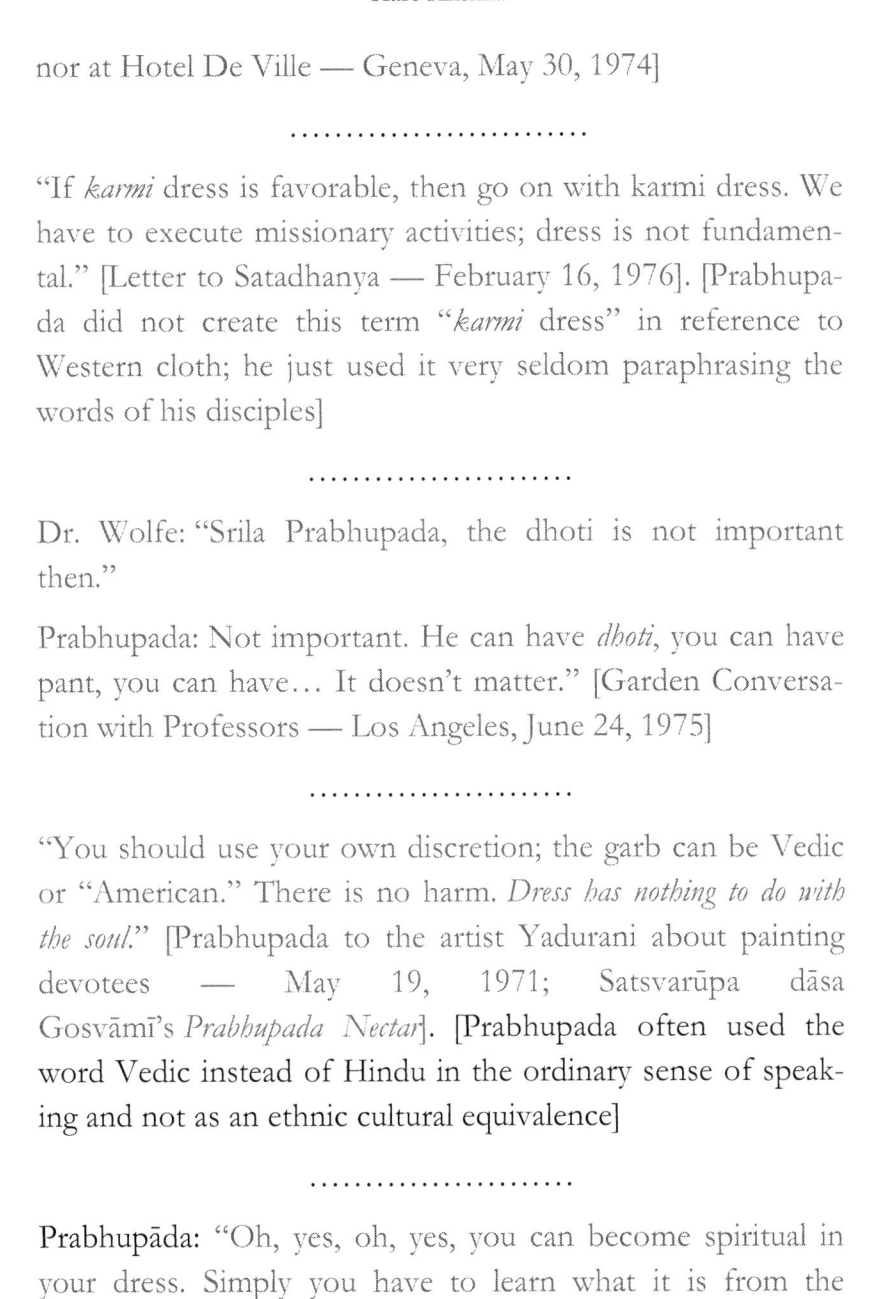

....

"If *karmi* dress is favorable, then go on with karmi dress. We have to execute missionary activities; dress is not fundamental." [Letter to Satadhanya — February 16, 1976]. [Prabhupada did not create this term "*karmi* dress" in reference to Western cloth; he just used it very seldom paraphrasing the words of his disciples]

....

Dr. Wolfe: "Srila Prabhupada, the dhoti is not important then."

Prabhupada: Not important. He can have *dhoti*, you can have pant, you can have… It doesn't matter." [Garden Conversation with Professors — Los Angeles, June 24, 1975]

....

"You should use your own discretion; the garb can be Vedic or "American." There is no harm. *Dress has nothing to do with the soul.*" [Prabhupada to the artist Yadurani about painting devotees — May 19, 1971; Satsvarūpa dāsa Gosvāmī's *Prabhupada Nectar*]. [Prabhupada often used the word Vedic instead of Hindu in the ordinary sense of speaking and not as an ethnic cultural equivalence]

....

Prabhupāda: "Oh, yes, oh, yes, you can become spiritual in your dress. Simply you have to learn what it is from the books. The dress is not very important thing…" [March 5, 1975]

....

"Householders may wear *dhoties* in the Temple, *or as they like*...It is not required to wear *dhoties*..." [Letter to Balai — September 12, 1968] "Better go and speak philosophy in your *grihastha* dress, not this dress, but you have nice coat, pants, gentleman. Who says no? I never said...Why this false dress? What is the wrong to become *grihastha*?" [Room Conversation — Bombay, January 7, 1977]

....

"*Sannyasa* [the renounce order or life] does not mean a particular type of dress or particular type of beard. *Sannyasa* means you can become a *sannyasi* even with your, coat-pant. It doesn't matter, provided you have dedicated your life for the service of God. That is called *sannyasa*." [ŚBh 7.6.1 — Montreal, December 6, 1968]

....

"Our *only concern* is to attract people to Krishna consciousness. We may do this in the dress of *sannyāsīs* or in the regular dress of gentlemen. Our *only concern* is to spread... Krisna consciousness." [ŚBh 7.13.10]

....

"You can become a swami even with your hats and coats. That doesn't matter." [ŚBh 5.5.3 Lecture — Boston, May 4, 1968]

....

"Regarding dress, I have already written to you that you can dress as smartly as possible to deal with the public, and dress is immaterial in Krishna Consciousness. *Consciousness is within*. I am a sannyasi, but if some important work requires, I dress myself just like a smart gentleman, I would immediately accept it. So, it is not a problem." [Letter to Gopala Krishna — March 9, 1969]

Srila Prabhupada stated on several occasions that he never insisted that his disciples and other members of the Hare Krishna movement wear Indian clothing. Here are a couple of examples:

Disciple: No, no. He's saying why are we dressing like that, like Indians?

Prabhupada: I have not said that you dress like that. You like, you do it. Did I say that you do it? [...] we are not concerned with the dress, we are concerned with the advancement of spiritual understanding, that's all. [Room conversation — Paris, June 1974]

....

Disciple: I'm just saying that it is a little difficult if they wear their dhoti.

Prabhupada: No, *dhoti*, I don't say. You have nice coat-pant. I don't say that you have to…I never said that. You have adopted it. (laughs) I never said that "You put on *dhoti*." [January 1977]

....

For Prabhupada, to carry out Shri Chaitanya's message for the welfare of human society was the fundamental principle.

"For *paramahamsas*, or *sannyāsīs* in the Vaishanava order, preaching is the first duty. To preach, such *sannyāsīs* may accept the symbols of *sannyāsa*, such as the *danda* and *kamandalu* [symbols of a person in the renounced order of life], or sometimes they may not. Generally, the Vaishnava *sannyāsīs*, being *paramahamsas*, are automatically called *bābājīs*, and they do not carry a *kamandalu* or *danda*. Such a sannyāsī is free to accept or reject the marks of *sannyāsa*. His only thought is "Where is there an opportunity to spread Krishna consciousness?" Sometimes the Krishna consciousness movement sends its representative *sannyāsīs* to foreign countries where the *danda* and *kamandalu* are not very much appreciated. We send our preachers in ordinary dress to introduce our books and philosophy. Our only concern is to attract people to Krishna consciousness. We may do this in the dress of *sannyāsīs* or in the regular dress of gentlemen. Our only concern is to spread interest in Krishna consciousness. (SB.07/13/9).

....

Well also have this well-known story.

"Prabhupada once saw a picture of Balavanta [a devotee] preaching into a microphone during a political campaign. Behind him sat the mayor and another candidate. Balavanta wore a suit and tie, *tilaka* (the symbol on the forehead of a Vaishnava), and tulasi beads… His hair was grown out. Around his neck he wore a bead bag…When Prabhupada saw the picture, he said that this is what we want, to preach in American dress. He said we should be known as American Krishnas." (Drops of Nectar, Satsvarupa Dasa Goswami)

....

Also, unlike what many today believe, Prabhupada did not expose spiritual science as the property of the East.

"Education may be wrong or right, but science is always the fact. 'Two plus two equal to four,'—that is equally good in the East and West, not that in the western countries, two plus two will be five…Similarly, to understand the science of God, it does not depend on the Western culture or Eastern culture." [Room Conversation with Malcolm — London, July 18, 1973]

....

"So far we are concerned, we have no such distinction, "East and West." [Bhagavad-gītā 13.8.12 Lecture — Bombay, October 2, 1973] .

....

"There is no question of 'Eastern' or 'Western.' *This is our manufacture, that Eastern is better than the Western.* We don't make such things as 'Eastern' and 'Western.' We test whether he's Krishna conscious. That's all." [Bhagavad-Gita 7.4 Lecture — Nairóbi, October 31, 1975]

....

Srila Prabhupada also urged his disciples to present the wisdom of the Vedas appropriately according to the time, place and circumstances. In his purport to Srimad Bhagavatam 1.9.9, Srila Prabhupada writes:

"Expert religionists know perfectly well how to adjust religious principles in terms of time and place. All the great *ācāryas* or religious preachers or reformers of the world executed their mission by adjustment of religious principles in terms of time and place. There are different climates and situations in different parts of the world, and if one has to discharge his duties to preach the message of the Lord, he must be expert in adjusting things in terms of the time and place."

....

"The teacher has to consider time, candidate and country. He must avoid the principle of *niyamāgraha* — that is, he should not try to perform the impossible. What is possible in one country may not be possible in another...The essence of devotional service must be taken into consideration, and not the outward paraphernalia..." [CC 2.23.105 Purport]

....

Dr. Hridayananda Dasa Goswami adds that Prabhupada, the founder of the Hare Krishna movement, often expressed his appreciation for the culture of India. Still, it is also a fact that when he saw that this could interfere with carrying his message effectively to others, he said that such cultural details were not significant. Therefore, dress, culinary recipes, and architecture are variable details. Prabhupada varied his statements on this, something he did not do concerning the essential principles of *bhakti*. Hridayananda Dasa Goswami concludes that if the members of the Hare Krishna Movement wish to practice and offer others a spiritual science, they must understand the crucial distinction between invariable fundamental principles and variable details, that is, between the essential and the peripheral.

Since Krishna is universal, the process of approaching Him must also be universal; it does not depend on the clothing, eating, and building style of a given culture. It is sufficient that our dress is clean and decent and our food is free from animal slaughter. The promoter of the Krishna West branch of the Hare Krishna Movement believes that this universalization of *krishna-bhakti* will open new doors for a currently surviving but fails to firmly spread its roots within Western culture, thus becoming more dependent on an India in the diaspora. He is of the opinion that unknowingly, the members of this movement have created a cultural bubble similar to the Amish phenomenon, living in a parallel world or "comfort zone," a world in which everything is favorable and compatible with themselves wherever they look. This distances them from a world very different from the days of the great Hare Krishna explosion of the sixties, a world to which they do not try to adapt but, ironically, aspire to transform for the welfare of humanity. So far, the nascent Krishna West version of the Hare Krishna Movement has caught the attention of many of its members.

In contrast, others still prefer a Hare Krishna model that they consider "classic." However, it is a fact that four decades after the departure of its founder, the harvest yielded by this model is very modest. For all the reasons mentioned above, many new generation members heed Hridayananda Dasa Goswami's words, the promoter of this reform: "Unless there is a modern Hare Krishna Movement, it will not work."

This book was completed in February 2018, in Shri Chaitanya's year 532, on the day of His advent.

Hare Krishna.

Made in the USA
Columbia, SC
09 February 2023